The **Oldie** *Annual II*

The **Oldie** *Annual II*

Edited by Richard Ingrams

BLOOMSBURY

This compilation first published 1994

Copyright © 1994 Oldie Publications Ltd

The publishers would like to thank the respective copyright owners
for permission to include articles and illustrations in this volume.
The moral right of the authors has been asserted

Bloomsbury Publishing Plc, 2 Soho Square, London W1V 5DE

A CIP catalogue record for this book is available from
the British Library

ISBN 0 7475 1899 8

Printed in Great Britain by St Edmundsbury Press

Editor's Introduction

The first *Oldie* annual having proved to be a modest success (reaching the giddy heights of No 69 on the non-fiction bestsellers' list), the publishers Bloomsbury have generously decreed that a sequel is in order.

This time we have decided to include three of Naim Attallah's interviews which have proved such an integral feature of *The Oldie*. A number of Pin-Ups pages have also been slotted in, in order to liven things up a bit. Apart from that the mixture is much the same as before with a strong emphasis on writers who in other circles would be regarded as amateurs – the actor Victor Langley describing Richard Burton's last film or Mrs Betty Gathergood recalling her adventures in Dr Johnson's House in Gough Square.

This is all to the good. In an age when most magazines tend to look the same, consisting of articles that you feel you have read several times before, *The Oldie* derives its individuality from the high percentage of articles contributed by the readers themselves – notably the enthralling series of encounters under the heading I Once Met. The Still With Us brigade is also well-represented, headed by the doyen of *Oldie* contributors, Hugh Cudlipp, whose account of his prostate troubles must rank as one of the funniest articles ever to appear in the magazine.

I would like also to single out for a mention *The Oldie*'s cartoonists – some of them veterans from the great days of *Punch* but others emerging, it seems, from nowhere, to grace the pages with their jokes. The quality has been exceptionally high and, alas, there is room only for a small selection here.

To savour the full delights of *The Oldie* it is necessary to buy the magazine. There you will also meet many of our regular contributors whose work is not represented in the annual. And as for those who still feel embarrassment about being associated with the title, I repeat the excellent advice of the Marketing Department – 'Say it's for your Dad.'

Contents

Herbert Ponting was the official photographer on Captain Scott's ill-fated expedition to the South Pole. **Beryl Bainbridge**, *who recreated the events in her novel* The Birthday Boys, *takes a look at Ponting's remarkable Antarctic film*

The Great White Silence

A UNIQUE DOCUMENTARY film was released this year by Academy Video, of footage shot by Herbert Ponting, official photographer to the 1910 expedition to the South Pole led by Captain Robert Falcon Scott. Originally shown in several episodes, it was issued in 1924 in a silent full length version, *The Great White Silence*, and subsequently re-issued in 1933 as *90° South*, with a commentary by Ponting himself.

Dear heavens, how the visual arts have progressed, and how those of us who remember the way things used to be, faced with such a bygone product, perceive the coarsening which technology and so called 'professionalism' have curiously accelerated. This observation is not an oversentimental response to all our yesterdays, but a reaction to the impact of momentous events captured on film 84 years ago.

The film opens with an introduction spoken by Vice-Admiral Edward Evans, formerly Lt 'Teddy' Evans of the ill-fated expedition, who stands in evening dress in front of a creased black curtain and briskly outlines the conditions under which the film was made. Though his voice is steady he plays pocket billiards throughout his brief address and concludes with the words, 'I hand it over to you, Ponto,' at which Ponting, also in evening dress and sporting a Hitler moustache, enters stage right. The two of them stand together for a moment, looking not unlike the Weston brothers about to take a final bow, and then the screen blacks them out.

Throughout, there are no manufactured dramatic effects, no odd camera angles, no distortions, and the music on the soundtrack is neither stirring nor particularly memorable. We see the *Terra Nova* leaving London Dock on 1st June, 1910, the banks of the Thames lined with well-wishers. We don't hear the celebratory hoots of the craft on the river any more than the cheers of the onlookers. One of the crew does a tap routine wearing his long combs and a bowler hat, and Anton the Russian dog handler flings himself about

in a spirited Georgian folk-dance; Captain Oates goes berserk with the hair clippers and gives one of his fellow officers a truly awesome crew-cut. Scott, who left the ship further down river because he needed to drum up more funds to pay for the adventure (he rejoined the ship in South Africa) smiles at the camera. He looks very young, very handsome; he has big eyes and fat lips.

Later, in New Zealand, we see the motor sledges, the dogs and the ponies being stashed aboard. The latter animals had come from Siberia, and it had been intended that Oates, the one member of the expedition who had a real knowledge of horses, should be the one to go off and pick them. In the event, he proved such an asset on board ship that he was kept behind and someone else sent.

Two days out of New Zealand a terrible storm hit the *Terra Nova*. We are given a glimpse of mountainous seas before encountering pack-ice and sighting the Great Barrier. The Ice Barrier, 10,000 feet in height and 500 miles long, looks like the cliffs of Dover, only higher and whiter.

Once landed on the west coast of Ross Island, the men unpack the food, the building materials and the livestock. The motor sledges, of which Scott had such great hopes, are slung overboard in wooden cases. The hut is built, the quarters made comfortable. Ponting films a football match, the habits of penguins and seals, a luminous study of the *Terra Nova* seen from a grotto in an iceberg.

Ponting left the Antarctic the following year, but he made a record of what it was like to strike camp and prepare for the night in a four-man tent. Apart from the clouds of tobacco smoke, one could mistake it for a boy scouts' outing; Petty Officer Taff Evans, Scott, Birdie Bowers and Uncle Bill Wilson hugger mugger over the primus stove, jostling for space, smiling. One almost forgets that later on, a year later, when five of them fitted into a tent this size, the temperature outside was minus 50 degrees and all of them were dying from frostbite, hunger and exhaustion.

Ponting wrote a book called *The Great White South*, with an introduction by Lady Scott. She writes: 'In his (Ponting's) book, which teems with appreciation of his Leader, there seems no word of his Leader's appreciation of him. That will never do. On 29th May, 1911, my husband recorded in his diary, "Ponting is the most delightful of men... he is an artist in love with his work. Tonight he gave us a charming lecture on Japan with illustrations of his own." '

In those days back-slapping was obligatory, of course; it was not gentlemanly to bring up differences of opinion or clashes of temperament between individuals involved in heroic exploits, particularly if, at the time of recollection, one of the leading contestants happened to be dead and buried, not to mention frozen.

Right from the beginning Scott was a bit off Ponting. He regarded him as lamentably commercial in attitude. Strapped for cash – it was not until the polar party perished that donations flooded in – he was outraged at the photographer's business sense. Having undergone six years' ranching and mining in Western America, two voyages round the world, three years in Japan – some months of which were spent attached as a war correspondent to the Imperial Army – Ponting struck a hard bargain as regards copyright. Moreover, when the great storm attacked the *Terra Nova* and it was all hands to the pumps, Ponting resolutely stayed below, fighting to save his photographic plates and chemical bottles from being dashed to smithereens.

Nor did either Ponting or Vice Admiral Evans think it necessary to draw our attention to the fact that the ponies were only fit for the knackers' yard, that the motor vehicles were a grievous mistake and worse than useless, that five men set off on the final dash for the Pole when only four had been catered for, and that insufficient supplies had been deposited for the return journey.

Quite right too! Ponting wasn't an investigative journalist, simply a superb photographer recording an epic and glorious enterprise.

Captain Scott in his study at Ross Island

George Bernard Shaw

THAT IS NOT strictly true. I met him twice, both times getting the same reaction – blue eyes blazing, stick held high and something being shouted. I am sure I represented the type of human being he loathed – namely a child.

We lived in the village next to Ayot St Lawrence in those far off days when parents took their offspring for longish walks. Shaw's village was very small, a straggle of cottages and middle-sized houses, a pseudo-classical temple and a ruined church. Not much else. A 17th-century cottage doubled as the post office, presided over by Gysbella Lyte who, like Shaw, had something of a reputation. Shaw's house stood darkly at a corner. In fact it was called 'Shaw's Corner'.

On my first meeting with the old man I was peering through his gate hoping to catch sight of him. I did. He appeared in the gloom of his drive waving his stick, eyebrows electrically alert, eyes flashing, shouting at me – 'Get away from my gate, urchin'.

The aura of temper hanging around this tall, skinny, knickerbockered man was enough to send any child running. I ran.

Our second meeting, perhaps a year later, took place in the dark lane leading to 'Shaw's Corner'. He had walked to the post office, no doubt to post more of his famous cards and was wending his way slowly back to his house. I was skipping along in the opposite direction.

I remember he stood still at the sight of a child having the audacity to be in his lane. Up flew the walking stick yet again, eyebrows unfurled, blue eyes hard as ice with annoyance froze me and an acid, high-pitched squeak issued forth. I was terrified and ran back down the lane to hide until he had passed.

When Shaw died his body was carried to Mr Blow, the undertaker in our village, and many important people came to view the great man. I was told that Shaw had died with his mouth open as if in speech – about to shout at somebody I expect! A small block of wood was hidden beneath his beard to wedge shut his mouth. An over-eager viewer knocked the bier, the wedge flew out and Shaw's mouth fell open. Consternation among the body-watchers. Was the old man still alive and about to utter again? **CHRISTINE PORTEUS**

An Oil Rig

The Oldie's classical columnist **Ross Leckie** *doesn't exactly have the kind of CV one associates with a doddering Latinist*

SWEAT OF MANY kinds is known to those who work on oil rigs. Not oil platforms, you understand, with their gymnasia, solaria, cinemas and fake French chefs, but oil rigs. They drill for the black black gold. If they find it, then great platforms are built. The rig, semi-submersible, discharges tons of water from its legs, casts off its many anchors, starts its engines and moves on.

The rig and the platform have as much in common as a trawler and the QE2. The 168 men who died a terrible death, drowned in a burning sea when the platform Piper Alpha blew up, might reasonably have expected the meejah at least to stop calling Piper a 'rig'. But that's just one of many things that people do not understand about the industry that paid for Thatcher's revolution. Another is that there was no 'economic miracle'. There was instead Advanced Petroleum Revenue Tax – and sweat.

The first starts at the heliport. It's a cold, a sad and sullen sweat. You're afraid of many things as you wait to board your helicopter for two long weeks in the grey North Sea. Have you paid the gas bill? Will you lose a finger on this trip, a hand? It used to help to be drunk, on surreptitious Smirnoff. But now they have breathalysers and you sit and sweat in sober silence. Perhaps it's the survival suits. Yards of poly-propylene that are supposed to keep you alive if the chopper ditches into seas at –15ºC just make you sweat as you sit not watching the safety video at a temperate 12ºC.

Some sleep as you thud, thud, thud your way across the sea. I sweat as I try to remember how you're supposed to get out of a helicopter underwater and upside down. I've done it many times, kicked in my window, struggled out and up to a raft and been afraid. But that was in a swimming pool, in a mock helicopter raised up by a crane and dropped, on an offshore survival training course. Those who've tried it for real can't tell you how it's done. They're dead.

Everyone sweats for the landing. Even the pilots, usually ex-Marines who've landed birds in Belize and in Borneo, take seriously the landing of a helicopter onto a helideck of 40 yards' circumference into winds of up to 30 knots. And so when 18 men peel off survival suits inside, the smell of sweat is strong and sour.

The next sweat is the best one, honest and clean. I am on the drill floor within 20 minutes of arriving, a roughneck running pipe. I have dug ditches in Uganda, piled bales in Perthshire, moved irrigation pipes in Israel, but nothing is as physically arduous as this.

You face, you know, a 12 hour shift. You will be allowed one half-hour break in which to get back to the quarters, clean up a little and consume as many calories as you can. The driller may or may not allow you a 10 minute 'smoko' after three hours. Some people get away with the larger calls of nature – you piss where you stand – but the only time I tried that one, the toolpusher, absolute monarch on an oil rig, was present. He was a big burly American called Red. 'You shit in your own time, boy, you work in ours.' I never asked again.

After two weeks off, the sweat runs free and you feel it running down your spine and the inside of your arms and you greet it as an old friend. It feels good to be back and you are caught up in the rhythm of the thing, sweating, 200 miles from Shetland on the Ocean Nomad 201.

The roughneck's sweat of fear is an altogether different one. It is a rushing, prickling, chilling, dry sweat that catches you first at the throat and passes like a bite of ice cream to your bowels. You are 'stabbing' a pipe, or trying to; that is, seeking to bring 120 feet of swinging steel to rest on top of another before you join them up and run them down the hole. The rig heaves suddenly, drunkenly. The pipe flexes, shakes you off and swings dementedly round the drill floor. One caught my friend Chris once, slap under the chin, and his teeth hit the wind wall yards away, a tinkling sound like gentle cymbals through the din.

Or when a tugger cable pulls you back, then you know that special sweat again. 'Not For Man Riding' say the signs on the heavy tuggers that haul up pipe. There are lighter tuggers for men. But when, 120 feet above you, your derrickman slips, you grab the first tugger you can to get up there, for once literally a *deus ex machina*, as quickly as you can. Sometimes, though – I don't understand the physics – the weight of the tugger's steel rope pulls you back, not up. You grab a strut on the derrick and bounce, bounce, bounce against your harness, fighting an implacable weight and the sweat courses across your body like the stirring of desire.

Sour sweat and sweet sweat, good sweat and fear sweat – they all go into the toil they call 'making hole'.

Cycling serenely through the streets of Beijing, **Adam Moore** *was suddenly thrown to the tarmac by a collision with a meandering Maoist, only to find himself cast in the role of imperialist aggressor*

Vicious Cycles

MY COMPANION Elaine and I were heading back to our hotel when it happened. The road was wide enough for a ribbon of cyclists and a broad band of cars, trucks and trams. I noticed, on my right, a grey-haired old man in his Mao suit sporting huge dark glasses (sunglasses which, incidentally, never left the bridge of his nose). The next moment I was sliding along the tarmac on my back with Elaine cycling into my groin. The old man was now on the left, although he too was horizontal, sandwiched between two bikes, one of which was mine.

I stood up and peeled the topmost cycle off of the old man, which allowed him to stagger up. He was, understandably, slightly shocked and that part of his face not covered by the sunglasses showed the effort of mind needed to comprehend this unexpected change in circumstances. A woman came over and stood making the appropriate noises to him. I picked up his bike and put it on its stand. I was not angry with him for knocking me to the floor, it had just been one of those things. I actually felt some concern about his condition. But he, although confused, was not on his way to join The Great Helmsman.

Now, my knowledge of Mandarin is limited to a few phrases picked up from a guide book. One of those expressions is *dui-bu-qu*, which I believe means 'Excuse me'. So I tried it.

But, as was often the case, I wasn't understood. The Chinese tongue having four tones which completely alter the meaning of a word, I could well have been rubbing salt into the wound.

The wound, it turned out, was a slight graze, about the size of a thumbprint, on the old man's elbow. Still, it was enough to hold the attention of both the victim and the pedestrian. We were, at this point, still only four people standing in the flow of traffic. Having exhausted my vocabulary, I decided it was pointless staying, so I mounted my bike and started to push off.

I was prevented by the iron grip of the old man, who had broken out of his hypnotic obsession with his own elbow. I was amazed and rather annoyed. There followed a totally pointless exchange of words – he evidently did not know any English. While I was indicating that the only injury was to his pride, the woman from the pavement quietly walked around to my bike, closed the wheel lock, (thus immobilising me) and handed the key to the old man.

I was stunned. From the figures dancing before me, it became painfully obvious that I was not going anywhere just yet and that it was going to be a long day.

Meanwhile the shouting, by the injured party and his new adviser, had started to draw a crowd. Cyclists stopped to hear what was happening, others stopped to see why the crowd had formed, and soon everything stopped because the road was blocked. Television is often blamed for creating an antisocial insularity in its viewers. I only wish that more people in China could afford sets. As it was, we were to be that evening's entertainment. Perhaps even that month's.

Back at the epicentre, Elaine and I were using hand signals to demonstrate that it was the old war veteran who had crashed into me, not vice versa. His adviser, though, was broadcasting to the newcomers, in their native tongue, what my crime was, whilst she indicated the poor, grandfatherly, patriotic freedom-fighter and recent victim of imperialist aggression. There was no escape now. Even if I had wanted to leave the bike and lose a $10 deposit, we would have had to fight our way through a dense mass of Chinese. Things looked bleak and rather worrying too.

A young lady from the crowd stepped

forward and said smilingly that she could speak English. We explained to her our side of the story. She translated. The old man and the woman, who had by now taken on the position of an expert witness, disagreed. I knew that the old in China are traditionally respected, so held out little hope for our cause.

'In China,' said the young lady, turning to translate for us, 'when you beat up old man, we beat you

'In China,' said the young lady, turning to translate for us, 'when you beat up old man, we beat you up'

up.' 'Oh my God,' I thought, 'we're going to be lynched.' We pressed our case again with rather more urgency. The old veteran proudly displayed his scar to the crowd. Home, England and trial by jury suddenly seemed far away.

Fighting for our lives now, we denounced the old man's graze and said that it did not prove who hit who, anyway. But a pound of flesh evidently was not his goal, as the message came back to us that he wanted to be taken to hospital. I pointed out to our interpreter the stupidity of such a request. Elaine, though, saw through his demand and called his bluff. 'Yes,' she said, 'we will take him to a

Chinese hospital, if he takes us to a Western hospital.' That shut him up.

A few minutes later the demand was changed to a more direct approach. 'He wants you give him money.' This was an improvement on taking our lives, but one which we were going to fight, on principle.

It was then that the policeman arrived, dressed in the usual ill-fitting green uniform. It quickly became apparent that he would be of little help to anyone. This officer was not one to take control of a situation. Instead, after hearing why the crowd had gathered and cut off a major road, he stood about grinning, waiting to see which side was

going to win before committing himself.

So it became an open contest to garner popular support. 'In China,' I told the policeman and the jury, 'there are many bicycle accidents. When Chinese hits Chinese, no problem. When Chinese hits foreigner, they want money.' That got us a few laughs. But only from the rear of the crowd. We needed more support from its centre.

Elaine, as ever, was more practical. 'Call the British Embassy,' she demanded. This shook the constable up. 'Call the British Embassy,' she repeated. Things were now getting too much for the local bobby. He was being forced into taking part. The case for our defence needed one more push.

Elaine came in on cue with a heart-wrenching outburst: 'We came here for our honeymoon, because we thought China was a nice country. But you are being cruel.' This fine, if utterly fictitious, performance (complete with sobs) decided the issue. The crowd's sympathy was won and the entertainment was, for them, brought to a satisfactory conclusion. The policeman authoritatively cleared a path and we were let out, although not without being told, 'Don't beat up old man again.'

Still somewhat unsettled, Elaine and I continued on our way. But for the remainder of our stay we were suspicious of any old man in a Mao suit – which is quite a neurosis to have in Beijing. I would add that if you are ever involved in a collision with an old Chinese man, don't stop.

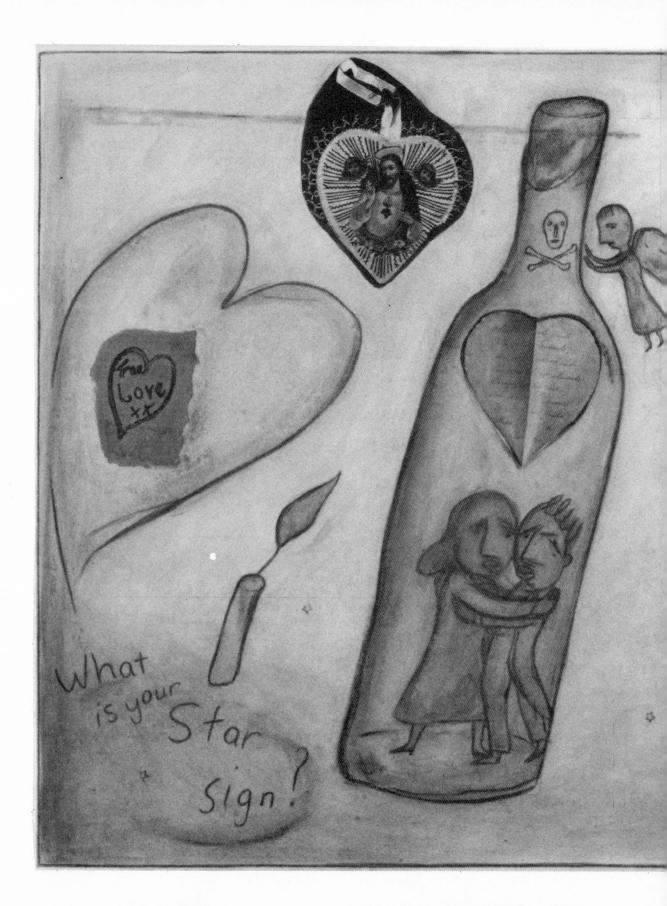

Sarzy

Forget tea and sympathy – Sarzy specialised in wine and psychiatry. In an ad agency in the Sixties, **William Trevor** *found himself working alongside this exotic amateur angel from northern Italy who ministered to the walking wounded on the fringes of London's Bohemia*

She stood, swaying, with a glass of *vin rosé* in one hand, a packet of Senior Service cigarettes and a crumpled sheaf of yellow typing paper in the other. Sarzy, she was introduced as: Frances Sarzano, middle-aged, half Italian, steeped in psychoanalysis, keen on birth signs, grinning and drunk on that Monday afternoon in 1960.

'Gemini,' I said when she asked me.

Nothing faltered in her face. There was no sharp intake of breath, no tightening of the fingers on the glass. Scorpio or Capricorn brought all that. Sagittarius turned the grin into a beam of delight.

Her father was a tailor who'd fled to England from the Fascist threat in Northern Italy, settling in Worcester Park. Her parents were now dead; Sarzy lived with a sister in Ewell, but often in the evenings did not return there, preferring to spend the night in the otherwise empty office building, stretched out on one of the account executives' sofas.

She was a smallish woman with a large bosom, dressed usually in a navy-blue suit. In the mornings she was spick and span, blouse buttoned, lipstick in place, exuding a determined air of efficiency. In the afternoons she looked as if she'd been exposed to a storm – hair awry, zips unzipped, her yellow typing paper damp with wine.

'What's the matter, love?' Sarzy would ask a lone man, unknown to her, on a bar stool. When he replied that nothing was, there'd be the quizzical glance, the sympathetic smile. 'Something's the matter, love.'

Often the man would turn his head away, or open a newspaper he had read already.

'Something's the matter, love,' Sarzy would insist again.

'Nothing's the matter.'

'Are you waiting for your wife?'

'I'm waiting for a friend.'

'When's your birthday, love?'

'Look, I came in here for a quiet drink –'

'Why don't you go home to your wife? Why don't you finish your drink and let me buy you another and then go home to her?'

She loved the thought of men going home to their wives. She loved the thought of other people's happiness, of children born, illness recovered from, duties observed, temptations resisted, the right alliances made when the stars were where they should be. A lifetime of copywriting had not made a cynic of her. She may even have believed what she wrote about Clark's shoes and VP wine. Happy endings had soaked into her consciousness. Mr Right was really there even if he had not yet approached her personally. The Colgate Ring of Confidence didn't let you down. Dr White came to the rescue on those problem days; there was Yeastvite for energy. Sarzy's saloon-bar conversations with strangers had dialogue in bubbles.

When I first knew her she had just stepped out of her office-bound world to become involved with the remnants of Fitzrovia and Soho. She was still to be seen returning twice in an afternoon from the Curzon Wine Company in Shepherd Market with a tightly-clutched bottle of *vin rosé* or Vouvray. Her hurrying footfall clattered on the uncarpeted back stairs and minutes later she distributed her largesse to anyone who happened to pass the open door of what had, until recently, been a stationery cupboard and was now her office.

She frequented the nearby Coach and Horses at lunchtime and in the evenings, but since her discovery of Soho she was more regularly to be found in the Caves de France or the York Minster, or the Swiss pub in Old Compton Street. Dylan Thomas was dead and so was MacLaren Ross, but the Scottish painters, Colquhoun and MacBryde, were still at large, setting a certain Bohemian tone. For his peregrinations through this beer-blurred underworld, Patrick Kavanagh had discarded the battered blue hat that had been so familiar on the streets of Dublin in favour of a cow-jammer's cap. Elizabeth Smart had long ago sat down and wept at Grand Central Station, and was trying to forget it. Hangers-on hung on in Jimmy's and the Colony and the Mandrake. Sarzy's generosity to the thirsty was widely enjoyed. Her particular friend was someone called Daria, whose *bons mots* were regularly quoted; her hero was Winston Churchill because he had won the war against the fascists.

She had once, and for years, been in love with a man she talked about, who had written persuasively about steel products, but unfortunately had had a wife and children to go home to. Now, it seemed, she was in love with Colquhoun, but unfortunately he was homosexual. He was there in the agency one afternoon, full of *vin rosé*, dancing with MacBryde. Everyone was invited to watch, the drawing tables in Joyce Peet's big top studio pushed back against the walls, artwork and unfinished roughs bundled away, the messenger boy with the Russian name urgently dispatched to the Curzon Wine Company.

Sarzy herself hurried off to fetch the more agreeable of the two managing directors, a man she was mistakenly convinced would appreciate Colquhoun and MacBryde. Blue-suited and portly, he arrived, but didn't stay long, muttering as he left that dancing homosexuals were not his thing.

Big Joyce Peet took the floor, and her example was followed by dispatch boys and typists and someone from Accounts. Sarzy kept darting off and returning with account executives who she believed would appreciate the Scotsmen. Then Colquhoun became testy because the dance floor had been invaded. He sulked in a corner and when he became abusive Sarzy said he didn't mean it, but MacBryde said he did. Someone fell into the typographers' camera.

After Colquhoun, Sarzy's affections were claimed by an out-of-work electrician called Charles, whom she almost certainly discovered on a bar stool somewhere. Charles was a huge man who rarely spoke and had a fondness for small bottles of high-strength beer. He also had a marital problem, which Sarzy was endeavouring to fix by

A lifetime of copywriting had not made a cynic of her. Happy endings had soaked into her consciousness. Mr Right was there even if he had not yet approached her personally

means of astrological readings and the expertise she had acquired in the field of psychoanalysis through being psychoanalysed herself.

Just before 5.30 one evening she was on the house phone, summoning me in hushed tones, as a matter of great urgency, to the disused stationery cupboard. Windowless and dank, it was just spacious enough to accommodate a narrow metal desk, a chair and a filing-cabinet. It also now managed to accommodate Charles, who was lying on the floor in a massive heap, most of him covered with newspaper.

'In case anyone comes in,' Sarzy said, covering the rest of him.

'Is he all right down there?'

She shook her head. But we must not do anything, she insisted, until everyone had left the building; then we must call an ambulance.

'What's the matter with him?'

'I think he's taken pills.'

Sarzy took pills herself: purple hearts, lifters, anything she could get. But I didn't think she meant pills like that.

'If he has taken something,' I said, 'we shouldn't just sit here.'

'It's only for ten minutes.'

So we waited. And when the departing footfalls on the stairs abated I telephoned 999 and asked for an ambulance. Sarzy poured *vin rosé* for both of us and lifted the newspapers off the man she loved. She smeared on lipstick, powdered her face, and lit a cigarette. She left me with Charles and went downstairs to greet the ambulancemen.

There were two of them, and a stretcher, which had to be left outside because there wasn't room for it in the stationery cupboard. There wasn't room for the ambulancemen either. We were touching one another as we stood there. 'What's up with him?' the taller man asked me. I said I didn't know.

The sheets of newspaper were still scattered on the floor. A one-bar electric fire which Sarzy had borrowed to keep Charles warm while he lay on the concrete floor had begun to singe the bottoms of his trousers. An empty Vouvray bottle was on its side in a corner.

'Hey, you!' the taller of the ambulancemen shouted into Charles's face. 'What's the matter with you?'

'He was threatening to take pills,' Sarzy said. 'I think he did in the end.'

'What kind of pills?'

She shook her head. He'd had a lot of trouble, she said, Pisces married to a Capricorn.

Charles's pockets were searched, but no pills were found. The taller ambulanceman roughly prodded his neck, then smacked his cheeks. Charles groaned.

'He's drunk,' the smaller man concluded furiously, red in the face. He was quivering with rage. All over London there were people dying, he said; there were people in distress, people in accidents, people who needed to be conveyed to hospitals.

Both men, having crouched over Charles for several minutes, were upright again. The taller one was glancing distastefully about him – at the sheets of newspaper, the empty bottle in the corner and the partially full one on the metal desk, the two glasses beside it. There was a smell of burning. A curl of smoke was rising from one of Charles's turn-ups.

'Did you think to alert the fire brigade while you were at it?' the smaller man enquired nastily. I turned off the electric fire and said I was sorry. The other ambulanceman sniffed.

'What's the matter, love?' Sarzy asked him.

'This turkey'll sleep it off is what the matter is. Next time just leave him to get on with it.'

Sarzy offered the men cigarettes. 'Please wait a moment,' she said when the gesture was ignored.

'For what, madam?'

'I'll fetch two more glasses.'

The ambulancemen didn't speak again. They picked up their stretcher and went. On the floor Charles began to snore.

Half an hour later when I looked in at the Coach and Horses he was standing at the bar. Sarzy was rooting in her handbag for something to pay for his extra-strength beer with.

Such lame ducks were her stock-in-trade – the sacked, the dodgy, the deadbeats of the Caves de France, the suicidal. When they didn't conveniently surface she created them: in a matter of minutes she could turn a care-free stranger into a mass of inhibitions.

Her head would roll a little to one side, her eyes acquire a shared-confidence look. Bubbling with encouragement, everything about her willed a confession of father-fear or mother-fixation, or revelations of destructive toilet training. Beneath a polished surface she often discerned greed or ruthlessness, even a whiff of evil. Others could do no wrong. 'A nice one,' she would say about a newly arrived young executive whom she had met for a moment in the lift. There was rarely a reason why some were good and others distrusted as future harbingers of grief or pain.

The agency's founder, Notley, was one of the good. Attributes of decency, straight dealing and honesty were affectionately applauded, a forthright Cockney manner endearingly dwelt upon. That the three former qualities were not always readily discernible to the less perceptive hardly came into it. Just as the much-quoted Daria was designated a wit even if her *bons mots* were not what the expression implies, so Notley's moral rectitude – sharing rank with that of angels and bishops – was stated as a fact.

'Do something for me,' Sarzy requested humbly when Notley lay dying. 'Light a candle for him.'

17

Because I was Irish she insisted on assuming I was a Catholic in spite of my frequent denials.

'Please,' she begged. 'On your way home light a candle.'

I began to explain, yet again, that I didn't have access to miraculous intervention through candles.

'Please. That church in Farm St, next to the little brown pub.'

The shared-confidence smile was there, the dishevelled head cocked challengingly to one side. She would sleep tonight, she reminded me, if I lit a last candle for Notley. It would take only a few minutes. It was what any good man would want.

Then she thought of something else and said: 'Light one for Tommy Kenyon too.'

Tommy Kenyon was not numbered among the chosen. But because he was in hospital recovering from something to do with the walls of his stomach, it wouldn't be fair – it wouldn't be right – that a candle shouldn't burn for him also.

Notley died. Tommy Kenyon was back in the office within a week, on a diet of milk drinks and slop. Although I hadn't lit anything for either of them, and constantly said so, Sarzy always believed I had, and that in doing so had offered up the candles carelessly, muddling them in some way. During the rest of the time I knew her she tended to bring that up.

Somewhere she found a dead cat and insisted that it was not entirely lifeless. She wandered from office to office with the remains of the creature wrapped in a duster, in search of someone who knew about feline diseases. She mentioned candles again, but this time I refused more firmly.

In the end they let her go. She had taken to interrupting afternoon meetings to enquire of the agency's clients what the matter was and may even have shown the dead cat to a couple of them. Men who manufacture wallpaper paste or nylon yarn do not take kindly to such interruptions, so Sarzy – after a vast number of years in the service of their products – was pensioned off.

Everyone missed her. Everyone said her heart had been in the right place: her persistence and her wild probings of other people's psyche had all to do with that. She suffered fools gladly, and didn't mind bores. She bewildered the conventional and the dull – two descriptions she would not have permitted herself to use. She was a woman about whom no ill was spoken, even by those whom she considered her enemies. Her tiresomeness was always forgiven: something about her made that seem natural.

Life in Ewell wasn't for her, people said; she would not survive there. But she did. She survived for another ten years, before the *vin rosé* and the Vouvray belatedly took a toll. There was a stroke, and then she died in a hospital for incurables.

ONE BRIGHT sunny day many years ago when I was living and teaching in Bishop's Stortford, a pretty young friend invited me to drive into Cambridge with her to do some essential shopping.

Her doctor husband was driving and, as parking was a problem, he put us down on the Backs and suggested that we should walk through the precincts of King's College into King's Parade.

My friend put her small son into the smallest of pushchairs and we passed through the massive gate. As we walked along the path we admired the beauty of the ancient lawn and the splendour of King's College Chapel in the sunlight. It was all so beautiful.

Suddenly the peace was destroyed by someone shouting 'Get back! Go away! How dare you!' I looked behind me to see if rowdy students were making a disturbance – and realised that *we* were the cause of this outburst of rage. A small, frantic old man in a long overcoat, cap and scarf was scuttling down the steps of an adjacent building, waving his stick in a threatening manner at us – two astonished young women and a startled baby.

I once met...

E M Forster

'Can you not read?' he screeched. 'Do you not read notices? You are not allowed in these precincts with a *perambulator!*'

I could read. I had recognised this angry little figure at once as Edward Morgan Forster. I had read all his books with great pleasure ('Only connect' his salient message).

I was not easily intimidated. Did I not deal with students every day of the week? My gentle friend was pink with embarrassment and totally silenced. I was not.

I said quietly: 'Do calm down or you will have a stroke.'

His mouth fell open in amazement and his entire manner changed. He said quite politely: 'You are not allowed in here with a *wheeled* vehicle. There is a notice on the gate. You must go back.' I replied: 'We are within a few yards of King's Parade and quite some distance from the gate through which we entered. Should we not wheel this small pushchair through the nearest exit?' 'Go on then,' he muttered, 'and don't do it again!'

I wish I had never met that most sensitive of writers, E M Forster.   **NONIE BEERBOHM**

The Oldie
SPORTS PAGE

A few weeks of strenuous long-distance drinking may not have been the best preparation for **David Conville** *to run against Roger Bannister, but then Lady Luck, in the shape of a lorry, intervened*

MY OXFORD CAREER was not glittering. It lasted eight weeks. My only achievement, besides an underwhelming performance for the St John's Mummers, was coming first in my college cross-country running trial. This caused surprise, as I was known to spend most evenings at Whites, a somewhat louche club made notorious by Kenneth Tynan, where I drank away that winter term of 1949 as the 'Harry Lime Theme' zithered on a wind-up gramophone. Not the best training for endurance running.

However, I was pretty pleased with myself to be St John's first string for the Varsity inter-college race, which would be run over a course of five miles, despite my friends pointing out that it might prove a doubtful honour competing against the likes of Chataway, Morgan, and Bannister. Although it was several years before he broke the four-minute-mile barrier, Bannister was already considered the best distance runner in the country. No chance of beating him.

The race took place on a cold, misty November afternoon, and started on a road on the outskirts of the city. Indeed, the first 200 yards were run on tarmac before the course took off into Scholar Gypsy territory.

The first strings of each college were lined up abreast across the road in alphabetical order, with their teams in single file behind them – John's wedged in between Exeter and Keble. The Exeter college runner on my left, a tall clean-limbed youth with a Christopher Isherwood haircut, seemed cool and detached. The Keble chap seemed as cold and nervous

Bannister's four-minute mile, 1954

as I was. Those were the pre-tracksuit days of blue knees and a great deal of jumping up and down before the off.

The road being narrow, the 200-odd runners were so jammed together that it was difficult for the starter to sort us out in the right order. Tension mounted with the delay. There were exasperated shouts of 'Why are we waiting?' – 'Make way there!' – 'Can't you wait?'.

Behind us an impatient lorry was edging through the pack of runners. Gradually the crowd parted, and the driver, thinking the way ahead clear, accelerated hard down and the lorry shot forward. Unfortunately, my Exeter neighbour seemed unaware of approaching doom. The lorry's wing mirror struck him a cruel blow on the temple, knocking him down unconscious at my feet with blood gushing from his head.

Sensation! There was a great wailing of 'Bannister's down!' – 'Roger's knocked down!'. Worried faces pressed round me as I cradled the stricken runner in my arms. Slowly he came round, but did not seem able to focus or know where he was.

My outward air of caring concern hid a most ignoble thought – 'If he runs in this state, I'll be able to boast to my dying day that I beat Roger Bannister.'

The famous athlete staggered to his feet, bleeding, dazed, and white. 'Don't worry, I'll run' – did I imagine he also said 'I can't let the college down'? It was heroic stuff, a Henty novel, a Newbolt poem – 'Play up, play up, and play the game'.

As we eventually lined up again, triumph seemed to beckon me with an insistent refrain repeating in my head, 'I'm going to beat Bannister! I'm going to beat Bannister!'

The starter fired his pistol. The race was on. Result: First – Bannister R, 68th – Conville, D. I followed the bloodstains all the way round.

'What does he mean, "A pint of ordinary bitter"?'

The Oldie Interview

SISTER WENDY BECKETT

Although she regards herself as socially inadequate, and spends her days in silence, seclusion and prayer, Sister Wendy has the gifts of a born communicator. **Naim Attallah** *is but one of millions to fall prey to her charm*

Portrait by **Jane Bown**

Sister Wendy, your family was extremely devout. Do you think in that sense it could be said you 'inherited' your faith, rather than came to it by a more personal route?

I would qualify 'extremely devout'. We were not a family who had prayers in common, for example. It was just obvious to me that my parents' faith mattered a lot to them by what they were, as opposed to what they said, and I'm sure that's how most children receive their religion, as opposed to their faith. They get their politics through their family, their religion through their family, but faith comes completely from your own depths and your own personal contact with God, and it is faith which fills out the bare bones of the religion. Faith is the spirit; religion is the body. I inherited my Catholicism, but the faith was a gift to me, direct from God.

How do you define God. Who is God?

God is mystery... we can't possibly know. The point really about being a Christian is that we believe only one person ever was able to look deep into the mystery and turn round and say to us 'it's father...' Jesus saw that the infinite mystery was the father, it was total supportive love, and we live in the strength of that. But we can never make a definition of God or have an idea of God, because then it is something limited. We can't define what by its essence is so infinitely beyond the concepts of our mind.

Why exactly is chastity so important? What has chastity got to do with God? He has after all created our bodies which are designed to function in particular ways, including sexually. That must surely also be a gift from God.

I agree with you totally. God gave us these beautiful bodies, and he loves all parts of them. Anybody who feels that the vow of chastity involves pain and frustration should not take it, because God does not like us to suffer. He takes no pleasure out of people making themselves frustrated and unhappy. But we only have so much psychic energy, and for myself I know I could never have had a deep emotional relationship with anybody, let alone a sexual relationship – even on the emotional level I couldn't have done it. All my energies are utterly absorbed in loving God. This is not everyone's vocation; obviously most people's vocation is to come to God through loving somebody else. I don't compare myself to Jesus, but I'm sure he couldn't have had a sexual or emotional involvement at very great depth, because he was so totally taken up with his Father.

Has chastity involved any degree of suffering for you?

No. I'm a totally fulfilled woman, and I don't miss a thing, but I recognise that it is not the normal way to God. The normal way is by receiving his gifts in gratitude and using them. But our vows are functional; they are meant actually to set you free for God. Obedience is to set you free from all the struggles of having a career and making your own decisions; poverty is to free you from all the hassles of earning and possessing; and chastity is to set you free from the psychic involvement with close friends and family. All your energies can then go out; if you're an active religious they go out to the world in service, if you're a contemplative religious they go out to the world in prayer.

Have you ever been criticised for doing what you do?

I may well be, but I don't know. People write saying how they love it, but the world may be full of people saying they think it's shameful. There was someone who wrote a letter after I was on the Terry Wogan show, saying she was very 'disedified' by seeing me showing off on the programme and telling dear Cliff Richard that he was mistaken in his Christian views, and she said that she looked for more humility in a

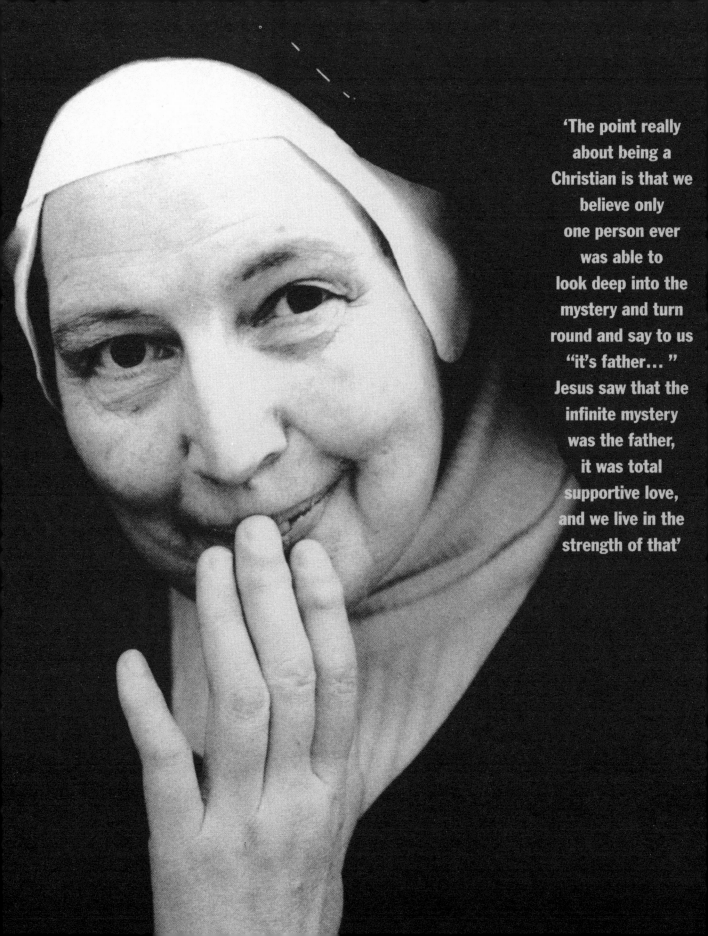

'The point really about being a Christian is that we believe only one person ever was able to look deep into the mystery and turn round and say to us "it's father..." Jesus saw that the infinite mystery was the father, it was total supportive love, and we live in the strength of that'

The Oldie Interview

nun. I wrote back to her and said I was very sorry I had disedified her and would she please pray for me to become humble.

How aware were you of the political situation in South Africa while you were there? Was it possible for you to help in any way?

I was completely unaware. I only knew the servants in my parents' home. My grandmother was a great benefactress of the African schools, and I can remember her buying a great box of sweets when I was about nine and taking me with her to distribute them to the African children, and it never entered my head that this was all terribly wrong. It was only when I was an adult that it came as an awful shock to me to realise that in fact the only citizens of my country were white. It just shows that you can live in a situation that's crying out aloud to God for vengeance and never see it; rather like the American southerners who say all their black servants are so happy. It shocks me now to think that we were so fond of our servants and we did not see the injustice of it all. I pray a lot, and I get very upset about South Africa, and although I tremble for them at the moment, there's no doubt whatever that it's got to be lived through.

How did it come about that you entered an order in Sussex, such a long way from South Africa?

The nuns with whom I went to school in South Africa were an international order in America, on the Continent, in England, in Africa and in Japan, but their novitiate was in Sussex which I entered 47 years ago on 1st February. I keep that day with great joy.

When you are in your caravan do you talk to anybody?

No, I don't. I don't live with the other sisters. After morning prayers, the sister who looks after me brings me some coffee and sits down and tells me what's going on. Perhaps I'll say to her that I need a new pair of socks, or something like that, but I don't chat. As soon as Mass is over I take my basket of provisions and go back to the caravan and I stay there all day in complete silence.

'Guilt and sin were words never mentioned in my upbringing, and when I hear people talking like this I just feel very sad. If this is the way they think, they've got the wrong end of the stick, they never have been Catholics'

But how is it possible to live in silence when you so obviously like people and enjoy talking?

This is going to sound very rude but I've never met anybody I'd rather talk to than be silent with God. That to me is the height of joy.

How did you reconcile your love for art, and its liberal expression, with the rather repressive teaching of the convent?

I was never taught repressively at a convent.

Would you dare in a convent, for example, to look at a painting of a nude and discuss pubic hair - as you have done in your books?

Yes, of course I would. I would expect all nuns to have reverence for the body God has given them. Anything else is narrow puritanism which has nothing to do with the faith. For some extraordinary reason this narrow puritanism seems to have taken over, but it's not Christian. Jesus speaks freely about excretion, for example, about faeces coming out, and He certainly didn't feel this wasn't quite nice. This fear of the body is a late development, and of course a lot of people have been taught it by the Irish, who have a real puritanical fear of the body. But I was lucky; I knew nothing of all this guilt that is supposed to cling to Catholicism. Guilt and sin were words never mentioned in my upbringing, and when I hear people talking like this I just feel very sad. If this is the way they think, they've got the wrong end of the stick, they never have been Catholics, because this is not the teaching of the Church. It is a version of it that is unfortunately favoured by people who like the tyranny of puritanism. God doesn't live in blacks and whites; God lives in the lovely fluid greys of the world, and He asks us never to accept black and white from above, but to look into our own hearts and see what is true.

Is the urge to live an entirely solitary life a strength or a weakness, do you think? Christ after all seems to have been rather a gregarious person...

I'm positive it's a weakness. It's a life only for the very weak who cannot stand the normal strains of life, perhaps the almost neurotically weak, who also have such a strong passion for God that they can impose upon their life the austerity that the life demands.

Is there some connection between the contemplation of works of art and the spiritual life? Is it an avenue to God?

For me it is, absolutely, and I think this is potentially what it is for everybody. Whenever you look at real art you're looking at something that's challenging you to be more wholly human, to enter more deeply into truth; and whenever you touch truth, you touch God. God is truth.

But I thought God was indefinable...

He is indefinable, but wherever there is beauty and truth, there is God. Yes, I put that badly, you're quite right to have corrected me. Truth and beauty don't encompass God but their presence shows us the presence of God, just as light shows us the presence of the sun.

'God is asking me to do this now,' you said in an interview. How do you know it is God?

You only know what God is asking of you through the circumstances of your life. The context of your life tells you. The Good Samaritan knew that God was asking him to succour the man who had fallen among thieves because he actually met the man. If he hadn't met the man, God wouldn't have asked him; but that's the only way God does speak to people, through the actual context of their lives. Whom does God ask you to love? The people you know, the people you live with. So we only have to look at our lives to know what we're called upon to do.

You have expressed some ideas which do not at first sight seem compatible with the faith. In what sense, for example, can homosexuality not matter, given the views expressed in the Bible and in the tradition of the Church?

Let me give you a parallel: the Church condemned Galileo for saying that the earth went round the sun, and not vice versa. Only when everybody, the man in the street, understood, and it was common knowledge that the earth did indeed go round the sun, not the other way round, did the Church accept it. The fact that

The Oldie Interview

Beauty doesn't mean pretty; beauty means something of the spirit which can show itself in a misshapen form. Beauty is often horrible, terrifying...

Top: The caravan in Norfolk that is Sister Wendy's hermitage

Above: On her recent Grand Tour, with Botticelli's 'Birth of Venus' in the Uffizi, Florence

Previous page: In Rome, with friend

the Bible seemed to say the opposite was meant to be poetry. Now, I don't believe the Church is the glorious unspotted leader, marching ahead of humanity; that's not the Church Jesus left us. The Church is a poor wounded creature and it's moved at the pace of the slowest. When the man in the street understands the full meaning of love, then the Church will understand it, and a lot of the present prohibitions will just dissolve. But they haven't dissolved yet, and I don't think it helps people for somebody who's totally committed to the faith as I am to say the Church as yet hasn't fully understood. I'll say it to a friend, but I don't think it's wise to say it in public, because it doesn't help the Church.

There will be many who see the campaign for the ordination of women as just another feminist effort directed by women with no interest in religion. Do you see it as principally a theological or a political matter?

I don't know very much about the ins and outs of it, but to me it's a completely theological matter, or perhaps I should say it's a matter of practical understanding of God's plans for His children, and in God's eyes gender is not very important. I don't think it's just a question of feminism. Men don't realise how terrible it's been for some women; the bright girl in the family who wasn't educated because her stupid brother had to get all the money; or the clever woman in a firm who could take responsibility easily and is overlooked because the men get it and make a mess of things. There is a lot of buried frustration and it'll take a long time for this to work itself out, but I think we'll see light at the end of the tunnel. Think how recently women weren't allowed to go to university, or to vote. We forget what enormous strides have been made to see women as fully

human; there are more strides to be made still, but we are making progress.

You were reported as saying of sexual activity: 'There is not going to be a personal involvement, but I would cheer it on.' That seems a remarkably liberal view for a nun. What did you mean?

I don't remember saying it, but if I did say it, I would have meant that for me there is no sexual involvement and never has been and never will be because God is complete fulfilment, but I'm delighted that the world is full of people who appreciate God's good gift to them. Of course sex is something to cheer on. Why did God invent it if He didn't want it to be something of delight to people?

You speak of art as giving insight into mysteries. Can you elaborate on that? What sort of mysteries are involved here, and what is it to have 'insight' into a mystery?

Art is working at a very profound level. It is almost by definition at the level of the mysterious. It is concerned with those things in us that are there but which we find it so hard to bring to the surface of our consciousness: the desire for goodness, the desire to be fully human, the desire for eternal life, the desire for happiness, the desire to make sense of suffering. A very great picture opens you up to a lot of these truths, perhaps not always consciously, but you're stirred at those depths, and if you have the kind of mind that wants to reflect upon what the experience has been, then you would have conscious insight into truths that perhaps you hadn't realised before you were faced with that great work of art. A work of art that leaves you untouched is not a great work of art, or you haven't opened yourself enough.

How do you think the idea of art as beauty correlates with paintings whose subject matter is ugly - of dead bodies, for example, or indeed of any picture in which the artist wishes to depict something ugly, like Goya's '3rd May 1808'.

There is a beauty in ugliness, you know. Think of Rembrandt's old people, with gnarled features, but absolutely lit up with wisdom. Goya was indeed painting something very ugly but he was showing the human spirit grappling with it – that's the beauty. Beauty doesn't mean pretty; beauty means something of the spirit which can show itself in a misshapen form. Beauty is often horrible, terrifying, with nothing of the attractive or the gentle about it; but it is equally beautiful.

You admire the skill (which you say you yourself will never attain) of being able to use words so exactly that no one will misunderstand them. Would you agree that the language of faith is singularly imprecise, that it is impossible for one person to understand what another means by 'knowing God', for example?

Absolutely. I agree totally. Not only have you a language difficulty here, you have a moral difficulty in that we only know as much of God as we want to know. Psychologists say that if you're faced with an unbearable truth, you won't bear it, you'll just block it out. And I can understand this. In a way, the truth about God is unbearable because it is so enormously large, and it's easy to see that people may not want to hear it. With the real God you're completely out of control the minute you look at Him. So where there's a difficulty of language, there's a difficulty of desire. Oh yes, the language of religion is absolutely hopeless. Everybody has a different picture in mind, and some are horrible. That's why I say I love atheists, because they're people who've thrown out a false God. They were perfectly right to disown the kind of God they thought was God. The point is they haven't met the real God yet, because if you meet the real God you can't possibly not love him. So hurrah for atheists.

What is your attitude towards death?

As a child I looked forward very much to dying. I thought how wonderful it would be to leap into the arms of God. Now I see it as the one chance to make a great act of faith, because we all go into the darkness in death. God says, 'Though he slay me, yet will I trust in him.' When God puts the knife to the throat, and I go into the darkness, I will be able to make an act of faith that I've never made before, so in that sense I'll be very glad to die.

The Death File

Equally convincing as a repressed butler in 'Remains of the Day' or a deranged killer in 'The Silence of the Lambs', **Sir Anthony Hopkins** chews over the gristle of mortality

My ideal way to go To be wide awake and fully aware of drifting away as I have heard others describe 'after-death experience'. Actually, I don't care how I go, but go I surely will.

My life expectancy I never think about it – but, now I've been asked – ninety-four.

My last words Bye all!

My method of disposal Cremation…

My funeral arrangements …with no service – no funeral arrangements and throw the ashes where you will (or perhaps put me in an egg-timer – let me do some work somewhere because I haven't done a stroke since I've been on this mortal coil).

My special effects Sunny day.

Memorial service Memorial services are an abomination and I refuse to go to them. This is my one passion – to avoid them. So if any member of my family breaks my last will and testament on this issue, I will come back and haunt them.

Who would you like to meet on the other side? My grandfather.

My thoughts on life and death If there is an after-life then this life is a dream so I may as well enjoy it and not take any of it seriously – which I don't any more. And, if there is no after-life and this is it, then I had still better enjoy it now, which I do. Anyway, I believe all of it is a dream, and one day I will wake up and say, 'What was that all about?' which incidentally is the question I ask every day.

Compiled by **Richard Middleton**

THE WORLD ACCORDING TO
Enfield Senior

ONE OF the pleasures of getting older is that one cares less and less about more and more. I never wanted a Lagonda, a Rolex or a yacht, but now I also do not want a racehorse or a house in the Dordogne. I do not want a holiday in the Carribean as there is always a frightful noise and nothing to do but sit on sand.

For lots of money I could get a grey vest, white shirt, woman's cardigan, ill-fitting blue jacket and a pull-over to tie round my waist, and if I put them all on and did not shave for three days I should look like the male model in the *Times*, or a tramp, and I don't want to do that either.

Going without things I do not want has become a constant source of virtuous entertainment, and if I were a reformed alcoholic I should spend a lot of time looking in the windows of off-licences. It was in this frame of mind that I was at Victoria station having an innocent and peaceful time wandering through the shops looking at all the things I did not want. It became a sort of litany: 'I do not want any patterned socks. I do not want any jockey briefs.' Then into W H Smith: 'I do not want the *Farmers' Weekly*. I do not want any Jilly Cooper.'

Then suddenly: 'Hallo, here is a lady sitting at a desk who wants £2 and my signature. She says she will analyse my character. But if

Where are you, Joanna Lumley? I want to give you £4 worth of Belgian chocolates

I give her my signature it will be easy for her to forge it. Is she that sort of person? Perhaps I need to analyse her character. Anyway I know quite enough about my own character to be going on with. But consumer spending helps the economy. Green shoots! Should I give her £2 and sign "David Mellor" or "Alan Clark"?'

I did not. I wandered on, chanting softly to myself, rather like Pooh Bear, 'I do not want to give away my signature. I do not want my character analysed.' Then suddenly: 'Chocolates!'

Now that was serious. When it comes to chocolate I can take it or leave it alone, but if my wife had to choose between me and

chocolates, she would choose chocolates.

They were Belgian chocolates, which was bad. Or rather, it was good, because she loves Belgian chocolates, but it was bad because they came from Belgium. Buying chocolate is good for the Third World, but buying Belgian chocolates is bad for the balance of payments. Well, it was only a small hole in the trade figures; I bought ten and they cost £4.

Then it hit me! Just as the girl finished sealing up the chocolates I realised: 'It is Lent! My wife will not eat these chocolates until Easter, which is weeks away.

What am I to do? Shall I have my character analysed twice, and pay in chocolates? No, I want to meet someone nice to whom I can give them. To whom would I like to give my chocolates?

Joanna Lumley! Where are you, Joanna Lumley? I want to give you £4 worth of Belgian chocolates. She is not here. I wish it was *The Oldie* luncheon, then I could go around giving chocolates to famous people.'

But the final solution to the chocolate problem was that I forgot them on the train and I expect they were mistaken for a bomb and blown up. As Kai Lung might have said, 'It is unwise for one of a forgetful turn of mind to place the Emperor's jewels upon the luggage rack of a river boat.'

A further point I wish to make is that my column has at different times been called cantankerous and even curmudgeonly, but it will be seen that on this occasion my thoughts were all directed towards the good of humanity, the benefit of the economy, the proper observation of religious festivals, and giving harmless pleasure to my family and people whom I admire at a distance.

It is not right to call a man of such an amiable disposition 'cantankerous' just because he gets irritated by foul-mouthed comedians, pornographic novelists, Andy Warhol, Dennis Potter, and one or two other things. 'Right-minded' would seem a better adjective.

'Agnes is leaving me for someone with more air miles'

IT WAS SPRINGTIME in New York City, 1918. At eighteen I had been studying music, drama, and, of course, singing for four years. I was a very ambitious student, encouraged by teachers and my parents.

I studied for two years with Fernando Tanara, the opera coach from Milan. A dear tubby man with a beard, he insisted that I learn at least six operas (vocally ridiculous at my age, but marvellous training for what was to come). Then he suggested that I sing for his friend, the director of the Metropolitan Opera, in order to get advice as to where I should be sent in Italy – some little opera house, 'now that the war was over'.

These opera houses were greenhouses really, where singers learned and blossomed – or failed. After several years, some lucky ones would be good enough to get to the big cities of the world. And so end at the pinnacle, the Opera in New York, Paris or Milan.

One May morning in 1918 it happened. Of course I knew the inside of the Metropolitan – its red and gold baroque magnificence – but now I saw it for the first time from the stage. It seemed a black infinity – a nowhere, awe-inspiring, frightening.

Somewhere near the stage five shadows were huddled in their seats, murmuring in Italian. One electric light bulb on a metal stalk stood by the piano, a spot of deliverance in the

my first job

Mary Ellis

distance of that huge stage, soaring up to the sky. Dear maestro Tanara sat on the piano-stool, waiting. A sickening silence.

Then I heard my own voice, disembodied, asking the black emptiness if I might have a table and a chair, to act my scene from Massenet's *Manon*. A deadly pause, before a loud, rasping Italian voice from the stalls asked an invisible stage hand to bring the requested items.

He also brought another rehearsal light and planted it near me, and gave me a wink and a thumbs-up sign. I was thrilled. I had wings! (No nerves – that would come later.) A deep breath, and I was away! Acting and singing 'Adieu, notre petite table' and enjoying every minute. How I did it, I will never know. At the end, I was trembling, and ready to faint.

Signor Tanara told me to sit down and wait. The light by the piano was

switched off. An almost palpable silence cloaked me. I saw Tanara leave the stage, looking grim. He joined the Italian ghosts in the stalls.

After an eternity, it seemed, he came back. The tears were running down his face into his beard. My heart gave a lurch. I must have failed him so miserably. He hugged me and his voice was choked with tears. All I could say was, 'Maestro, I'm sorry, so sorry.' Then it came – the shock: 'But *cara*, listen. They gave no advice. They offer you a four year contract, here!'

Four years! To sing all the established 'young' roles – a debut in the première of Puccini's *Triptych*; Mytyl in the new French opera of *The Bluebird*; and particularly Gianetta in *L'Elisir d'amore* with Caruso, Scotti and Barrientos (the dream of every young singer was to sing with Caruso); Siebel in *Faust* with Farrar – and so on.

I gathered up enough voice to go to the edge of the stage and say 'Thank you, thank you' and had just enough strength to walk off the stage without falling down. I heard their soft laughter following me.

My long life in the theatre (because it came to pass that after those first four magical years I defected to the real theatre) started as Nerissa in *The Merchant of Venice*. But music is still in my bloodstream – and every new 'job' still has the thrill of that first one. The magic persists – even at ninety-three.

THE OLDIES   **TONY HUSBAND**

Darling can you come home....

It's the tortoise...

... He's run away...

PARTNERS – and how to

Can West ruff a singleton or must dummy finesse? **Kjartan Poskitt** *fails to explain*

ARE YOU one of those people who can roll the front of their tongue into a U-shape? Some people can and others can't, it's simply a question of genetics. The same is true of playing bridge, apart from the fact that those who can do it always assume that those who can't must be desperate to learn. 'Come and make up a foursome,' they say lightly, 'you'll soon get the hang of it.' If you are too cowardly to decline, you'll quickly realise that what you've been offered is thirteen cards and a persecution complex. For you, then, here is a guide to surviving the evening.

The first point to register occurs as soon as the four of you sit down. Take careful note of the person sitting opposite to you. This person is your partner. You are called 'we' and the other two are called 'they'.

In games such as Monopoly or the 100 metres sprint, you can only let yourself down. Alternatively, when you mess up in large team games, at least your team mates have each other for consolation. The trouble with bridge is that you have one partner who is going to stare at you and you alone. 'We' can be very miserable.

The other thing about bridge is that those who play it take it so damn seriously. As soon as you've completely messed up a hand, one of several things may happen, depending on your partner.

The Know-All Partner (which in bridge is most of them) will slither round the table for a post mortem. This involves asking you to recall every one of the thirteen cards you had. You will then be told exactly in what order you *should* have played them. Naturally this information is terribly useful should you happen to pick up exactly the same hand again, but at odds of 635,013,455,971 to 1 against, don't hold your breath. Besides, even if it did come up, you can bet trumps would be different.

The Haughty Partner simply goes 'tch' and smiles weakly at 'they' for sympathy. If you are with an Aggressive Partner, wear shin pads.

For the uninitiated, bridge is a bit like whist in that you're trying to take tricks. One mammoth trap to avoid is taking a trick if your partner already has it in the bag. 'They' will snigger and 'we' will sulk. Happily, bridge has one huge saving grace. For each hand of cards, one player gets to be 'dummy'. Being dummy is bliss. All you have to do is put your cards face up on the table and slope off for a drink. This leaves your partner wondering how he or she got stuck with a dummy hand that holds nothing higher than a nine.

ILLUSTRATION BY STEVEN APPLEBY

The odd thing is that you'd think being dummy should be pretty popular, and in any normal game you would take turns at it. However, in bridge, with a bit of almost undetectable cunning it's quite easy to make sure it's usually you. The secret is in the bidding.

Bidding in bridge boils down to betting on how many tricks you are going to get. Many dull books are devoted to this subject but what they never cover is the blessedly simple way of maximising your time as dummy. When the bidding starts going round, say 'no bid' when it comes to your turn.

avoid them
lever Wanted to Know about Bridge

E EVENING:

GASP!! Sorry.

— Nude players.

ne thousand points to us, I think!

iv — A bridge-building competition.

However, if your partner has said anything apart from 'no bid', then take note. Suppose your partner has said 'two hearts'. Simply add one to the number and repeat the same suit. In this case you would say 'three hearts'. If your partner goes on to say a different suit, again add one, but move to the new suit! Should 'they' start saying higher numbers than you, keep repeating your partner's last suit but raising the number.

If this rule is adhered to, your partner will always win the bid and you will always be dummy!

NB For complex technical reasons, you must never go over seven or you'll blow it. Also, you should remember to pick up your cards before you start bidding or else it will look suspicious.

Sadly the dummy wheeze can come unstuck if your partner never bids, and you may be forced to play your own cards. You may then care to resort to one of the following emergency proceedures:

1 Select the biggest card in your hand, preferably a trump. When a couple of tricks have gone, have a coughing fit and drop the card under the table. Play on until you've run out of cards and then 'notice' that everybody else has one left. This has two effects. Firstly, the hand will be scrubbed. Secondly, and certainly more entertainingly, the psychological effect on some bridge superbrain wondering where the king of clubs was is not to be underestimated.

2 Pretend to get locked in the lavatory, but rather than hold the evening up, insist on playing your cards under the door. It's just possible that your gamesmanship might be admired even if you are unable to do the basics like follow suit, deal, pass the cheese straws, etc.

3 Finally, if you've got a bit of real nerve, try the bluff. If you really are playing with demented bridge freaks you'll see that after the bidding they only play one trick. Then they throw down their cards announcing: 'That's yours, all those are good, the lead then takes the ace into the dealer's left, and you get the last one. 1,200 points above the line to us, I make it.'

What rot, eh? However, nobody likes to question the wisdom of statements like that lest they be regarded as mentally sub-normal. Consequently anyone bold enough can join in.

If you are feeling unsure, you can enhance your credibility by conceding that 'they' have won! Your partner will not mind losing if it's generally thought that he or she regularly plays with someone of the calibre to declare: 'That one and a short follower leads the response to a triple demand point slam, of course you'd duck the finesse for the follow through giving you vulnerable preference half play. More gin anyone?'

Follow this up with immediate congratulations on the overshare turn bidding and you're away. There's just one snag that you must bear in mind. Such a combination of sporting manner with modest brilliance is rare. You may be invited to play again.

PRESS

Roy Greenslade

MY FIRST newspaper office was located in a little house which backed on to Barking station. Our desks rattled when the fast train from Southend to London passed. All the typewriters were filthy, with keys that stuck and ribbons that refused to turn.

The editor was both illiterate and pedantic, a combination which provided me with unending material for satire at his expense. He was also decent and honest, qualities I only later realised were more important and enduring.

On my first day the editor introduced me to the local cinema manager and the undertaker. During the following years I met both of them almost every week, one for openings, the other for closings.

I was also taken by the previous junior reporter – relieved at last to have moved one notch up the rung – to Ilford station. Now it would be my daily task to transport a package of articles, pictures and adverts to the guard on the Chelmsford train, hoping he remembered to off-load it.

After six months serving my probation I was indentured as an apprentice-journalist and went off every Friday to the West Ham College of Further Education to learn shorthand from a Mrs Robinson, practical journalism from a Mr Humphrey and English from a Mr Compton.

Strange, you might think, that names from more than 30 years ago should come so easily to mind. They remain more vivid than the years in between because, whatever I pretended at the time, I really enjoyed myself. Schooldays were not the best of my life; the *Barking Advertiser* days were.

Those happy memories floated back when I attended the Regional Press Awards. Before making presentations

to the winners, Neil Kinnock spoke of local newspapers as 'a great public service'. I think the hyperbole is still justified in spite of the profit motive and the inevitable move towards monopoly. But during my years at the *Advertiser*, it was hard to realise I was playing a key role in fostering our nation's democracy.

I recall drinking gallons of beer with policemen in pubs, after hours of course; yawning through interminable council committee meetings about the siting of bollards; being deafened in empty dance halls by groups of pimply teenagers who dreamed of following the Beatles to stardom.

The closest I got to the democratic heart of our nation was none too uplifting either. True, the local MP did take me to debates at the House of Commons and introduce me to a host of the Labour government's shining

they should be placed in the paper, how the pages should be designed. Bill would arrive in the morning quoting a *Daily Express* intro as though it was a Shakespearean couplet.

And all the time – at inquests, school speech days, football matches, boxing tournaments, factory gate union meetings, election rallies, Rotary dinners, charity dances – I never stopped learning. About the community, the law, the activity of journalism. I discovered not only what was permissible but what was desirable, the only way journalism can both enhance people's lives and impinge on them. Local newspapers cannot afford to mistreat their audiences.

In my final year of apprenticeship I convinced myself it was forced labour, crossing off the days until I would be free to take the next step towards Fleet Street. I don't

I was unaware how or what I learned. A bit of advice from the other reporters at Barking magistrates court helped. The editor's heavy sighs when he read my copy gave me clues

stars. But his name was Tom Driberg and his idea of maintaining close relations with the local press consisted of taking the rawest young male reporter to Soho's Colony Club, filling him with drink and offering him a bed for the night in his Wimpole Street flat. And Tom would never have thought of claiming he liked to share beds merely to save money.

Discovering how to escape Tom's attentions was all part of the learning process. Acquiring the skills of journalism and of life went naturally together.

I was unaware how or what I learned. A bit of advice from the other reporters in the press box at Barking magistrates court helped. The editor's heavy sighs when he read my copy gave me clues.

My immediate seniors, Lesley and Bill, who are both top-flight journalists today, criticised and corrected. Our conversations were all about how to get stories, how to write them, which was the most perfect headline, where

regret leaving when I did, but I am indebted to the process which ensured that I must learn slowly and thoroughly. College was probably less important than the on-the-job training, but together they were invaluable.

I therefore find common cause with Nick Davies, one of Britain's finest investigative journalists, who has become so alarmed at the lack of enforced training that he argues we are witnessing 'the final disintegration of an old profession'.

Journalists who fail to spend at least two years in the provinces, he wrote in the *Guardian*, have no idea how to do their job: 'They don't know one end of a libel law from the other, they can't do shorthand, they don't know the difference between a feature and a school essay, they have never been taught how to run an investigation or even an interview...'

Hear, hear! Enhancing the professionalism of journalism is a public service. Its opposite is a public scandal.

Crawling Back to Mary

In Tinos, they go to heaven on their knees. Words and pictures: **Nick Baker**

NOT MANY TOURISTS come to Tinos, a Greek island in the Aegean just north of Mykonos. But on 15th August every year it is filled with thousands of pilgrims and gypsies who debouch from the ferries for the Festival of the Virgin Mary. In 1822 an icon of the Virgin, or Panagia, with miraculous healing power was found at the top of the hill above the port. The Greek Orthodox Church built a huge basilica, the Panagia Evangelistria, on the site and it became a centre of pilgrimage for those seeking cures.

I was in Tinos in time to watch their arrival. Pilgrims with cases, gypsies

carrying huge bundles and rolled-up rugs. Many gypsy families drove off the ferries in Japanese pick-up trucks loaded with plastic stacking chairs and staggering sheep. They sold the chairs and ate the sheep.

Gypsy girls looked spectacular in full-sleeved long dresses of glittering man-made fibre, like beautifully wrapped Christmas presents. Gorgeous silver and black patterns, gold, cerise and vibrant metallic blue flashed like sun on sea. Older, fatter women went for black and white designs. Young gypsy men had long black hair curling over shirts of material like crazy curtain fabric.

If you are a pilgrim seeking a cure or particular blessing this is what you do: get off the ferry and start crawling on hands and knees towards the basilica over a kilometre away at the top of the hill. (You'll need a minder to help you negotiate the traffic.)

Most pilgrim crawlers seemed to be women aged between thirty and sixty but I did see several youngish men in jeans and a lot of teenage girls. One

tiny hunchbacked woman of about thirty passed my chair quite quickly. Some women in black dresses followed, knees bandaged against the tarmac, hands encased in yellow washing-up gloves.

Once past the bandstand the pilgrims face the main crawl up the hill, about a one in ten. On the unshaded, crawling side of the road, minders can buy icons printed on blockboard with added gold leaf, blue glass eyes to ward off the Evil Eye, little replicas of breadboards used in the early Christian Church and long candles wrapped in dull red paper. A 5ft candle cost 1,000 drachmas – about £2.60. I was told that they were no sooner lit in the anteroom at the Church doorway than snuffed out, dropped through a trapdoor, melted down and recycled for the long haul up the hill again.

Also on sale are little tin rectangles embossed with parts of the body – legs, arms, torsos (female), whole figures, even a house. The idea is to hang the effigy of the bit that needs healing in the basilica and for the icon's miraculous power to attend to the rest. I had

a bad sty in my right eye. The tin eyes were all left ones, but I bought one anyway. It was so nice that I kept it – and the sty.

Near the top of the hill a runner of harsh grey carpet rivetted to the road gives some comfort to the exhausted pilgrims. I saw one young man with two 5ft candles and an icon tied to his back inching his way up on his stomach. Next day he was limping towards one of the ferries carrying a bazouki.

Later, when the crowds had gone, I went in and looked at the Panagia icon. It is under glass and completely obscured by silver beads and jewellery. There were flowers all around and metal sculptures of ships hanging above. I saw one or two cartridges with bullets hanging there, too.

On the morning of the festival my girlfriend and I stood in the line of people waiting in the middle of the street for the procession bringing the icon down for the seafront ceremony. Boy Scouts and Girl Guides came past on both sides bearing Greek flags, followed by the town band and

bearded priests in black hats, escorted by marines casually swinging fixed bayonets.

An acolyte said something crossly out of his beard at me and pointed to my hat. Ah, of course! I whisked it off as four sailors appeared carrying the icon under a silver dome on a long wooden stretcher over the heads of the people. The police herded us under the stretcher, a bit like sheep-dipping. Hands touched the framework, mouths kissed it. I ducked underneath and was ejected out the other side between lines of marines and unsmiling police.

I noticed a dark patrol boat slide into the port; then a small group came walking quickly from the quayside. I had been told that deposed King Constantine might seize this chance to meet his people while on his two-week sail-about in the Aegean. But I hadn't done my homework. Was that him in the sunglasses, smile and blue suit or was he the small man with the

slicked back hair? Many Greeks near me looked sullen or uncertain, others smiled, waved, took photos. Later I identified the former King clearly in a photo I took.

One thing I am sure of. The former King of Greece, Constantine II, 'Tino' to his friends, Mr C Glucksburg to others, the deposed ex-Ruler of the Hellenes, walked up the hill to the Panagia Evangelistria. He did not go up on his hands and knees in yellow washing-up gloves.

Miles Kington

MEMORIES OF MEL

WHEN I STARTED writing for the *Independent* they lent me a small word processor called a Tandy 200, which you could plug into the telephone system via a modem to send your writing down the line to the *Independent*'s mighty computer so that the sub-editors would, a moment later, be reading it on their screens. This was fine when I was at home. When I was out and about, it wasn't so easy.

If, for instance, I was coming up to London in the train from Bath, I would often try to write a piece in the 100 minutes the journey took. Fair enough. But when I got to London, I then had to find a friendly place which would allow me to plug the damned thing in to their BT socket. I traded on *Private Eye*'s charity once or twice, but one day, when en route to Bush House, I had the brilliant idea of popping into Mel Calman's Cartoon Gallery in Museum Street and asking to borrow their socket.

Pat, who was in charge when Mel wasn't there, saw no reason why not, and was in fact curious to see how the thing worked, so she allowed me to lie full-length on the floor and scrabble around with the fittings at wainscot level. I was halfway through transmitting my article when Mel walked in and found me crouching in a corner like a man trying to fiddle an electricity meter.

'Is that Kington down there?' he said in amazement. The scene repeated itself many times, with a varying script. I don't know how it always came to pass that Mel should enter when I was halfway through my little ritual, but he always seemed to, and one strong memory of him will always be that of a bearded face peering down and a voice saying: 'Oh God, is that Kington again? Will he be here long? Does he need feeding…?'

> **I don't think I could ever again think of attacking a rival without laughing**

Now that Mel Calman has died, life seems a bit greyer.

I didn't know him that well, but I knew him a little over a long period. I can remember sitting next to him one morning in Valerie's, his Old Compton Street haunt, and asking him for advice about my marriage so I knew him at least that well. This must have been in 1980, as that is the year my first marriage broke up, and I was full of those conflicting emotions of bitterness, fraughtness and all the other things which are useful ingredients for a broken marriage.

'You're looking a little upset,' said Mel. 'What's up?'

'We're trying to make the job more customer friendly, Thornley'

'Tell me one thing, Mel,' I said. 'Do you think physical revenge is justified in matters of the heart?'

'No,' he said calmly. 'I tried it once, and it didn't work at all.'

'??' I said.

'Oh, it was some years back when I was pretty certain that my loved one was having an affair with a specialist in Harley Street. Well, I was going through Harley Street one day when I saw this man letting himself in to his place of work. I rushed up the steps to his posh front door, called out his name and started beating at him with my fists, somewhat ineffectually. He just took hold of my wrists, pulled my hands down and said: "Now, Mel, let's not externalise our emotions, shall we?" And d'you know something? It's impossible to go on beating a man up under those circumstances…'

You'll notice that he hadn't answered my question directly, and yet he had indirectly, and I don't think I could ever again think of attacking a rival without laughing. You'll notice also that the role he assigned to himself in that story was very like that of the little man in his cartoons, yet that wasn't how he came across to me in life. If nothing else, he was the only cartoonist I ever knew who could organise things. Most cartoonists find it hard enough just to get themselves on the right train home; Mel not only organised his Cartoon Gallery, but was the moving spirit behind full-blooded efforts to set up a national museum of British cartooning.

I once saw him give a talk at the Edinburgh Book Festival and it was one of the best monologues I ever

heard. He was equally grave and assured when talking me into joining a panel of judges for a competition run by the Californian Prune Board. It never occurred to either of us that there was something faintly ridiculous about discussing prizes for the best drawing of a prune.

His worried look of certainty, his amazement at finding me on his floor yet again, his incredible niceness to everyone… I shall miss him a lot.

Naomi Sim

LYRICAL BALDERDASH

AN *OBSERVER* journalist recently quoted a friend who told him that writing a novel is easy. You simply get up in the morning, climb three flights of stairs to your study, open the window and throw yourself out.

That has been a great comfort to me. I have wanted to write a novel for a long time and now I know that my failure is not due to lack of talent or imagination, as I had supposed. It's just that I live in a bungalow.

I've only done this and that this morning. Time-consuming, boring, and when you stop there's nothing to show for it. But as I did it I found myself humming 'My Grandfather's Clock' and thought again about the words. Do you recall them?

'My grandfather's clock was too tall for the shelf so it stood ninety years on the floor.'

Question: How tall was it? No one is suggesting that it was a grandfather clock – it was simply too tall for the shelf. It was probably about four feet high, five at the outside. Now, don't fidget; concentrate and listen to the next line.

'It was taller by half than the old man himself, though it weighed not a penny-piece more.' Question: How tall was his grandfather? A five-foot clock would be very heavy, so Question: How fat was his grandfather? No, don't go away. There's more.

'In watching its pendulum swing to and fro many hours he had spent as a boy.' Many hours? Question: How bright was his grandfather?

And the clock is remarkable too. 'For it struck twenty-four when he entered at the door with a blooming and beautiful bride.' Question: How

> **It's extraordinary what can be found if you examine some of our familiar songs more closely**

did his grandmother come to marry this short, fat imbecile? Of course she was blind, poor girl. It's the only explanation. She is never mentioned again in the song although her husband lived to be ninety and she must have produced at least one child. I think, myself, that she miraculously recovered her sight and left on the same day with the man who came to repair the clock.

It's extraordinary what can be found if you examine some of our familiar songs more closely.

What about 'Did you not hear my lady go down the garden singing? Blackbird and thrush were silent to hear the alleys ringing.' Have you ever *counted* the decibels it would take to make an alley ring? Blackbird and thrush were silent. I should damn well think they would be. They'd be gripping their perches for dear life and have their wings stuffed into their ears.

And what about that poor man stumbling about in the snow outside the palace of Good King Wenceslas gathering winter fuel? The king asks his page if he knows him and is told, 'Sire, he lives a good league hence underneath the mountain, close against the forest fence etc'. So what's he doing there? If he lives right against

'The media appear to think you're guilty'

the forest fence one thing's for sure. He hasn't struggled for a league through all that snow just to gather fu–u–el. I think he's a spy, but almost certainly unemployed.

If I think of any other songs that would bear examination I'll wake you.

David Ransom

GROVELLING FIRST CLASS

'HAD A NOVEL experience the other Friday,' said my son as he sat down to breakfast just after Christmas. 'I got to the station to find the Station Master, the girl from the ticket office, and the guy who cleans the lavatories all waiting for me.' 'What for?' I said, not wishing to be distracted from a typically riveting account in the *East Anglian Daily Times* of a mystery pig disease. 'The train had been three and a half minutes late on Thursday,' continued Christopher. 'They were there to apologise.'

'Apologise?' I said incredulously. 'Yeah. And on their hands and knees too. They grovelled before everyone who used the station that morning, handing each of us a written apology. Pretty impressive.'

'Do they always do this?' I asked. 'Always,' said Christopher. 'Mind you, they don't have to do it very often. The previous occasion was well over two years ago. It's the shame, you see. The only way to expiate the guilt is by formal public apology, with lots of bowing and scraping,' he went on. 'Actually, the bit of paper's quite handy. It's so unusual to be held up by the train that you can't use it as an excuse for being late for work. That's why they give you a chitty. So you can show it to your employer.'

'They're punctual, then?'

'I should coco,' said Christopher. 'You can set your watch by them.'

I put down the *East Anglian* and poured another cup of coffee. 'By the way, Christopher,' I said, 'when are you leaving?'

'The plane takes off at 10.30 am on Tuesday morning, so I need to be at Heathrow around nine,' he replied. 'Fine. I'll drop you off at Ipswich station on Monday evening.'

'What do you mean?' said Christopher angrily. 'Can't I go up on Tuesday morning?'

'Well,' I began, 'you could…'

'I get it!' Christopher cut in testily, 'I've only been home a few days and you want to get rid of me already. Christmas comes but once a year. I come home but once a year, and you want to throw me out quicker than the gin bottles!' 'Look here!' I retorted, 'you just won't make it…' 'I suppose you don't want to get out of bed to take me to the station on Tuesday morning?' 'Don't be ridiculous,' I sighed wearily. 'It's just not sensible to assume that you will get to Heathrow by nine o'clock.'

'You're joking, aren't you?' he said. 'It's only 70-odd miles to London. There must be half a dozen trains from Ipswich, any one of which should get to Heathrow in time.'

'Yes, of course there are,' I replied. 'But I wouldn't bank on it.' 'But doesn't BR claim a "to the minute" service?' cried Christopher. 'It might claim it, but it's more of a "to the day" service,' I said. 'You're not in Japan now, you know.'

YAKUZA or crime syndicates in Tokyo publish 'in-house' magazines. Features about learning from oldie criminals' experiences, poetry and opinion pieces are the norm. A recent issue of *Asakazi* (*Morning Wind*) contained a piece by a crime boss who, as a member of the All-Japan Anti-Drug Movement, advised readers to steer clear of trafficking in the capital – despite the fact that most syndicates peddle drugs overseas in places like Hawaii or Australia. **SIMON STOCKTON**

ALTERNATIVE BIOGRAPHY
DIRK BOGARDE

THE SPEEDWAY champion and tragedian's original ambition was to be a film star. In 1947 he was placed under contract by J Arthur Rank and seemed on his way. But then came the movie *Once A Jolly Swagman* (known in the US as *Maniacs on Wheels*) in which he played a dirt-track rider. Bogarde was captivated by the glamour and excitement of speedway. He wanted to do the real thing rather than pretend. He was soon riding professionally for Tamworth and, from 1952, for Cradley Heath. His good looks and courage made him the darling of the crowds.

Between speedway engagements Bogarde resumed his career as an actor. In 1955 he was Midlands champion and a much-praised Freddie in *The Deep Blue Sea* at the Alexandra, Birmingham. In 1958 both careers nearly came to an end when he crashed badly at Gothenburg and also in Strindberg's *The Father* in Stockholm. Only two years later, however, came his *annus mirabilis* when he won the World Speedway Championship at Coventry and immediately afterwards drove to Stratford-upon-Avon to open in *King Lear*. 'His Lear,' wrote Sir Harold Hobson, 'leaves Sir Laurence and Sir John spitting out cinders on the starting line.' **PHILIP PURSER**

Honor Blackman

picks her top six

1 Nelson Mandela
A courageous man who suffered imprisonment with stoicism and emerged apparently unembittered. He walks a political tightrope with great skill.

2 Mikhail Gorbachev
He moved history along by terminating the Cold War. And he has a beautiful voice – a joy in a time of nasal and unresonating politicians' twangs.

3 Maria Callas
What a gift! What work to perfect it. Sadly, I never saw her but thanks to recordings that glorious voice will live for ever.

4 Spencer Tracy
The greatest screen actor. I met him once in Hollywood and wouldn't leave him my phone number. Mad? No. Married.

5 Helena Kennedy
Feisty Scottish barrister, spearhead of Charter 88. She gives one hope that the legal profession might one day catch on to the way 90 per cent of people actually live.

6 J Atkinson Grimshaw
Artist, 1836–93. For the enormous pleasure his work has given me. The moonlight, the water, the mud… And he dared to give up the steady job and go for it.

Right: Honor Blackman, glamour personified

Windows of the Soul

Spectacles are a multi-million pound industry, so a way of improving your eyesight without artificial aids is not likely to be advertised in every opticians.

John Gibbens

talked to Eveyln Sage, Britain's oldest teacher of the Bates method

PERFECT SIGHT *Without Spectacles* was the promise made by Dr W H Bates when he first published a layman's account of his eye treatment methods. This one short book remains the standard text on the Bates method, though many more have been written. He quotes in an epigraph an inscription from Florence:

*Here lies Salvino degli Armati,
Inventor of Spectacles
May God pardon him his sins*

Bates's most celebrated pupil was Aldous Huxley, whose sight was restored from the verge of blindness, and who wrote an account of his cure in *The Art of Seeing*. Art, as an antithesis to Nature, is perhaps a misleading word for the Bates method. Insofar as it implies dedication and application it's a fair description, though. As Miss Evelyn Sage says, the people she can't really help are those who aren't willing to work.

One man who called her up from Sydney and then flew over to see her went home disappointed when he discovered that the miracle on offer was one he had to perform himself. The key to success, Miss Sage makes

clear, is 'relaxation of the mind' and, as she told her Australian visitor, 'I can't change your mind.' 'They think money can buy them everything,' she goes on. 'Money doesn't buy anything worth having really, does it?'

Evelyn Sage is the oldest Bates teacher in Britain and, in all probability, anywhere. She was born in the reign of Queen Victoria, in 1900, and at the far end of the century she is still practising in the house she has lived in for 60 years in East Finchley.

The eldest child of an analytical chemist and a headmistress, she left school at sixteen to join the Bank of England's loans department as a clerk. Thirty-two years later, still at the Bank, she was dealing with sums in millions, where the repercussions of the slightest mistake could be vast. The strain began to tell, and she started getting headaches. 'I went to get some glasses, and in a fortnight they blinded me.'

It was then that she heard of the Bates method. She was taught by Madeleine Fousset, a pupil of Bates himself, and by two of Miss Fousset's pupils, the sisters Marie and Olive Scarlett. She solved her own problem and discovered a métier in the process.

She left the Old Lady, having fulfilled the 30-year term of service she first signed on for, took the Bank's pension with thanks, and after two years' training set up her practice. In the 45 years since then she reckons to have helped people 'from two to eighty-two' as well as training most of the other Bates teachers in London.

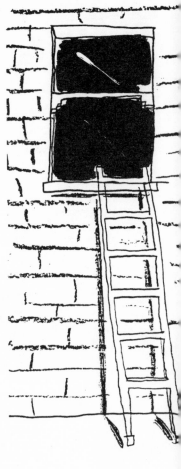

Like most nonagenarians, she regards her longevity askance, unsure why she should have to stay and lose nearly everyone she has known. But she is unequivocal about her choice: 'I've really enjoyed my life,' she says emphatically.

Physical frailty means she has a 'country cousin', sent from an agency in Horsham, to live with her. As for the rest, her mind, her eyes and her smile remain wonderfully bright and clear.

I asked her about her most spectacular successes and she told the story of a man who'd been looking after an estate in Belgium. 'They had elephants to pull

'I question not my Corporeal or Vegetative Eye,' wrote William Blake, 'any more than I would Question a Window concerning a Sight. I look thro' it & not with it'

their trees about, and one hit him in the face. He went to St Mary's in Paddington and they told him, "You're blind in the left eye and you'll soon be blind in the other one." He said to me "Am I blind?" and I said "No, you're not blind." He *wasn't* blind. And he still sees.'

Another woman came to her with blepharitis: 'The eyes stick so they bleed, when you open them in the morning they bleed. They look awful. She came in that door and I thought, Lord! I knew what it was she'd got. Any rate, she's quite pretty these days. I saw her last week. I said to her, "Why *do* you come and see me?" And she said, "Well, I'd feel lost if you weren't here. I feel as long as you're here, I'm safe".'

How is it done? With a series of simple exercises, the aim of which is relaxation. 'It's because people will *try* to see that they can't see,' she says. 'The moment you try, you lose.' By allowing the eyes to work in their own way and breaking down the habits forced on them by stress, people's vision can be improved remarkably.

Bates, who developed his method over long years of practice as an ophthalmologist, records some startling results in his book. But the oculists as a profession remain unmoved: 'They can't bear us,' says Miss Sage. 'If they can hurt us, they will. I've had them tell people not to come here because I'll ruin their sight.' And of course the Bates method is not calculated to gain the support of the opticians' trade.

Those who wear glasses are told to carry on wearing

them when they feel they have to, but Bates believed that lenses as worn by most people, to adjust the focal length of the eyes, are unnecessary. He particularly abhorred the practice of putting young children into glasses, and it was this that first impelled him to try improving their vision through exercise and relaxation.

As he saw it, the case for glasses was simply based on wrong assumptions about the way the eyes work. Whether or not Bates's anatomical ideas are right, the fact remains that his methods have been proven in practice, and the results sit far better with his model than they do with the conventional one.

The accepted wisdom is that the eye focuses light from near or far sources onto the retina by adjusting the thickness of its lens, and that long or short sightedness are the result of deformation of the eyeball, so that the lens can no longer make sufficient accommodation.

Bates pointed out that the eyeball remains, even after death, a flexible organ, quite capable of adjusting its length. He records cases of patients who had had their lenses removed as a result of cataracts, whom he taught to see both near and far – an impossibility if the lens is the eye's only means of focusing.

Likewise presbyopia or 'old-age sight' (the condition for which so many people as they reach middle-age are fitted with reading-glasses) is supposed to be caused by hardening of the lens, so that it no longer adjusts

properly. Yet so prestigious and orthodox a figure as Prof David D Michaels, a clinical ophthalmologist at the University of California, admits in his 1985 reference work *Visual Optics and Refraction* that hardening of the lens has never been demonstrated.

Long and short sightedness are not, Bates argues, the result of wrong-shaped eyeballs but of the muscles which surround them holding the eye in a particular habitual position. Persuade them to relax and the focal length of the eye will adjust itself naturally to whatever is required of it.

One is reminded of William Blake's dictum in *A Vision of the Last Judgement*: 'I question not my Corporeal or Vegetative Eye any more than I would Question a Window concerning a Sight. I look thro' it & not with it.'

In her own unobtrusive way, Miss Sage, like Blake, is a radical. 'I wasn't made to do that sort of thing,' she says of her years in the Bank. 'I know what I want to do in life and I've tried to do it.' Like Blake's, her work may have been overlooked by the world at large, but then it is our persistent *overlooking* which she has dedicated the second half of her long life to correcting.

The latest edition of Dr Bates's book is 'Better Eyesight Without Glasses' (Thorsons, £4.99). Aldous Huxley's 'The Art of Seeing' is published by Grafton (£6.99). A good basic introduction is 'The Bates Method' (Optima, £5.99) by Peter Mansfield.

Modern Life

What is...
Corporate
Identity?

TAKE A BENIGHTED middle-manager, all dodgy vowels and stroppy body-language in his grey shoes and chain-store suit. What does he want? He wants, above all else, to be American. Each new manifestation of half-arsed American lunacy soaks into his brain like canteen tea into a cheap biscuit. Picking through the bestiary at random, let us contemplate Corporate Identity.

You'll agree that it's silly. Corporations, by their nature, have no identity. They are what they produce. Beyond that, who cares?

But this does not suit their executives, who are deeply insecure and lack purpose. They want to be recognised, to be loved, and to look busy.

To these joke people, corporate identity is a blessing. It's a creepy off-shoot of the insane American urge towards anthropomorphism. They

do it to animals. They do it to food. You get singing hamburgers, dancing broccoli, hot dogs with faces, saying 'Hi! I'm so-o-o-o tasty! Eat me!' And they do it to corporations.

You cannot put a face on a corporation, so they do the next best thing. They give them logos. The word – an abbreviation of 'logotype', from the Greek *logos* (a word), and *typos* (an impression) – used to mean a company's name and address set up in one block of type.

Now, however, it means a face. Or, at least, what executives hope will serve the purposes of a face, which are to be instantly recognisable and to disguise what is going on within.

It does not, of course, work, just as politically correct language does not work, because of the inherent permeability of symbols. The meaning keeps leaking through; the leak-proof word or logo has not yet been discovered, and probably never will be.

So, when British Rail decided to revamp its Inter-City 'services', it dropped the old double-arrow logo on the grounds

that nobody could see it without their blood pressure going up. They replaced it with a silly bluebird. Why? Presumably because hucksters with clipboards produced 'market research' to suggest that bluebirds make us all go 'Aaaaah...' and would, by association, make us feel warm and comfy about British Rail.

Of course, it doesn't work. Now our blood pressure goes up when we see the damnable bluebird, or the trumpeting cissies of British Telecom, Labour's rose, or the Tories' fire-

brand. Image-building symbols follow the laws of thermodynamics. If a stinking organisation adopts a fragrant logo, the smell travels but one way. Soon, the logo begins to stink.

But while symbols may be permeable to meaning, executives are not. The alternatives – of pulling their socks up, resigning, or simply blowing their brains out – does not occur to them. One after another, they fall for the compulsive fix of a new logo: Cable and Wireless's leprous circle, presumably meant to represent the state of the earth. Mercury's excitable electrocardiogram crashing into a blob. The Royal Mail's ugly orange-on-red letters, in an oval box, lest we become confused and forget that the Post Office – sorry, Post Office Counters Ltd, pardon me I'm sure – is now an Independent Business, and in our confusion try to post our letters down the drain, or cash our Giros at Debenham's.

As in the 80s, people suckered into buying their council houses declared their owner/occupier status with a fancy new door, so each newly-privatised institution

'Just practising, Miss Belgrove'

40

YOUTHSPEAK

must commission a new logo. The Institute of Hygiene and Tropical Medicine now has an incomprehensible daub instead of the simple dignity of its venerable name. The Defence Research Agency has turned its initials into a picture of a crippled snake sniffing another snake's bottom.

Every polytechnic newly allowed to debase the name of 'university' has acquired a fancy logo with all the pathetic, unconvincing bravery of a 1930s factory-girl in Woolies' rhinestones. Manchester Airport has adopted a parachute as its symbol, and what fun the creatives, yah?, at the agency, right?, must have, like, had selling them that one, okay?

Even respectable firms fall for it. My venerable barber used to sell almond shaving-cream in tubs which said 'Almond Shaving-Cream' on them. Now the tubs say it in tricksy-tweezy 'olde' lettering, with balderdash about 'His Celebrated Establishment' to boot. Peter Ackroyd can get away with that sort of stuff. A barber shop can't – except, of course, to Americans.

But is it worth getting cross about? Yes, I should say, because so many of these logos are standing lies, like a thug putting on a suit to impress the beak.

Because as long as horrible managers think they can fool the public by altering appearances while leaving reality unchanged, their contempt for us will continue to grow.

Because every pound paid to a mincing 'image consultant' for a hospital logo is a pound less spent on the sick.

Because it is nasty, vainglorious visual pollution.

And because, if enough of us get cross enough, we may live to see the joyous day when they strip the aptly-named 'Wally' Olins, *eminence cerise* of the corporate identity business, of his bow tie and silly specs and burn him at the stake. His crime? Heresy, of course: propagating the belief that *in principio erat logos*. **MICHAEL BYWATER**

Winnie the Pooh

IN 1940, when I was nine, I was evacuated out of London, though my parents didn't use that word, implying as it did a scared East End child with a label attached, allocated to a resentful but dutiful volunteer in the country. I was sent, without a label, to stay with friends of theirs in a village near Seaford on the south coast. This was to escape the blitz, although that part of Sussex was in the direct path of German planes unloading their unused bombs on their way back across the Channel.

The house belonged to W A Darlington – the theatre critic of the *Daily Telegraph*. The Darlingtons had a daughter, exactly my age, and also called Phoebe. For nine months we shared our lives and, rather surprisingly, a governess. They also had an older daughter, Anne, who stayed in London because she was in the ATS and sometimes came down for the weekend in her glamorous uniform. (How I wanted to be a Brownie!)

The Darlingtons were close friends with the Milne family, and I knew that *Now We Are Six* was dedicated to Anne because 'now she is seven and because she is so speshal'. (Alright, sickening now, but charming then.)

One day Phoebe and I were taken to visit Anne in her flat in London. We were helping to wash-up the tea things, and just by chance I looked under her kitchen sink. There, in an enamelled washing-up bowl, were Pooh, Piglet, Kanga and Roo. I don't remember seeing Eeyore, but perhaps he was there. Tigger certainly wasn't.

They were instantly recognisable. E H Shepard had drawn them from life, as it were. Anne explained, in a matter-of-fact way, that she was looking after them while Christopher was away fighting the war. They lived under the sink because it made a good air-raid shelter for them.

I was allowed to pick them up, but was too surprised to actually play with them. They seemed to be taken for granted – no-one had mentioned that Pooh and Piglet would be in Anne's flat. I had just found them, and it seemed bad manners to make too much of a fuss about them.

They were rather battered and balding and had obviously belonged to another child and been much loved. But, like every other *Winnie the Pooh* reader, I, too, had played with them, loved them, and shared their adventures in the Forest. I even knew how they thought, and what they talked about.

It was all rather disturbing – like bumping into Jo March of *Little Women* (my favourite book at that time) in Harrods, or meeting *Huckleberry Finn* in Hyde Park. I heard much later that Pooh, Piglet and Kanga survived the war, and used to tour America in a glass case. I wonder where they are now.
PHOEBE WINCH

All my teachers at school were as the walking dead compared to my father who, though he did all my maths homework for me for five years, was not my official teacher at all. He was what is called 'a famous schoolmaster', a housemaster of Sir William Turner's, a 17th-century grammar school turned public school in the late 19th century, which I did not attend, being a girl. It had great pretensions and was famed for its 'Results'.

A dreadful headmaster of my father's first years had remorselessly sacked any master who could not produce 98 per cent passes in the School Certificate. He paid them almost nothing. There were few jobs about. It was *Decline and Fall* time. The stress was awful.

For 17 years boys passed through my life in multitudes, and through our house which was across the road from the school itself. Every evening and at the weekends for several hours my father's voice could be heard ringing out from behind the dining-room door, where he gave extra coaching in maths and physics. He did this for 47 years, dying at ninety-two. To his funeral came old, old men in floods of tears who had been golden lads just after the first war.

My father taught eccentrically. 'I could get a cow into Cambridge,' was his cry. 'I have a little girl at home who can do quadratic equations and she's only five.' (Oh, what a lie.) Across at the school he would begin his lesson at the foot of the main stone staircase, chanting mathematical rules, the classroom above falling utterly but expectantly silent by the time he reached it.

Long before I was born he had stopped the very thought of any boy cribbing by jumping from desk-top to desk-top about the room, which he found excellent exercise. Gales of laughter issued from his classrooms and floated down corridors.

Every form was always the worst he had ever had. There was 'no hope for any of them' and he marked their books in a way that would nowadays

Master in the

He was a schoolmaster both brilliant and beloved, who specialised in 'healing the thick' and claimed to be able to get a cow into Cambridge. But he couldn't teach
Jane Gardam *maths*

ensure instant dismissal by order of the parent. 'FOOL!' he wrote, 'DROP DEAD! Do you want to be KILLED?' A life-long opponent of capital punishment – one of the servants on his father's Cumbrian farm had been executed for murder in 1919 – he would sometimes write 'YOU DESERVE TO HANG'.

Everyone always passed, or if very occasionally there was a failure my father was silent for a week. In the second war some of his boys taken prisoner in Burma survived, they said, only because they re-taught themselves physics from his remembered voice. It was a Cumbrian voice to the end – easy

House

to mimic. He was a tiny man, a mixture of Chaplin and Woody Allen but with Celtic blue eyes. He also was said to have a Celtic sixth sense and could guess the next year's public examinations' questions with ease.

His speciality was with thick boys. 'I heal the thick,' he said, and was very successful with those who needed a mathematical qualification to reach medical school. 'God knows how many people I've killed,' he said. He was adored.

I and my brother were his two failures. Mathematical paralytics. My brother now runs his own farm successfully – a difficult arithmetical job – and I coped with logic and Latin at university so we can't really be dim-witted, but our father could not comprehend our numerical terror before his lightning mind. Even now, four years after his death, I can't read my bank balance or my royalty statements without shaking and, whatever I know I've paid in I always expect my card to be confiscated by the machine. My father kept note of every farthing, halfpenny and sixpence – though he had few enough – all his life, and was in endless consultation with his bank.

He was atrociously mean – the result of an anxious childhood and a cruel father – and was never known to give a present; but gave me more than a present when he had me privately coached in Latin for university entrance. Still afraid of his own father, he was particularly gentle with us as children. I believe that his childhood insecurity went very deep. When I later won a small postgraduate award he said that he was pleased because it had 'done him good in the staffroom' where he had been a respected fixture for over 30 years.

When I began to write fiction he was utterly mystified ('Why couldn't you be a teacher?') and couldn't get on with my books at all, except for the bits about Cumberland ('You're not as good as that fellow Bragg, though mind you he's more of a misery – very slow') and one short story about a repentant daughter, which he said was wonderful.

He sank into terrible depression in old age. We grew further and further apart and only found common cause in his last years when he took to growing roses. (He'd always been a chrysanthemum man – I had not dared compete.) Once he even asked my advice on pruning, and before he died gave me £100 for my ailing rose garden, 'In my memory,' he said.

It was a staggering sum, but I resented the reason for it. I didn't want to see his critical face among the black spot and the thrips, and I bought a hundred pounds-worth of manure instead, planning to buy new roses of my own. Needless to say it was the manure that at once did the trick.

PETER BAILEY

ALTERNATIVE BIOGRAPHY
ROY HATTERSLEY

'HARD-HEARTED Hatters,' the popular pantomime and club comedian, was born Roy Hattersley into a Sheffield family active in local politics; the young Roy was for a while drawn to the Labour cause himself. The lure of the bright lights proved too strong, but he never forgot the passionate debates he had overheard as he played with his toys on the kitchen floor while the grown-ups 'set the world aright with the aid of no more 'n a sup of tea and a slice of seed cake'. His music-hall act 'Silver-tongued Slobberchops' was modelled on a favourite uncle of these boyhood memories.

It was on the club circuit in the Eighties, however, that Hattersley evolved the character with whom he would thenceforth be identified. 'Hard-hearted Hatters they call me,' he would sing as he bounced on to the stage brandishing a replica of the Chancellor of the Exchequer's red despatch box, 'Hard-hearted Hatters's the name'. Audiences convulsed with laughter as he went on to enumerate the taxes he would impose on the rich once Labour were returned to power. As that party suffered its string of electoral defeats, unfortunately, the famous 'turn' lost its piquancy, and in 1992 Hattersley retired to write humorous novels. **PHILIP PURSER**

'The views expressed herein are not necessarily those of the management'

IN THE MID-FIFTIES and in my late twenties, when Entre Deux Mers was six shillings a bottle and parties in London were as plentiful as blackberries, I thought of myself as a poet. Other, shrewder heads regarded me as a layabout. A plot was hatched to find me a respectable job, various strings were pulled.

Soon I found myself at the premises of the publishers William Heinemann, facing a man whose nerves seemed to be as ragged as my own – Rowland Gant, the editorial director.

We recognised each other as kindred spirits instantaneously – literature lovers, loners, possibly loonies. We talked for an hour, at the end of which he said that the post of assistant editorial director was mine, if I wanted it, for £350 a year. Mentally calculating how many bottles of Entre Deux Mers that represented, I accepted and we shook hands.

Afterwards it occurred to me that he had asked me neither which university I had been to and what degree, if any, I had obtained, nor what form my military service had taken. (I had been to Oxford, read English Literature and done alterna-

my first job
James Michie

tive service as a pacifist; he, I learned later had never been to a university and was an ex-parachutist.)

One key feature of this delightfully old-fashioned 'job interview' which sticks in my memory is that at one point he suddenly asked me what the capital of Nicaragua was. I said that I hadn't the faintest idea, but could quickly look it up. He seemed satisfied with my reply. As we parted, I asked him why he'd thrown the question at me. 'Ah, that's the Managua Test,' he said. 'If you'd known the answer, I'd have been too scared of you to be your boss.'

One of my jobs was to take over the blurbs, which had been the province of Major Gyde, the sweet but unsuitable publicity director, whose prose had been deteriorating. 'This is more than a mere biography,' he had recently written, 'this is the man himself.'

My own first effort, I remember, was scarcely better. I described the plot of some leisurely historical novel as 'moving with the stateliness of a saraband'. For support, and out of politeness, I showed it to Gyde. 'Good God, no, dear boy. Never suggest slowness. Say that it goes at a rattling good gallop.'

Next time round I tried to inject a bit more snap: 'Did you know that in Alaska the water from firemen's hoses sometimes freezes before reaching the flames?' 'No, I didn't,' groaned Gant, 'and I don't think I want to.'

Slowly I learned the tricks of the trade. Dear old writers whose punctuation I polished, whose spelling I de-Americanised, whose jacket copy I laboured over, where are you now?

The name Barbara Goolden floats into my mind – the only author, apart from J D Salinger, whom I edited but, by tacit agreement, never met. She was a gallant lady who had been a domestic servant and was supporting a child by churning out banal Home Counties novels involving very small catastrophes and a great deal of cheerfulness. We printed 5,000 of each in hardback and usually sold out, with the help of Boot's and W H Smith's lending libraries. I shudder to imagine her royalty statements by the late 60s, after I had left the company.

I nearly went much earlier, over the 'Elastoplast Incident'. I was entertaining, generously as was my wont, Anthony Burgess and his then wife to dinner in a restaurant. Over the brandy Mrs Burgess threatened

AN AMERICAN entrepreneur has invented a wrist watch that runs backwards and can be programmed to match the owner's predicted life expectancy. This is achieved by starting with the owner's age at the time of purchase and then calculating how much longer he's got left by reference to actuarial tables. A weighting can be added for life-style, diet, family longevity and other risk factors, in exactly the same way life insurers calculate annuities and insurance premiums.

GRAHAM BALL

playfully to bite my ear. Her husband, ever the model of manners (I see his face urbanely set and the smoke curling from his cigarette), attempted to defuse her impulse: 'No darling, I really shouldn't bother. It's of no gastronomic interest.'

But bite it she did, so that it bled lightly, which is why my next expense account invoice contained the item: '50 pence – Elastoplast', which was duly queried by the parsimonious managing director. But Gant was delighted. 'You've come through your baptism of fire,' the war hero said. 'I'll see if I can get you another £500 a year from that tight-fisted garden gnome.'

And, as it was opening time elsewhere, we linked arms, did a soft-shoe shuffle

44

and sang our scabrous version of 'Happy Days Are Here Again', as we always did at closing time.

WHEN ROLAND GANT left Heinemann, I became the editorial director and could no longer avoid the simultaneously grown-up and juvenile world of office politics. I had to deal with two gnomes, one wiry, the other portly – Dwye Evans, the managing director, and Frere (even his friends and his wife didn't use his Christian name), the chairman. The two men clearly detested each other.

It was rumoured that Frere had joined the firm at the invitation of Mr Doubleday, its then owner, and that Charlie Evans, Dwye's father, the London boss, had at first refused to recognise the young Frere as an employee, so that he was forced to hire a motorcycle and sell books from door to door until his status was confirmed from New York.

At any rate, Frere could not readily bring himself to mention Evans by name – 'him over there,' he would say mockingly, pointing with one hand in the direction of Dwye's office and swinging his corded eye-glass slowly to and fro with the other.

At first I attempted to ingratiate myself with both of them, but it soon became obvious that I was destined to be 'Frere's man'. Being a natural publisher, Frere liked odd, creative people, and this luckily included me. He also disliked, as I do, all cumbersome procedure.

If I read a book I wanted us to publish, I simply went to see Frere, described it and suggested terms to offer.

'Buy it, dear boy,' he would almost invariably say, and off I went to the author or agent, who was pleasantly astonished at the celerity with which Heinemann appeared to transact business. No need for a reader's report, nor an editorial committee with interminable clashes of taste, no need for a consultation with the sales side. Sheer simplicity!

Sheerly simple, too, was the fact that had I chosen the wrong books, I should soon be drinking Entre Deux Mers again in farthest Fulham.

When he sent me on my first trip to New York, Frere was typically unexpected. 'Go for six weeks,' he said. 'Get to know them, sort them out, charm the hind legs off them (they're mostly donkeys). I don't care a frozen hoot whether you buy a book or not.' For pride's sake I bought just one – Robert Fitzgerald's translation of the *Odyssey*.

'The blighter waited until they were asleep'

where Graham Greene and J B Priestley were both directors and literary advisors. Greene thought it a masterpiece and Priestley said he would resign if the Bodley Head published such filth. The rest, is history.

Two more vignettes of Frere. One day he summoned me to his room,

Over the brandy she threatened playfully to bite my ear. My next expense account invoice contained the item: 50 pence – Elastoplast

He seemed pleased, but I detected a trace of disappointment at my conformity.

I can recall only one occasion on which Frere vetoed my enthusiasms. We published Nabokov's *Pnin*, and were therefore the first to be offered *Lolita*. Frere had just been through an obscenity prosecution over a novel which would probably be required reading at some schools today, and he had a thirteen-year-old daughter. He jibbed.

The book was then offered to the Bodley Head,

which I entered with nervous speed. 'Sit down. Relax, James.' (After five years it was Christian name terms for him.) 'You're first-rate, you know, but you do some things too quickly. Look at my letter trays.'

I looked: there were four. 'The first I call *Urgent* – that means I'll answer within a week. The second is called *Think About It* – which means exactly what it says. The third is *Let Them Wait and Wonder* – you should do a bit more of that, if I may offer a word of

advice. *Pas trop de zèle*, you know.' 'And the fourth?' I asked, interrupting overquickly. 'Ah,' he said, 'that's my favourite. It's *Give Them Enough Rope and They'll Hang Themselves*.'

On the other occasion it was I who requested an audience. I announced that I wanted three months' sabbatical without pay – an outrageous demand in the 50s. 'Why?' I said that it was because I had never read *War and Peace* and that, though I had read Classics, I had never been to Greece, and I was determined to do both.

There was an immense pause, then: 'Well, dear boy, I'll expect to see you here again at 9.30 on 20th June.'

I made for the door, stammering my thanks. He raised one hand and swung his eye-glass with the other. 'You may like to know that if you'd said that you were overworked, or having a nervous breakdown, or your marriage was going wrong, I'd have said, "Get back to your desk, young man!"'

Trouble at t' Waterworks

Be warned – any male who lives for long enough will eventually come a cropper in the prostate area. **Hugh Cudlipp**, *no exception to the rule, found that the cure for his problem included a 'digital', a grandfather clock and a Christmas tree*

ILLUSTRATION BY JOHN STOREY

SHALL WE DISPOSE of the statistics so that we may then enjoy the fun? The *Macmillan Guide to Family Health* informs us that 'routine tests show that nearly every man over forty-five has some degree of enlargement of the prostate gland: harmless growths of normal prostate tissue are a natural result of the ageing process... [It] rarely becomes troublesome before the age of fifty-five. Serious urinary troubles due to this disorder affect one in ten elderly males.' Statistics concerning the possibility of cancer of the prostate are equally reassuring: 'Rare in the young but increasingly common with age. About 15 per cent of all forty-year-old men have this relatively low-risk form of cancer. At the age of eighty virtually every male has it. But it causes the deaths of fewer than one man in 1,000. If you are over fifty when you discover you have developed the disorder, you will most probably die from some other, unconnected cause.' In other words, midnight muggings, midday car encounters or armed robbery are a far greater danger to your health and longevity in this age of enlightenment.

My acquaintance with the prostate problem began on 17th October, 1963. It was not mine, or one of the family's: it was, if you will pardon a little name dropping, the Right Honourable Harold Macmillan's, a prostate of some political significance, indeed the sole cause of Lord Home of the Hirsel changing his address to 10 Downing Street, peering over his half-moon spectacles like a startled barn-owl at an equally bemused nation.

On that day in 1963 I was trapped in a dental chair at 83 Harley Street, a torture chamber presided over by the late Mr Reginald Jack Pickett. While drilling with skill but abandon, he extolled the virtues of the Tories, belaboured Labour, advised the 'work-shy' unemployed to get on their bikes, and urged the restoration of hanging and flogging forthwith. Assent or dissent was, as usual, denied me because my mouth was stuffed with cotton wool, my lower lip and gums were frozen by a local anaesthetic, my eyes

were bulging and hands clenched. Whereupon Mr Pickett's receptionist announced that Lady Dorothy Macmillan was on the phone to speak to me urgently from Downing Street. Mr Pickett was impressed, standing to attention, dental drill at Present Arms.

Her Ladyship asked me to express her gratitude to my secretary for divulging my whereabouts, then exploded. 'The *Daily Mirror* this morning is *dis*graceful. It is not true that my husband had his prostate trouble for several months. He was *rushed* to hospital on 8th October in acute *pain* for an immediate prostate operation, *yet* your Cassandra is suggesting it was all a put-up job to enable Harold to slither [her word] out of the Premiership on the spurious grounds of ill-health. You know *perfectly* well he is not like that.' She was polite but forceful.

The political atmosphere was polluted at the time by the Vassall and Profumo scandals and Government morale was at zero. Cassandra's allegation was that Mac the Knife had done a bunk, 'cutting up his colleagues badly', choosing the most awkward moment on the eve of his Party's annual

conference. 'Mac the Knife treated 'em rough in the six years he had presided over the Cabinet,' he wrote. 'In the role of a sick Samson he seems to have treated them rough right to the bitter end... All indications are that Mr Macmillan had his prostate trouble – a most common complaint in elderly males – for several months. It was not very serious as we can now see from the fact that he is on his feet again and it doesn't seem to have been a sudden emergency from the medical point of view.'

Lady Dorothy explained that getting on one's feet again sooner rather than later was in keeping with modern medical advice. I was able to convey to her by waggling my upper lip that if she would send me a letter I would gladly publish it in our next issue. Mr Pickett, now standing At Ease, inquired whether the matter was important.

'Yes, Mr Pickett,' I said. 'Lady Dorothy wanted my personal advice on an important confidential matter. Drill on,

> **My prostate did not make the front page. There was no Cabinet crisis or change of archbishops and they did not fly the flag at quarter-mast at Buck House**

Mr Pickett.' He relished the sadism of having the *Daily Mirror* in his dentist's chair but I knew he would never allow that pinky newspaper to sully his homestead.

The headline next day, LADY DOROTHY TELLS *MIRROR* THE FACTS, restored the peace. Maybe Supermac had not told Dot, but had told others, that he had been aware of the problem for several months or more. During September he had discussed with the Chief Whip the procedure for choosing a successor in the event of his own resignation through ill-health. Cassandra's slur that Macmillan was welshing was equally adrift. Until the operation he fully intended to speak at the conference the same week. Dammit, a few decades later President Reagan after two prostate surgeries was still listening on the hot line to Margaret Thatcher.

What occurred suddenly on 8th October is succinctly explained in the *Macmillan Guide to Family Health*, published ironically by Mac the Knife's own family business.

'If severe enlargement of the prostate remains untreated, the muscles of the bladder may no longer be able to overcome the resistance to urine flow and may suddenly or gradually fail to function. Sudden failure occurs when, all at once, the bladder ceases to expel its contents. This condition is called retention. It is very painful, and requires emergency treatment. Gradual failure, which is more common, occurs when the amount of urine that can be expelled decreases little by little.'

I am addressing my homily to the 'Eric, or Little by Little Brigade.' I joined the Prostate Club this year, nudging eighty, but the consolation prize of a hernia in 1981 familiarised me with consultant-communication, hospital ceremonial, and hospital wine cellar facilities. My prostate did not make the front page. There was no Cabinet crisis or change of archbishops at Lambeth Palace and they didn't fly the flag at quarter-mast at Buck House. The revival of my interest in the subject was inspired by a two-column ad in the *Observer* and other quality newspapers with an over-abundance of over-mature readers:

New Book Reveals How to Get PROSTATE RELIEF
If you suffer prostate problems such as
• getting up at nights to urinate
• urgency and frequency
• delay and dribbling
• pain and discomfort
YOUR PROSTATE: What Every Man Over Forty
Needs to Know... NOW!

Realising I was thirty-nine years overdue I applied by first-class mail for this excellent book. The author is Chet Cunningham (whom I'll call 'Chet' for short), with a foreword by Dr Israel Barken, MD, Fellow of the American College of Surgeons, Board Certified Urologist, whom I will call 'Israel' – instant intimacy is natural in prostate circles. The medical artwork is by Shirley Turner, RN: the drawings are intimate stuff, though only in black and white. You can

'*Before you go, have you noticed the super strong suction of the SupaVac?*'

take it from me that Shirl knows all there is to know about men, side view and frontal, from the navel to the knee-cap. The authors are obviously not itinerant quacks flogging cure-alls to suckers or hypochondriacs.

The book is movingly 'dedicated to all of those men who ignored the symptoms, refused to believe the diagnosis and failed to act quickly enough to save their own lives. May the rest of us learn from their experiences. May we all survive "the prostate years" and not die until we're ninety-five doing exactly what we want to do!'

Israel's foreword is professionally impeccable. He writes: 'I recommend this book, not as a substitute to seeking medical advice, but as a resource that will make you a better partner with your urologist on the patient-physician team, and as a tool that will enable you to make better, more informed medical choices.' It was Chet's jaunty intro (it's an American book) that got me weaving: 'Let's face it, men, the years sneak up on us quickly, far too fast for most of us. It's like the hero in *On Golden Pond* said to his family: "I'm not surprised that I'm eighty years old. But I am surprised that I got here so fast." If you're a man over forty you can't afford to miss reading this book. The prostate is often where cancer strikes men in their later years.'

I was in my GP's surgery in no time, reciting my symptoms. Thanks to Chet I was already versatile in uro-speak. The nomenclature is intriguing – a 'steady stream', a 'sluggish stream', a 'dribble'; traipsing to the loo three times a night, not everyone's idea of fun, is euphemised, indeed romanticised, as 'nocturia'. BPH is uro-speak for Benign Prostatic Hyperplasia, meaning that the prostate has enlarged. Waterpipe is apt BUPA hospitalese for urethra, which is partially strangled because of this enlargement.

'*Another pint of virtual reality please, gorgeous*'

The doctor confirmed my amateur diagnosis and advised an appointment with a urologist, a specialist (for those who like to know what's what and who's who) in the scientific study of the urine and genito-urinary tract and of changes in its anatomy and physiology. There are probably urologists who are short, bald and bandy-legged, five-times-a-night nocturnal prowlers themselves. The gentleman I had the good fortune to encounter was everything that can be encapsulated in the word *distinguished*; tall, handsome, intellectual, exuding professional authority, personal charm and confidence. If Lady Thatcher had clapped eyes on him in her heyday he would have been appointed a Cabinet minister, or Our Man in Washington, or governor of the Bank of England before sunset.

There is one item on the agenda for dealing with the prostate affair I should explain to you over the port now the ladies have left the room and the children have gone to bed. Chet is his usual chatty self about this ritual. 'The first exam,' says Chet, 'will be the digital one.' Digital? Accompanied by a digital CD recording of Simon Rattle conducting the CBSO in Mahler's Second ('The Resurrection')? I looked up 'digit' in Paul Hamlyn's *Encyclopaedic World Dictionary*, and it said: 'a finger or toe'. Good God, was this going to be a David Mellor toe-job? The indispensable *Macmillan Guide to Family Health* makes the point abruptly, referring to an examination of the prostate gland 'by means of a gloved finger inserted into the rectum'. My GP and I know each other far too well to indulge in that sort of lark, but now that I was on the medical rollercoaster my fate was in their hands.

'Since the prostate is right next to the rectum,' Chet explains, 'it can be palpitated. In this slightly uncomfortable digital exam the doctor is checking to see if your prostate feels enlarged. He is also finding out if there are any hard spots or lumps on the two lobes he can touch.' So be it: a man's gotta do what a man's gotta do.

My appointment was at 1545 hours. Chet would be the first to agree that there is nothing to beat a good lunch and a bottle of Mouton Cadet before a digital. The urologist ignored the neatly typed list of symptoms I had composed after my studies, preferring to do it his way. It was a pleasant, enlightening teach-in. I realised, however, that consummation was approaching when we strolled nonchalantly to another room dominated by a casting couch, as they call it in showbiz, and an antique grandfather clock with a magisterial tick-tock, tick-tock, tick-tock.

A wave of the hand indicated that pantaloons should be removed, and then, as if we were exchanging tips for the four o'clock at Goodwood, came the order that I should lie on my side facing the wall and relax. Relax! One knows, in this compromising position, while relaxing, that it is possible to protrude one eye from its socket like a lobster and swivel it to achieve a surreptitious view of what is happening behind one's back.

I heard the twang of a surgical rubber glove stretched over a hand, and then at the moment of truth the bloody grandfather clock boomed out the hour of four.

Boing-g-g-g...   Boing-g-g-g...   Boing-g-g-g... Boing-g-g-g!

Between the first *Boing* and the second, I thought of England; between the second and third I recalled a joke somebody told me about the subtlety of loveplay in Australia ('Brace yourself, Sheila'); between the third and fourth it occurred to me that if it got around in certain quarters that it could all happen on the National Health there would be a prostate epidemic and our national deficit would be nearer £60 billion than 50.

The urologist made no comment. No 'Ah-ah-ha', or 'Oh', or 'Blimey!' or 'Coo-er!' When my wandering eye returned to its socket I mentioned in an off-hand sort of way, as I glanced nervously at the grandfather clock while re-occupying my pants, that I was glad I hadn't made the appointment at twelve o'clock, whereupon a judicious smile flitted across the urologist's lips.

His verdict that an operation was advisable sooner rather than later led to a friendly chat about our mutual professional and social obligations. I was booked to go to Spain over Christmas – a mere frolic, back early January. He was committed to attend a European urologists' convention towards the end of January, a serious annual occasion for the interchange of research and information, mingled with some pleasurable sporting distractions. It is held in a ski resort and I later heard from a medical friend that the occasion is known as 'Pee and Ski'. 11th January was pencilled in our diaries.

'Read my lips: You live next door!'

Now came tests prior to my arrival at the hospital mutually selected for my graduation into The Prostate Club. The *Macmillan Guide* had again forewarned me of what I was about to receive and endeavour to deliver. The 'urinary stream' is measured by 'a gadget called a urine-flow meter' (or, I guess, a pissometer when the patients are out of hearing). IVP, which is uro-speak for intravenous pyelogram, follows an important test to assure the urologist that the familiar symptoms are in fact due to an enlarged prostate and not to urinary-tract disease, also that other organs have not been damaged by delay in treatment.

The frightening half-audible chats between medicos and nurses at the foot of the patient's bed, interspersed with expressions of concern such as 'Really?' and 'Hm-m-m-m-m', are now among the medical relics. The BUPA hospital where I sojourned for my five-day prostatectomy – five-star service, menu and wine cellar, daily newspaper order requested in advance – believes in telling the patient the truth in lucid Before and After pamphlets; you know what has happened, what is happening, and what will happen; you also know that your friendly urologist, who performs his principal miracle of transforming a drought into water when you are out for the count, is hovering in the background at all stages.

Sooner or later, after he has removed the tissue causing the prostate enlargement by traditional surgery or, as in most cases nowadays, the more modern method of TUR (transurethral resection), you emerge from the anaesthetic and wake up in the bed you don't remember leaving. Same room, same friendly staff, same TV set, but the decor has changed.

You find yourself the centre of an elaborate set-piece of Heath Robinson paraphernalia of horizontal and vertical bars which initially encourages the illusion that you are playing a bit part in the last act of a mad modern opera on satellite communications, or have been abandoned in the telephone exchange in Dodge City.

I know you are busy, so I will end with my Fool's Guide to what my nurse called 'The Christmas Tree' and 'The Shopping Bag'.

Medical Module I consists of two plastic bags resembling hot water bottles hoisted a few feet above your head on something resembling an elevated coat-hanger. The pamphlet – my comments are in italics – explains:

'You will find a tube called a catheter in your waterpipe (*you don't feel a thing*). There will also be some fluid suspended beside you (*the hot water bottles on the Christmas Tree*). This fluid (*clear saline fluid, in fact*) will be passed continuously via the catheter into your bladder to ensure that the catheter drainage does not block as there may be some blood and urine present: the bladder irrigations drains into a bag at your bedside (*The Shopping Bag!*) and it should be removed at the consultant's request, usually 24 to 48 hours later.'

Medical Module II is simply called Infusion. A plastic bag resembling another hot water bottle and also suspended above your head-level contains clear fluid which passes through a tube into your arm, compensating for the six hours of fasting before the op. This gadget is removed as soon as you are able to eat and drink normally, in my case the morning after the op.

The departure from hospital was a cosy occasion with the recitation by a nurse of eight commandments, one by one. Six were medical, including when I would again be meeting my urologist, an occasion to which I looked forward in the absence this time of the grandfather clock. I was advised it was important to keep drinking four to five pints of 'mainly water-based fluids' for at least two weeks, quite an intake even for the Gold Medal drinking professions of journalists, doctors and lawyers: alcohol allowed in moderation, etc.

I noticed that the nurse omitted Commandment No. 6, to which I turned as soon as she left the room. It said: 'You may resume sexual relations after one month.'

THE OLDIES — TONY HUSBAND

Burton's Last Film
A Butler Remembers

'Ellis Island' was an American TV film about the immigrants who flooded into the United States at the turn of the century. The cast included Richard Burton as Phipps Ogden, a ruthless politician, and Faye Dunaway as his beautiful, faithless wife. **Victor Langley**, *cast as the Ogdens' English butler, kept a diary of what turned out to be Richard Burton's last week of filming*

I WAS UNDER CONTRACT for the whole week and the film company had booked me into an hotel in Luton where most of the cast and crew were staying. I was a bit worried by the fact that I had never seen a copy of the script. I had just been given bits of it, where I had dialogue to speak. I had learned these words, but had been told that I would be included in further scenes and, ominously, that 'Any lines you need to speak will be given to you on the day.' I had complained to my agent that my part seemed rather vague and ill-defined, but he replied 'Don't worry, you are only there to add tone to the proceedings.'

Monday 16th July 1984

The first person I see when I arrive at the location is Brook Williams, the son of Emlyn Williams, and himself no mean actor. For many years he has subordinated his own career to work as an assistant or aide to Richard Burton. 'How are you Brook?' I say. 'Fine, fine,' he replies. It is quite obvious that

Victor Langley as The Butler in 'Ellis Island'

he does not remember me, and I don't intend to remind him. I have brought him an old movie magazine called *House of Hammer*, which contains a large still of him being strangled by a zombie in *The Plague of the Zombies* (1966). He is delighted with it.

I go to my caravan parked in a field about two hundred yards from Luton Hoo. I see that my costume has arrived and am debating with myself whether to get into it or not when my thoughts are interrupted by the arrival of a gold coloured Rolls-Royce which bumps over the uneven ground and pulls up near a large and luxurious caravan. The chauffeur opens the passenger door, and out step Richard Burton and his wife, Sally. They are followed into the caravan by a small entourage of make-up, wardrobe and hairdressing assistants. Twenty minutes later Richard Burton emerges made-up and in full costume.

I spot an actress whom I know approaching my caravan. 'What's she doing here?' I wonder – 'She's not in the cast.' Then I remember I have seen her name somewhere as the Dialogue Coach. 'Would you like any help with your American accent?' she asks. 'No thank you,' I reply, 'I am not playing an American.' 'Oh,' she says, clearly non-plussed. 'But I thought you were the butler?' 'Yes, I am, but he's an English butler.' 'Ah,' she says.

I am not used at all during the day.

Tuesday 17th July

Work hard all day. Meet Faye Dunaway in the morning and do first scene with her. She is charming and beautiful, but hard. I introduce her to the major domo of Luton Hoo because she is keen to see the collection of Fabergé jewellery. Brook Williams still does not remember me, but is slightly more friendly.

I have a scene with Kate Burton when she returns to the mansion. The director, without telling me, has filled Kate's suitcase with bricks, so that when I come to lift it and carry it into

the house, I will stagger under the weight. Well, I'm not having any of that. I am not a weight-lifter, neither am I particularly keen to rupture myself. I explain the position to Jerry London.

'Yeah, well I kinda thought it would look more real, you know,' he says. 'Yes, I dare say, but I am afraid I won't lift it,' I reply. I am polite but firm. I start to undo the suitcase to take the bricks out, but unfortunately break the catch, so the suitcase won't be able to be used anyway. I mumble my apologies, but although he does not say anything, I can see the director is annoyed.

We come to the scene. I am supposed to rush forward as the car comes to a stop and open the passenger door and say 'Welcome home, Miss Vanessa.' *And... Action!* I rush forward and grab the handle, and it comes off in my hand... Even the director laughs. The scene goes to five takes.

Wednesday 18th July

Still haven't been introduced to Richard Burton and now the wedding scene, but whose wedding? Faye Dunaway is helpful and explains the

plot. Seized upon by Second Assistant Director, who says 'Governor, will you stand next to Richard Burton – ' I reply that I have not actually been introduced to him yet. 'Oh dear, haven't you?' We go over to him. 'Sir, may I introduce you to your butler, sir; this is Victor Langley, this is Yates, sir.' We shake hands.

He says 'May I introduce you to my god-daughter, Kate II. We call her that so as not to confuse her with my daughter Kate.' I talk to the girl who is an extra in the wedding scene. Where does she go to school, how old is she, will she be an actress? Yes, she might. Is she good at English? She says she likes Scripture and Religion. Burton says, 'That's English in a way.' I agree.

Brook Williams appears from nowhere and finally recognises me. He tells Burton of our involvement with *The Sea Wolves*, the film we were in four years before in India. Burton says, 'Yes, I was going to do it. I liked the book, didn't like the script, let (Gregory) Peck do it.' I say, 'We were all very sorry you didn't come, you would have had a wonderful time in India.' He sighs. 'Nearly all the people in that film were old friends of mine.'

At this point the wedding scene is ready to go. I have one line to Faye Dunaway which I have been trying to memorise, having been given it 20 minutes ago. 'Excuse me, madam, Mrs Byfield is feeling unwell and she is looking for her husband.' (Who Mrs Byfield is and why she is unwell, I don't know.) As I come into shot I turn to Faye Dunaway and say 'Excuse me, madam... ' No reaction. I try again. Again no reaction. The camera tracks past, Faye Dunaway quite unaware of my existence. 'Victor, did you give the line?' asks the director. 'No.' Dunaway says, 'If I don't pay any attention just tap me on the shoulder.' We do it again. Alright.

Have really finished for the day, but am not released, so watch scene between Greg Martyn and Burton on the terrace. From where I am it does not seem to be going all that well. Brook Williams is sitting close to the camera, the script on his knees, his whole body tense, silently mouthing the lines. Richard Burton does not look at him but a current of understanding seems to flow between them. This time the director is satisfied.

Thursday 19th July
Day off. Sent back to London by agent for television commerical interview. Complete waste of time, as usual.

Friday 20th July
Richard says 'Hello love, did you go to the party last night?' 'No,' I reply, 'I wasn't invited.' Kate says 'That's because you weren't around yesterday.' Third Assistant says he was so drunk he woke up in his room to find all the light bulbs on the floor. Burton, much amused: 'Well, I've been to some parties in my time, but nothing like that ever happened.'

He then tells the story of how he was staying at the Dorchester and Stanley Baker was so drunk he went into a coma, so he took him outside and although it was pouring with rain and very cold, he stuck him in a vertical position in the flower beds by the entrance, but Baker kept falling back onto the muddy earth.

Eventually Burton managed to get him into a sitting position, although, of course, his face and clothes were very muddy. Burton then went back into the suite, thinking that the cold and rain would revive Baker and that he would come back inside shortly.

Burton fell asleep and when he awoke it was about 9am and still raining. Richard could not remember clearly what had happened to Baker. He searched the suite and then suddenly remembered the flower bed.

Stanley Baker was still unconscious, sitting in the same position covered in mud. Burton summoned help and they got him upstairs. They thought he was dead and were about to ring 999 when he began to show signs of revival. After a hot bath and tea, he rapidly recovered with no apparent ill effects.

Burton is very proud of his daughter. He says 'She's only been doing it for two years and she's gone straight to the top in the theatre in New York.' As if on cue, she appears. She is very affectionate and keeps kissing him. I notice that he cannot put a jacket on. He can put one arm through one sleeve, but he cannot get the other one through unless helped.

Outside again, talk to Brook, Richard, Sally and Faye. Burton – 'I was convinced there would be a war at the time of Cuba.'

'Bay of Pigs?' I say.

'Yes, I was driving through France to get back to England by boat. I was driving through these towns and villages with hardly anyone around. Whenever I stopped the French were terrified, huddled around radios. Get back to England, nobody worried at all: "I say old boy, what's the Test Match score?" '

Pretty early finish – back to hotel 5.15 pm. Have dinner with the costume designer, Brian Cox, tell him about play I have been researching and which I will write as a collaboration with another actor. I explain the historical background at some length to Brian and we spend the whole meal discussing it.

At some point I am aware that the other diners in the restaurant are all members of the film crew. They listen silently to our conversation, the whole room seems to hang on every word.

Suddenly they all get up and walk out and as they do so one of them turns to me and says: 'Your voice is so loud we can't stand it anymore, we're leaving, and anyway what you are talking about is so boring.' The entire restaurant is emptied. The manageress looks very embarrassed. I am stunned into silence.

Brian Cox says 'Victor, they're only ordinary working men, they don't understand what we've been talking about.'

I say 'No, my voice is too loud, I must apologise.' I go outside and

apologise. They seem mollified, but I must have ruined their evening.

Saturday 21st July
The last scene is the Thanksgiving Dinner. We do the first take which is the master shot. It is also Richard Burton's close-up. 'Richard, we are right in on you,' says Jerry London.

Master shot completed and intercutting. All that needs to be done are the close-ups on Greg, Kate and Faye. It will be necessary for Richard to read his lines off camera, but he will not be filmed any more.

Richard says 'OK, I'll just nip back to the caravan, have a shower and change into something casual.' He comes back wearing rust-coloured lightweight trousers and a grey short-sleeved shirt. He reads the lines off. He looks happy and relaxed.

Then it's a wrap. The director shouts out in an excited voice 'Thanks guys for a great week's work.'

It's 6.30 pm. Richard Burton stands up and says 'Never in the history of the cinema has a supporting actor been treated so royally. Thank you all very much.'

Sunny Side of The Street

*The engagement of the Rev Bernard Morton to Emily Bishop came to a sad end, but for **Roland MacLeod** (below, left) playing the smitten clergyman was a time of unalloyed happiness*

JOINING THE CAST of *Coronation Street* is like marrying into the Royal Family. There is such widespread affection for the programme that, if your character has but a smidgen of pleasantness about it, a cloak of public affection and goodwill automatically descends on your shoulders.

Jobbing actors who have wrinkled the foreheads of commuters struggling to place the fairly familiar face in context, or who have been approached with that tentative line, 'Haven't I seen you somewhere?', once they grace the cobbles of 'the Street' are not only credited with the name of their character but often surprised to find that their own names are known as well.

Granada TV has set aside a building called Stage One for *Coronation Street*. Here are the dressing rooms, make-up and wardrobe, the studio itself and the Green Room where the actors meet, drink tea or coffee, exchange gossip and sit together quietly rehearsing scenes. I was welcomed into this world with unaffected warmth and felt as if I had been a cast member for years, not days.

It was a September morning when I was first shown into a small, nondescript room with a sink and gleaming water heater at one end. Nearby stood a half-empty jar of coffee, a box of tea bags and a tin of biscuits. It was the sort of room known to actors throughout the country, but this was the antechamber of delight.

A door was opened in the corner and as the sunlight flooded in I stepped into – Coronation Street itself. Immediately in front of me stood the corner-shop, empty at that time owing to the sudden death of its owner, and at the end of the Street, which was smaller and shorter than I had imagined, stood the most famous public house in Britain, the Rover's Return.

The actor who plays Richard III at his local theatre can slough off his hump and walk briskly down the High Street without hearing cries of 'How many princes have you murdered today then, Richard?'; Hedda Gabler can contemplate a toy pistol without blanching; the *Coronation Street* actor is never totally free of his 'alter ego'.

We rarely know how our characters are to develop more than a week ahead. Every Tuesday scripts for the following week are distributed. Most people take a cursory glance at the story-line and then return to their preparation for the current week.

Tuesday morning is devoted to a quick run-through and positioning for all three episodes. On Tuesday afternoon and Wednesday morning the scenes are worked over in more detail and run through one or more times. Wednesday afternoon is the technical run. Thursday and Friday are filming days. Saturday is usually a day off while Sunday and Monday are set aside for filming on location or on set.

I was originally engaged for five episodes to play a vicar of liberal persuasion, with a sense of humour, who clashes with the irascible Percy Sugden at a wedding and thereby meets Emily Bishop. There was no sign in the first episodes that this was anything but a pleasant and, possibly, passing friendship.

As the story developed and each scriptwriter added his own layer to the character, it became apparent that he was a priest of the Anglo-Catholic wing who was becoming increasingly disillusioned and doubtful about his vocation. At the same time he was increasingly attracted to Emily Bishop, a woman of a naturally good disposition with a quiet strength and common sense.

Viewers will now know the end of the story and non-viewers will not be interested, so I will not go into the details except to say that I was told of the unhappy outcome, as a matter of courtesy, some six weeks before.

'Events' as Harold Macmillan called them, are the staple of all long-running serials. The life of an actor is a series of small births and deaths as he moves from one job to another. My overriding impressions of *Coronation Street* are of enormously hard and dedicated work which, despite the relentless pressure, continues to produce a programme of great quality, and a friendliness and warmth which pervades the whole of Stage One and, I believe, shines out into the living rooms of all its devotees.

IT MUST HAVE been around the early 1930s that the gentleman char came into my mother's life. I helped her in the house after school, as had my older sisters, but they were now out at work. How she coped, in that old, cold, inconvenient, no-amenities house was truly amazing.

We were a family of ten, with huge appetites, and we frequently brought hungry friends home for meals. My mother could stretch a meal quite miraculously. We lived in Limehouse, close to the docks (the area now featured in the TV soap *EastEnders*).

One day a friend who lived near Whitechapel's Rowton House, a hostel for the homeless, brought 'Laurel' to our house. His real name was not known; 'Laurel' was the label attached to him by the East Enders with whom he came into contact. He was prepared to clean our house for the going rate of half a crown a day, plus a midday meal. The money just about covered the cost of a bed and possibly some cigarettes.

I came home early one afternoon and there he was. The tall, slim, narrow-faced 'charman' certainly did bear a resemblance to Stan Laurel. When he spoke, it was not what he said that startled me, it was the way he said it. His speech was what we at that time called Oxford English, cultured, correct, plum-in-the-mouth English. I was too

George Orwell

young then to hide my surprise at his posh accent. He smiled, bowed slightly, and then further astonished me by kissing my mother's hand and saying, 'Goodbye, queen of the kitchen.' Turning to me he added, 'Your mother is a fine lady and a splendid cook.'

My mother was consumed with pity for the poor man. She told me that he had scrubbed all the floors, cleaned the twin outside lavatories and polished the blacklead cooker to a mirror finish. 'That well-bred gentleman worked so hard I had to make him stop for a rest.'

Then, quite suddenly, Laurel vanished. He was seen no more in our part of the East End. He was just another of the anonymous men who overnighted at the doss house.

After the last war, I came upon a book written by George Orwell. In it was a photograph of the author, taken when younger. The man was Eric Blair, and I recognised him. He was my mother's Laurel; it must have been during his period of tramping around London, doing any work that came his way, that he did his East End charring.

George Orwell was reputed to have said that the women he admired most were the hard-working, uncomplaining mothers of at least eight children. I like to think that he included my mother in this. She certainly fitted the description.   **STELLA JUDT**

'It may seem laughable to you, members of the jury, but…'

WILFRED THESIGER

One of the great travellers of our age, and one of the finest of all travel writers, describes his disenchantment with the 20th century and the 'civilised world' and his love of the wild places of the earth, in conversation with **Naim Attallah**

Portrait by
Jane Bown
All other photographs by
Wilfred Thesiger

Your life has been defined in terms of travelling… where do you now regard as home?

I suppose Maralal, in Kenya. I've been in Kenya on and off for over 30 years, and now that I'm older and have stopped travelling seriously, I'm based there.

Presumably you still feel English. How important is your Englishness to you?

All important. I wouldn't want for a moment to be anything but English and I have a profound admiration for the English. I will also never entertain any running down of the British Empire. When people – whether they be English, or Americans or foreigners – criticise the Empire, they are quite unable to give one instance of brutality or oppression, apart from Amritsar which was General Dyer's personal error of judgement. That aside, there were no other examples of real oppression, which is an extraordinary tribute to the British.

Probably you feel as much at home in Kenya as it is possible for a non-Kenyan to feel. Do you think this dimension of 'otherness', so to speak, of the outsider looking in, has made it possible for you to value their way of life in a quite unique way?

I am less involved in Kenya than I was with the Bedu from the Rashid in

Southern Arabia, for example, or indeed with the Marsh Arabs. I'm happy in Kenya, I like being with the people, but I have not studied them or done any anthropological work among them. I just live with them.

Your autobiography is called 'The Life of My Choice'. Do you consider it to have been a very privileged life?

I haven't thought of it in those terms. It's been exactly what I wanted to do all my life, and if something went wrong at any time, it invariably led on to something better. I don't think it's been privileged, because when I travelled with the Bedu in Southern Arabia, in and around the Empty Quarter, it was probably as hard a life as any human beings lived, including even the bushmen. I was determined when I went there that I wanted no concessions; I wanted to live on equal terms with them, face the challenge of the desert as they did. If ever they tried to ease things for me, I tended to react rather badly, and this earned me their respect and their loyalty.

But are you very conscious of the fact that if you hadn't had private resources this way of life would not have been possible for you?

I never had anything in the way of private resources. My uncle paid for me at Oxford and we were a poorish family until my grandmother died. Then my four brothers and I got about £300 a year. When I joined the Sudan Defence Force they paid me another £400, and since there was nothing to spend it on it accumulated. But it's never been wealth.

You were born in Abyssinia and your early experiences in Addis Ababa seem to hold the key to your adventures in later life. In your ambition to travel and explore, were you never deflected by the years of traditional public schooling at Eton and then at Oxford?

No. From the start, it was what I was determined to do. The event which had the most profound influence on me was when the Shoan army came back after the big battle of Segale. I still remember in detail the triumphal re-entry of the army into the town: the embroidered hats of the drummers, a man falling off his horse as he charged

The Oldie Interview

by, a small boy lifted high on shoulders – he had killed two men, but seemed little older than myself. At that time there was nothing Western or European about Africa; it was at its most barbaric and most colourful, and that made a great impression. Then in India there was all the pomp and ceremony of the viceregal court. We stayed with maharajahs, we were taken on a tiger shoot, and so when I came to school in England I rather longed to get back to the adventurous life.

Later, in the summer of 1924, Haile Selassie, at that time the Regent Ras Tafari, visited England. He'd been very close to my father who'd helped him a lot during the revolution, and he asked my mother and myself to meet him. We had tea and spoke in French, and he expressed sorrow at my father's death. As I left the room, I turned to him and told him how I longed to return to his country. He gave me that very sweet, gentle smile of his and said: 'You will always be very welcome. One day you shall come as my guest.' Four years later at Oxford, I received a personal invitation from Haile Selassie to attend his coronation. I was to be attached to the royal party, the Duke of Gloucester's, and that had a profound effect on me. Haile Selassie had remembered the fourteen year old boy and that touched me greatly.

Did you come across the colonial attitude in your compatriots, or anything which smacked of superiority?

I was extremely lucky because when I was in the Sudan I was under a very remarkable District Commissioner who had travelled and lived with the Arabs there. His overriding consideration, and that of his men, was the welfare of the people they were ruling. There were no British businesses, there were no settlers, just the governing administration. It would have been different in Kenya where the colonists had settled.

Between 1930 and 1940 you did a great deal of hunting big game before there was any threat of extinction. You believed then that men have an inborn desire to hunt and kill – do you still believe that?

Yes, I do. I think it goes even to the extent of killing other men. It's well submerged in our civilisation but if there is a war then it emerges at once. During the time I was in the Sudan, I suppose I shot far more lion than almost anybody has ever shot – 70 in four years. I never shot a lion with a bait, or out of a car; they were all on foot or ridden down on a horse. I was charged 16 times and knocked down once, and all the time I wondered whether I'd get away with it again. I believed they would kill me in the end, but I had the same sort of urge as those people who ride in the Grand National – they feel they'll break their necks sooner or later but they can't stop doing it.

But why did you kill these poor lions?

Poor lions! You wait till you've been charged by a lion as I was! Also lion were very numerous and were regarded as vermin by the Sudan government. You were allowed to shoot as many as you liked. Besides, if a lion came and raided the encampment and killed one of your cows, it was a matter of honour that you collected the men and together you went out in the morning on horses and rode the lion down. The lion was brought to bay in a patch of thick bush and after making sure it was going to stay, the men went in shoul-der to shoulder. They had no shields, just their spears, and inevitably they were charged. Generally while the lion was killing one of them, they killed the lion, but I remember one time when they went out on their own they had seven casualties, four of them fatal.

Your travels in the Empty Quarter with a handful of Bedu companions were amongst the most dangerous you undertook, and yet you regard this period as the supreme years of your life. What made them so wonderful?

Being with the Bedu, observing their qualities. The Bedu were the only society to which I could apply the term 'noble'. They had a nobility which was almost universal among them. Of course you can say that some of the British were noble – Auchinleck for instance – but you wouldn't call the British a noble race, at least I certainly wouldn't. The ordinary man you meet in the street has no nobility about him at all. But the Bedu were different; they were always anxious to excel, to be known as more generous, braver than anybody else.

In your autobiography you write: 'I have no belief in the sanctity of human life.' But isn't that at the basis of what we might call civilised values?

It probably is. But then I don't think I have what one might call civilised values.

You have always held Haile Selassie in very great regard, and indeed you helped restore him to power after the Italian occupation of Abyssinia. Yet in 'The Emperor', Kapuscinski portrays him as an autocrat who ruled by terror and insisted on absolute loyalty...

That's absolute balls. This is something I would challenge very strongly. Back in 1932, for instance, there had been an attempted coup by Ras Hailu, the hereditary ruler of Gojjam, who was jealous of Haile Selassie and wanted to reinstate his son-in-law Lij Yasu as Emperor. The plot failed and Ras Hailu was arrested. Any other ruler would have confirmed the sentence of

You wouldn't call the British a noble race, at least I certainly wouldn't. The man in the street has no nobility about him at all

Previous pages: Migrating wildebeest in the Serengeti

Left: Women and children of the cattle-herding Samburu tribe at South Horr, Kenya

The Oldie Interview

death passed on him for treason by the high court, but Haile Selassie merely fined him and imprisoned him. Later when Italy invaded Abyssinia Ras Hailu collaborated with the Italians and plotted time and again against Haile Selassie. In every other country in Europe collaborators were imprisoned or executed by their countrymen, many for offences less grave than Ras Hailu's. But Haile Selassie proclaimed that past offences must be forgiven, and merely sentenced him to house arrest.

A propos the UN's censure of human rights in the Middle East, you are reported to have said: 'Who the hell are they to judge how other countries should behave? Why should America be able to impose its values on the rest of the world?' But shouldn't there be basic standards of humanity in all societies?

I don't think you can impose them. What would the Americans have said 60 years ago if the British had threatened to break off relations unless the blacks were given the vote? They would have answered – as Moi in Kenya answered – this is an internal affair, and has nothing to do with you.

But if something is morally wrong, shouldn't it be morally wrong for all people in all places?

I don't think you can apply it like that. If other people in other countries do not have our moral standards, I don't see that you can impose them. Just as it is no good trying to force Christian ethics on a lot of pagans.

You have said you are 'reconciled' to the modern world. Is it not more resignation you feel in the face of something unstoppable?

I suppose it is. I deplore all the material manifestations of our civilisation. Radio and television are extremely pernicious. I remember the moment when I heard the Americans were walking about on the moon, I had a feeling of desecration and despair; despair at the deadly technical ingenuity of man.

But as an explorer, wouldn't you like to know what is beyond our planet?

No. It's right out of my world. One of the things I liked to think when I went to live with the Rashid and others was that nothing in their lives would be altered by my coming. Even though they benefitted from maps which I made, I did not want to change these people. When I travelled among the Danokil, they were killing each other and castrating each other, but as far as I was concerned they were perfectly entitled to do so. I shot lion, they killed other human beings, and I didn't feel, by God, it's about time somebody civilised them.

At the end of your autobiography you say that you have felt the need for human company all your life, and wherever possible have avoided solitude. Why do you think you have found the deepest friendships in races other than your own?

SUMMER FAYRE

Possibly as a result of my childhood. A psychiatrist would say it was because I was rejected by my contemporaries when I was a boy. When I went to my prep school I was pitchforked into an alien environment with an extraordinary life already behind me. I had no idea of the conventions that were so rigorously observed by small boys in England, and when they asked me about myself I started telling them about tiger shoots or travelling with camels. I found myself ostracised as the most appalling little liar. I was driven in on myself, and I longed to get back to Abyssinia.

Have you regretted never having been married?

No. I've had some very close women friends, but I have had very little sexual interest in women. I did meet a girl when I was about nineteen or twenty and I felt that I really could have become very attached to that girl, but then I thought, if I do it will wreck my life. My whole life has been with men and boys – of course I'm not talking sexually now. When I was travelling I didn't often see a woman. Perhaps if we arrived at a camp there would be some women there, but then we'd be off again into the desert leading an entirely masculine life. Marriage would have crippled me. If I had been married there would have been children whom I would have had to educate at Eton or wherever, and there would have been no money left for me. Also, I spend only three months a year in this country – no wife would have tolerated it.

You haven't had much time for orthodox religion. Has there been a religious dimension to your life?

No. I find it very difficult to believe in a God or in an afterlife. I can't see why we're any more important than the ants. I think man has created God in his own image.

PIN-UPS

Dawn French

picks her top six

1 Charles Dance
I admire his courage and
fortitude. He has found
success despite obvious lack
of eyebrows and lips. A
brave, brave man.

2 David Owen
He has lovely hair and I find
his peace plans fantastically
sexy.

3 The Pope
~~Censored – Ed.~~
A great

4 John McCririck
Suave, elegant
Renaissance man. I
just simply cannot
find a single fault.

5 Jimmy Krankie
I don't know why,
but this young lad
has always had a
strange effect on
me. He makes me really get
in touch with the woman in
myself. He makes me feel
like I've been to Paradise,
but I've never been to me. I
want to discipline him – soon.

6 Martina Navratilova (Ms)
I want *her* to discipline me.
Soon. I know she could.

Right: Dawn French

Scorching rubber and screaming engines are a heady stimulant, and once you've got the bug it's hard to kick. Hankering

A Vroom of one's own

after a further dose, racing ace **Frank Barnard** *rashly took up a fellow enthusiast's offer…*

At four in the morning the alarm clock went off. It was wasting its time. I was already awake. The familiar knot of apprehension in my stomach tightened a turn or two. I hadn't raced a car for years but I found myself victim to the same old emotions; the need to do well and not make a chump of myself; lurid imaginings about the hazards that lay ahead…

I had met Ted at a Sunday morning drinks do. 'Do you know Ted Figgis?' someone said. 'He's a racing driver.'

Ted flushed modestly and said: 'Ah, yes, uh, well… ' A stocky, owl-like figure, he pushed his hand through cropped grey hair and then paused, his palm on the top of his head, in an attitude of uncertainty and indecision. It was an attitude I was to get to know well.

Ted did drive at the occasional club event but he was more interested, he said, in the technical side. He ran an aged Formula Ford single seater, the kind of car in which Ayrton Senna and Nigel Mansell started their careers.

'Trouble is, my reflexes aren't what they were,' he said, dropping a chipolata to prove his point. 'I hear you've done a bit. How about you having a go?' And so I found myself dusting off my old helmet, discovering that my overalls had mysteriously shrunk and trying to remember which gears you used for which corners at Brands Hatch.

A blanket of silence lay over the suburbs of Reading as I drove to Ted's bungalow. As I turned into the street I heard the crash and grind of metal on metal. Lights were on in adjoining houses. In Ted's drive the small single-seater was half on and half off the trailer.

'Anything I can do?' I said.

'Couldn't quite see,' mused Ted. 'One minute I was winching her on, the next minute something slipped.' He leaned on the racing car and it crashed down another foot, the clang and racket shattering the dawn. Somewhere, houses away, a distraught voice shouted: 'Do you mind?'

Oblivious, Ted positioned himself at the back of the car and, leaning forward with a grunt, tried to man-handle it onto the trailer. The exhaust pipe hit him squarely on the forehead and he staggered back, a neat black circle imprinted just above his eyebrows. 'Doesn't seem to want to go,' he said mildly.

Ten minutes of huff and puff had the car secured. During the jiggling back and forth I noticed a disturbing amount of play in the steering; but rather than start the day on a downer decided to mention it later.

For a mild, devoted-to-Vera kind of man, Ted drove like a demon. 'Wow,' I said, hoping the hint would strike home, 'this outfit can certainly shift.' 'Oh yes,' said Ted and thrust his foot down on the throttle, encouraged.

One mile down the road, I could see a junction with traffic lights. The lights were green. The speedometer needle flickered upwards – 78, 79, 80… Ted stared ahead, like a man who has seen a vision. Half a mile down the road, I could see the lights were just changing.

'Ted,' I said, 'Ted… ' 'Not sure we've tied the racer down properly,' said Ted, glancing in his rear-view mirror. 'The old trailer seems to be fishtailing a bit.'

He was still glancing in his mirror when we thundered across the junction against the red light, doing 84 miles an hour. 'Fishtailing's like the sound barrier,' said Ted. 'You can accelerate through it… '

'Don't know when you last raced at Brands,' said Ted, 'but I'll teach you what I know. I've never been what you might call an ace but I've had my moments.' He told me about his moments and they spanned most of the racing circuits of Britain. He'd driven at them all, but hadn't finished a lot.

At Donington it had been a keen young chap who banged wheels and put Ted into the armco. At Snetterton he'd been caught out by rain – 'just steered straight on'. At Silverstone he'd moved over to let someone

ILLUSTRATION BY DAVID LYTTLETON

NEE OWW NEE OWWWW ERR RRR PKWKKH!

through and hit the pit wall. At Mallory he'd been black-flagged for a loose exhaust and only noticed when it fell off and took out the leader. At Thruxton his camshaft snapped on the grid, blew a hole in the block and deposited a lake of engine oil which meant the race had to be stopped. 'But,' as Ted observed sagely, 'that's motor racing.'

We were off the M20 now, swooping up Wrotham Hill to West Kingsdown. The blue RAC signs began to appear, 'Brands Hatch'. The stomach-knots took another couple of turns.

In the paddock Ted selected a spot with a steep slope to it, bisected by a stream of water from a toilet overflow. 'It's quieter here,' said Ted. 'You sign on and I'll get the car to scrutineering.'

It was good to be back, queuing to get my competition licence checked and sign a form that said that if I got

killed it was my fault. The banter and nervous laughter hadn't changed.

In the scrutineering bay a glum, baffled Ted was being told we couldn't race the car. The official with the toothbrush moustache and leather armband was completing a litany of shortcomings including, I noted, play in the steering. For someone interested in the technical side Ted seemed to have missed a lot.

'Now most of this can be put right,' said the official, 'but your basic problem's your firewall.'

'Why's that?' said Ted.

'You haven't got one,' said the scrutineer. 'The regulations have changed since you last raced this thing. Aluminium firewall between fuel tank and cockpit, that's mandatory.'

'Ah well,' said Ted, starting to turn away, 'that's motor racing.'

'If we put one in,' I cut in, 'surely we could race?'

'If you can put one in,' said the scrutineer, 'before practice starts, I'll check you through.'

Forty minutes later we were back. Our firewall incorporated some aluminium sheets begged off a tired technician in a huge transporter, and a wastebin liberated from a nearby fence, dozens of rivets, and yards of tank-tape.

'Yes, well,' murmured the scrutineer. He twitched his moustache. 'You'd better get your skates on. They're calling up your practice session. And get it done properly next time.'

Practice was the usual blur of noise and movement: blaring engine, howling tyres; inside the helmet, heat and sweat, my visor fogging from gasping breath; catch it, watch it; God this is fun and then the flags and end of session, easing off and droning down the pit road, hot and pappy tyres flicking up the grit and gravel. What was my time? Halfway down the grid, a midfield place – but not last.

It rained. One hour before the race it rained. We sat in the Granada, windows misted up, listening to Radio 2. Ted hummed along to the 'Donkey Serenade', then clapped his hands to the top of his head. 'Oh dear,' he said, 'oh dear.'

What Ted had forgotten, he said, was the tyres on the car were almost worn out. Good for a dry race, but now, well... We got out of the car and Ted found the set of OK tyres. 'I'll do the wheel nuts,' I told him, 'and you get the jack.'

'I haven't got a jack,' said Ted. 'I make do with a piece of wood.'

Ted went to look for his piece of wood. I felt wetness on my face and was not sure it was rain.

'Don't worry,' said Ted. 'Here it is.' He waved the length of wood cheerily and snapped off the Granada's radio aerial.

In Formula One it's a bad wheel-change that takes more than six seconds. Ted's record was 35 minutes and we didn't break it. Finally, with bloodied knuckles and bursting lungs, we stood there by the car, fresh tyres in place. Ted turned a quizzical eye to the sky. 'I think it's brightening up… Still,' he added, 'it gave us something to do.'

I was on the grid. The car quivered round me. There was a little play in the steering but so what? I'd made it, I was here. In a moment the Formula Fords would be released on their warm-up lap to re-form on the grid. Then, red light, green light, go.

To my right I noticed Ted perched on the pit wall. Good old Ted. What a great bloke… Who else would let someone else drive his car?

The great bloke was standing now, with his hand on top of his head. He looked like a silent movie actor in receipt of bad news. Ted crouched down, then went on all fours.

A marshal joined him; then another. The first one hurried off. Suddenly a third marshal was kneeling by my cockpit. 'Sorry, mate, you're not going anywhere. You're dropping oil. Pull into the pits.' I sat frozen in the car, still strapped in, visor misted, hands clasping the wheel, going nowhere.

We were back on the M20. Ted was humming along with *Melodies For You*. 'Just a mist,' he said 'as you drove onto the circuit… Could have sworn it was oil, but maybe it was fuel from the breather tube. I always put too much in the tank because once I ran out in the middle of a corner at Lydden and caused a bit of a contretemps. Nasty business. Still,' he added, 'I'm glad it turned out to be a false alarm. One less job to do for next time.'

Abruptly, from behind us, came a screech and a thud. The trailer crashed down to the right. A wheel passed us in the centre lane, going well.

'Oh dear,' said Ted, fighting the Granada to a halt on the hard shoulder. 'Oh dear, oh dear. We've lost a trailer wheel and I haven't got a spare.'

He stood for a moment, wreathed in the stench of hot brake pads and burning rubber.

'Well,' I said savagely, still in the Granada, 'that's motor racing.'

'Absolutely!' he said brightly, leaning across me to turn up Mantovani. 'Now where's that piece of wood?'

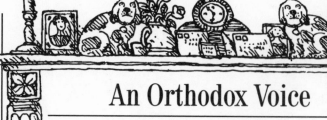

An Orthodox Voice

Just a Coincidence

AN AMERICAN woman I know told me of something strange that happened when she was a little girl. It was a few years after the War, and she was sitting with her father in the local soda-bar, enjoying an ice cream. A man came in, and the father recognised him as an old comrade whom he had not seen and barely thought of since they were in the Army together. He rose to greet him, but then realised that it was the wrong man and sat down disappointed. A few minutes later another man came through the door, and he indeed was the father's old Army friend.

I once kept a Coincidence Diary, noting down all the things of that kind which happened day by day; and I found, as others had done before, that the more I noticed them the more frequently they occurred. If I thought about someone he would immediately call or write; words I had previously never heard of repeated themselves in twos or threes; the clues in my crossword began giving personal messages; long lost objects reappeared in places where they should always have been; and if I wanted a reference to any subject, I had only to pick up a book lying on someone's table, and there it was. Life became so nervously intense that I grew tired of it, gave up the diary and sank back into normality.

I think that during that period I was in a state of Primordial Perception, the state in which our primitive but highly sensitised ancestors lived. To live well, or at all, they had to be alert to the clues and hints which nature provides, and know how to take advantage of them. They rode their luck, not fatalistically but as they themselves made it, through the forms of sympathetic magic which develop naturally from the primordial mode of perception.

That is not a state in which one can comfortably live today. It clashes painfully with the modern way of perception, and those who discover or fall into it are liable to end up in the madhouse. Today one must muffle one's perceptions, or the battery of signs and stimuli to which one is exposed would be overwhelming. We have our own special sensitivities, crossing the road without looking, for example, or understanding what a book is about just by scanning through it.

It is quite a relief that we no longer have to worry much about ghosts, witches, hobgoblins, ominous birthmarks or a strange shape that has appeared in a cloud. We can live pleasantly by modern reason and custom, without having to rely upon luck and coincidences.

Yet the primordial perception is always at hand, and in times of shock or intense need it can take over, exposing its recipient to the underlying reality of our existence. Solzhenitsyn gives a good example in his description of a communist prison in Moscow.

In the next-door cell was a famous physicist who was working out some formula or other and needed certain mathematical tables in order to continue. He did not exactly pray for these tables, but he certainly very much desired them. His desire was answered that week when the library came round. They just gave you two books at random, usually items of party propaganda; and the physicist received one of these, together with the very book of mathematical tables he needed. Knowing this to be a miracle, he quickly memorised the figures, and the next day an inspector came round, saw the book of tables and angrily confiscated it.

JOHN MICHELL

High Force, Co Durham

High Force could be in South America. Standing below its foaming, boiling mass which falls with a roar from the 70ft high sill into the deep dark pool of burnt umber coloured river, you expect Daniel Day-Lewis dressed as a missionary to appear from behind a rock. Instead you meet the occasional back-packing rambler in lightweight rainwear, which makes a feeble swishing sound compared to the waterfall's thunder. The path which winds down from the road lost many of the 100ft high trees which shaded it in the devastating hurricane of 1992, but there are moss-covered crags with stalwart beeches clinging to them by octopus-like roots and ash saplings on vertical cliffs above the great River Tees.

This is not South America but County Durham, the Land of Prince Bishops and always a different domain, a county Palatine set apart from England and Scotland. The Tyne marks its northern boundary and the fair Tees spreads its pools and tumbles through the south. At Scotch Corner, where the A1 strikes onwards dragging its hurried victims in steady streams, you can turn westwards and make for Greta Bridge, one of the most beautiful in all England. It spans the River Greta in a simple elegant sweep and was designed in the 18th century by John Carr of York for the owners of the house and sylvan park of Rokeby, whose Grecian entrance gates stand beside. Just beyond is the Morrit Arms, a coaching inn which has long been my favourite stopping place. Dickens stayed here while researching *Nicholas Nickleby* and the bar is covered in murals painted in 1946 by Gilroy, the originator of the Guinness advertisements.

Rokeby's park is sliced through by the dual carriageway A66, but once that is crossed the journey up the valley of the Tees to High Force begins, past the glorious yellow ochre coloured house of Rokeby, its plain Palladian façade looking straight into the morning sun, reserved and elegant. Velasquez's 'Rokeby Venus' (who was said by Augustus John to have the most slappable bottom in the National Gallery) once hung here, bought by J B S Morrit in 1813. He wrote to his close friend Sir Walter Scott about the hanging of 'my fine picture of Venus's backside' which he had placed in a suitable high position so that 'the ladies may avert their downcast eyes without difficulty and connoisseurs steal a glance'.

On up the valley the spectacular ruins of Egglestone Abbey stand on a plateau above the Tees – a few cottages edge the small sheep-grazed green beside it – but the image of a quiet idyll is soon hit for six by the sight of the Bowes Museum – a vast château, plucked from the Loire and dropped by the Tees in the 19th century. It is positively startling and houses the most wonderfully eclectic collection of art and artefacts, all thanks to George Bowes, the bastard son of the Earl of Strathmore.

The museum stands on the edge of Barnard Castle, one of the best market towns in England with wide streets of handsome houses, some of the local pinkish-grey stone, some white stuccoed with black-painted window surrounds. A beautiful octagonal market-cross commands the view down the steep hill called the Bank and the great Norman ruined castle rises up dramatically above the river.

Out from the town the road leads on up verdant Teesdale which secretes its treasures of spring gentians, birds-eye primroses, cinquefoils, nine species of lady's mantle and in the high pastures 'double dumpling' orchids. There are farms on the hillsides all around and a cattle market smelling of disinfectant beside the bridge which leads over to Middleton on Teesdale. A fine little town with some proper shops – general stores selling shrimping nets and potatoes, a family baker, butcher and chemist, a fishing tackle shop and an unforgivably ugly Co-op with red shiny plastic facings. There are big beech and sycamore trees down the 'Horse Market', a huge pinnacled Methodist chapel and the grandest of arches leading to nothing but a few cottages and fields.

Leaving Middleton, the capital of Upper Teesdale, the country becomes bleaker with outcrops of the dark resistant Whinstone rock which form vertical cliffs, scarps and waterfalls. The Cauldron's Snout, a spectacular cascade, is hidden in the hills, and near Low Force Europe's earliest suspension bridge spans the Tees. But it is High Force, the largest and mightiest waterfall in England which caps all.

ILLUSTRATION BY JOHN O'CONNOR

SuperGran

Imogen Lycett Green *went to India in search of Penelope Betjeman – writer, traveller and grandmother extraordinaire*

My earliest memory of my grandmother is of her ample figure lurking near some daffodils in her garden at The Mead, Wantage, encased in brown gaberdine jodhpurs and an Aertex short-sleeved shirt under a mauve and white cotton apron. Her hair was a silver grey helmet, fringed and bobbed around her wrinkled face. It seemed wrinkled at the time, although later I found out that it was smoother than other people's. The silver hair was shorn neatly in a straight line at least an inch above her dark currant eyes, and before she went out she would comb it down firmly.

Her voice was loud and high-pitched and slightly nasal, and she said words like 'gawn' for gone and 'gel' for girl, and she laughed with a resonant boom. She had a girlish laugh too, and often got an attack of giggles so violent that tears would run down her cheeks and then she'd plead, 'Stop! Stop – I can't *bear* it!' Another distinctive sound she made was her elephant's trumpet-call nose-blowing, which she did at regular intervals into the handkerchief she kept up her sleeve or in her bloomers. Standing at the end of the garden, she was probably feeding her ducks and I was five and a little fearful of her.

By the time I was nineteen, she had become my friend and mentor and the fear was almost gone. In the intervening years she could not have squeezed in more gold stars for grandmotherhood. We called her GrandmamaElope and she taught us to sit on ponies and to jump fences, and then she took us hunting. She taught us how to make brandy snaps and lemonade, how to grill sausages over a fire and to cook a béchamel sauce. She read us the ancient Hindu epic, the *Ramayana*, before we went to bed and she taught us how to say Hail Marys and the Lord's Prayer.

We were ticked off about our manners, our cleanliness (she taught us how to wash our 'smalls' by hand) and about waste. She was a recycler by instinct long before green meant anything but the colour of grass, and if we left the tap running while we washed our teeth we were reminded of little children in Africa.

Despite her sometimes schoolmistressy strictness, visiting GrandmamaElope always promised adventure. When she

had moved to New House, near Hay-on-Wye in the foot-hills of the Black Mountains (her 'Hereford Himalaya', she called it), we would ride over the ridge of Hay Bluff into Wales and have a cheese sandwich and a bottle of ginger beer in the pub. We would trot home in the dusk, avoiding bogs on the mountain and singing hymns to frighten away ghosts. She would pretend there were Rakshashis (demons from the *Ramayana*) in the Forestry Commission Christmas tree woods behind her house, where we went to collect logs for her wood-burning stove (nicknamed 'the Crem' by my grandfather, to whom the the logs' gloomy fate in the furnace seemed poignant).

Later on she sent me Cadbury's Dairy Milk and en-couraged me through my exams with notes like: 'I think you might allow yourself just one bar of choc??? *No reply*

30s when her father, Field Marshal Lord Chetwode, was Commander-in-Chief of the British Forces. She had returned in 1963, after my mother was married, and was bitten by what she called her Indian Bug again. Thereafter she returned almost every year for months at a time, studying temples, leading tours, and making friends.

She then took me to India in 1985, when she was seventy-five and I was just eighteen. It was to be an Educational Tour. After three months exploring the hills and the temples and the festivals and sculptures and the trains and the cities, and the food and the literature of the Indian sub-continent, with her beside me, jogging my mind to attention and directing my gaze and, above all, making life richer by her inspiration (not to mention her jokes), I began to love to learn.

My last memory of my grandmother was of her waving from a train at Birmingham New Street station when I was nineteen. It was a grim day in February and I felt bereft as her beret-clad white hair disappeared from view. I was at university there and she had come from Hereford to spend a cultural day with me admiring the Pre-Raphaelites in the City Gallery, before lunching on quiche and orangeade. We talked about the merits of chocolate éclairs over lemon meringue pie. She was off to India again to lead another tour through the Himalayan foothills.

When she died while leading that tour out of the Kulu valley on an April morning not three months after our edifying art tour in Birmingham, I minded terribly. I decided the memory of her must be preserved. I promised myself I would write about her. She had often been asked to write her biography, but she was too humble to try it. She could not see the use of writing down the details of her past, and she couldn't think who would want to read about her, as she assumed (on account of her own preference) that most people would rather read about horses or India.

At the time of her death she had begun a book about her life with horses, and she also planned to write about her time in India between 1928 and 1933 before she married John Betjeman. Neither project was completed, however. Procrastination was her greatest vice, she always said, and really she much preferred collecting logs in the forest to writing. (Though she did, in fact, write two brilliant books for John Murray, one about a riding tour of Spain and one about the Kulu valley.)

When my time came to stop procrastinating and to act upon my intention I knew the only way to conjure up her spirit again was to return to India. I travelled for six months in her footsteps from Manali in the North, all the way south to the Palni Hills. I had only a vague idea how the book was going to emerge, but I felt her at my shoulder all the way around, and knew that if I just opened my eyes and took my notes, the structure would materialise. Magically, it did. It's about India and horses and God and her, and I hope in Heaven she's happy with it.

The book in question is 'Grandmother's Footsteps' (Macmillan, £20)

required. Much love and I am still saying a daily decade of the Rosary for the successful outcome of your 'A' Levels – Gr Elope.'

My grandmother's most important lesson only filtered through to my teenage mind after she had died in 1986. I realised that by the unconditional friendship she had extended to each one of us, she had taught us to communicate across generations; that one of the most creative things you can do in life is to keep asking questions, to keep making friends with people of all ages and denominations, to Keep Being Interested. Never, she said, *never* lose your will to learn and then you will never be bored or unhappy.

She had directed her intellectual curiosity back towards India, where she had been as a 'gel' in the late 20s and early

The Meeting-House

A Short Story by Jane Gardam

There should be nowhere less haunted than the Quaker meeting-house on High Greenside above Calthorpedale in the north-west.

To get there it is best to leave the car on the by-road and walk up through the fields, for there are six gates to open and shut before you reach the deserted village of Calthorpe, which stands on a round lake that is shallow and silver and clean and still. The hamlet's short street and its empty windows and door frames are nearly blocked with nettles, its roofs long gone missing. A century ago poor farming people brought up broods of children here on tatie pies and rabbits and broth, and very occasionally some pork. The pigsty – one lank pig to a village – lies above the ruined houses. Behind the sty you take a track up the fell until you hit a broad grass walk, nibbled to a carpet by sheep since James the First's time and before. You come to two stone buildings, to the right of the walk in the tussocky, shiny grasses. They are attached, one house bigger than the other.

When you get near you see that the smaller building is empty. A dark doorway gapes. There is not much roof left. But the creamy stone is bleached and washed clean by the weather and there are wild flowers and grasses round its feet.

The bigger building is one tall room within, and is almost the oldest Quaker meeting-house in England. George Fox himself is said to have preached here shortly after his vision of angels settling like flocks of birds on Pendle Hill. Its floor is the blue-white flagstones of the dale and there are three tiers of plain, dustless benches. The walls are dazzling white limewash, and on a high stone shelf is a small paraffin stove and two now unused candlesticks. The Friends bring a medicine bottle of paraffin up the fell for making tea after worship, but they don't bring candles, for the meeting-house is only used on summer mornings now. It is a secure little place, and bare. If walkers look through the clear glass in the windows they see nothing to steal.

The view from it is wonderfully beautiful, and as the Friends sit looking out through the windows and the open door across the dale to the purple mountains, a grassy breeze blows in. If Quakers believed in holy places this would be one of them. They do believe, however, in a duty to be responsible about property and thus it seems odd that the building alongside the meeting-house should be derelict. But it had never been the corporate property of the Friends, being part of the estate of a local farming family who had been Friends for many generations, and had used the little house as a lambing-shed and springtime home of a shepherd, who had doubled as the meeting-house caretaker.

These days are done. The farm has passed now to a consortium at York, the sheep are brought down to low pastures and shepherds today have motor buggies and houses below the snowline. The meeting-house caretaker was now Charlie Bainbridge, who had walked up to High Greenside for years at all seasons once a week, and he had seen the smaller building left to fall gently down. Bainbridge, a huge old man white-bearded and white-haired, was a still fellow who walked very upright without a stick even with snow on the ground. He said the long pull up to the meeting-house was what had kept him healthy.

Hawks on the ridge watched Bainbridge for years as he moved on a weekday morning across the valley floor, passing through the six field-gates fastening each one after himself; passing through the nettle-stuffed village, passing the muck-hard pigsty and away up beyond it to the broad grass track. On the common garth wall before the two buildings he sat down each week, ate his dinner out of a paper parcel and watched the weather coming and going. Larks and lambs in season, curlews at every season. Far too many rabbits. Disgraceful multitudes, he thought, remembering hard times and good stews of old. In winter there was often a stoat turned white, a rusty fox dipping a black paw in snow. In April there were rainbows, often far below him and sometimes upside down. In May, a madness of cuckoos. A preserved, and empty country.

He would consider the rain as it approached, watch the storms gather, the flashlights and searchlights of sun piercing purple clouds and turning the fields to strobe-light, elf-light emerald. He sat waiting for the rain to reach him and wet him, the wind to knock him about. Until it did, he sat untroubled, like a beast. Then he got up, opened the meeting-house door with the seven-inch iron key that lived under a stone and plodded about inside, maybe sweeping

around a bit with the broom that lay under the benches. He looked out for cobwebs, trapped butterflies, signs of damp. Accumulated silence breathed from the building, wafted out onto the fell, swam in again like tides. Silence was at the root of Charlie's life.

So that when he was walking up one day and heard canned music he was jolted. He thought it could only be picnickers or bike boys cavorting about from over the west. They'd been seen about sometimes before. But then he saw that there were two big piles of rubble in front of the smaller building and clouds of lime dust floating in its dark doorway. Banging and crashing began to drown the music, and then a dirty man came through the doorway carrying more rubbish and slung it on the tip. A child appeared, and then a very thin young grubby woman. The child was whining and the man aimed a kick at it. The woman swore at the man and the man said, 'Sod you. Shit.'

The woman said, 'Leave it, will yer?'

Then the three stood looking at Bainbridge. 'Good day,' he said.

They said nothing. The man lit a cigarette.

'Can I help you?'

'Ye canna. We's 'ere. We's stoppin'.'

'Are you to do with them at York then? The farming company?'

'We's 'omeless,' said the man, 'we's Tyneside.'

'See?' said the woman, and the baby stepped out of its plastic pants and defecated beside the rubbish.

'I come here,' said Bainbridge (in time), 'to see to the meeting-house. We don't use it often but it's our property. We are Quakers. The Society of Friends.'

'No friends of ourn,' said the man. 'Ye'll not shift us. Ye can't force us.'

'We wouldn't force you,' said Bainbridge, 'it's not what we do. We don't have violence. But we have a right of way in to the meeting-house across the garth.'

'Not now you haven't,' said the man, setting light to the rubbish.

Bainbridge left. He had never been a talker. Once or twice he had come across such people as these and had tried to understand them. Sometimes he had watched

'I had that Rolf Harris in my cab this morning'

things about homelessness on somebody's television set and had always given generously to appeals for them that dropped through his door. But confronting them had been shocking, as shocking as meeting fallen angels, bewildering, frightening, disgusting and against natural order. When the Elders of the Meeting went up to High Greenside to investigate a few days later Bainbridge stayed at home and planted onions.

The squatters at once made their position quite clear: they were not going, a point they made clearer still to the owner of the building who came over before long in a Merc from Harrogate. The owner, however, was not deeply worried. When he found that the family was not an advance party of vagrants or New-Age travellers or a pop-music festival that might take root over his fields and settle there like George Fox's angels – fornicating, druggy, aggressive angels ruining pasture and stock – he said that at least the place was being used. The glass front door off a skip, the new metal windows set loose in the walls, the plastic chimney pot painted yellow and crazy tarpaulin slopped on the roof were matters for the National Park, not him. Carrying off an 18th-century rocking chair that the family had found in the rafters and also painted yellow, the owner said that he would of course have to tell the police.

'You do that.'

'I will. Oh yes. Don't you worry. I will,' he called, and a Doberman who had been drooling and lolling with the baby in a broken chicken-wire playpen leapt at him with slippery turned-back lips and man and chair fled down to the dead village.

'I'll give yer summat in rent when I'se in work, see? The wife's bad, see? She's had a tumour,' the man shouted after him. 'She likes it 'ere, see? Right?'

Next, a number of the Friends went up to explain to the family about the Sunday meetings and how, each week, they kept an hour of total silence at High Greenside. The music behind the glass door screamed and blared, the baby cried and it took a long time for the woman to answer their knocking. It was noon but she was in her nightdress.

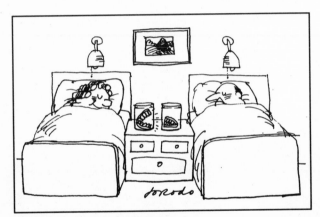

'We sit in silence once a week. From 10.30 until 11.30 on Sunday mornings. Only on six Sunday mornings. Only in summer. You are very welcome to join us.'

She said, 'Oh yes – yer comin' in?'

The flagstoned floor was still covered with lime dust and the sheep droppings of years, and heaped up with torn plastic bags of possessions – cracked shoes, rags, bottles, jars. There was a mattress with greasy coats across it, and a new-looking television set and video recorder standing bewildered by the absence of electric plugs. In a little black hearth a fire of wormy, sawn-up floorboards from the room above was burning, but the room was cold. The woman coughed and behind the door that hid the stairs the Doberman boomed and clawed.

'You can't be very comfortable here.'

'It's OK.'

'We could help you. We have brought you a few groceries. And some runner beans and a stew.'

''E'd never.'

'Well, tell him we called. And about the silence on the Sundays?'

She wrapped a terrible matted cardigan more tightly round her bones.

''E'd never listen. 'E's that wild. One thing one minute, another the next.'

When they arrived the following Sunday the Friends found parts of old scrap-yard cars dragged across the garth and barbedwire fastened across their door. After negotiating all this and opening up the meeting-house, they conferred, standing close together and thoughtful. The dog slavered and scraped inside the lambing-shed windows.

But seated soon on the familiar benches, their door open to a paradise morning, the dog quietened and the silence began. A different, answering silence from the house next door became almost distracting.

Or perhaps insolent; for the following Sunday the entry to the meeting-house was blocked more thoroughly, this time with old roof beams; and after they had struggled through these and silent worship had started, two transistors on different wavelengths were set outside on the party wall. An ill-tempered political argument fought with a programme of musical requests, both at full strength.

The next week it was a petrol-engine chainsaw. For an hour its lilting scream, like cats in acid, seared the brain and ears and soul, and a young Quaker who was a summer visitor from Leeds ran off down the hillside.

The noise was switched off the minute the hour ended and the Clerk of the meeting, speaking slowly, said to the man lounging outside, 'By law, you know, you are meant to wear earmuffs when you're working one of these.'

The next week the man did wear earmuffs but the Quakers sat again in pain. 'What have you against us?' they asked as they locked up – taking the key now with them. Even Bainbridge looked shaken and drained. But the man said nothing.

The next week the saw broke down. The scream jolted and faded and died. It was a few minutes into the meeting and the man outside began to swear. He kicked and shouted, shouted and kicked, then stormed down to below the pigsty and shouted and kicked the tin-can of his old pick-up van into action. Soon it could be heard exploding its way down through the fields.

The two transistors kept going when the sound of the pick-up had faded, but their clack now was like balm and

'Look! Meals on wheels'

blessing after the saw; and a greater blessing followed, for soon they were switched off. The depth of the Quaker silence then was like hanging in clear water.

After a time, the child appeared in the open doorway quite naked – a queer, grey, dirty, sickly thing standing in the bright air. He tottered forward and flopped down and old Bessie Calvert, a gaunt stick herself, took him up on her lap where he seemed to have no energy to do more than fall asleep.

When, in a few minutes, his mother stood in the doorway looking for him, Bessie moved a little and touched the seat beside her and the woman, in her nightdress again, threw her cigarette in the grass and came in. She sat sideways, twisted away from the people, staring sulkily out of the door, but she sat and when the car was heard returning she did not stir.

And when the man and dog stood in the doorway she did not look at them. The dog's great chain was twice round the man's wrist and the chain rattled heavily as the dog dropped down to the ground, its chin on its paws. The dog sighed.

Then the man pulled the dog away and they both stood outside in the garth, the man leaning up against the meeting-house wall.

'Good day,' said the Quakers passing him by at the end of the hour (there had been no tea-making this summer) holding out their hands as usual, one after another. As usual the hands were ignored, but leaning against the wall the man gazed far away and said nothing. He looked very tired.

As they went off down his voice came bawling after them. ' – next week, mind. Not an end of it. See what we do next week. Settle your silences. You'll not get rid of us. You's'll never be rid of us. We's after your place next.'

But the next week nobody was there. All gone. Family, dog, car, television set, chainsaw, the few poor sticks of furniture, the new padlock on the pathetic glass door that now stood open on the foul mattress, piles of nappy bags, flies and a mountain of sawn wood. A jam-jar of harebells stood on a stone sill with a note under it saying, 'Sorry we had to go. We'd got started to like it up here.' In the paper the following Wednesday the Friends read that at about the time they had been reading the note the whole family and its dog in their wretched car had been killed on the M6 just below Tebay.

Quakers accept. Grief must be contained, translated. Friends do not as a rule extend themselves over funerals. But three of the Quakers from High Greenside did attend this one far away over in Cumbria, and later on Charlie, Bessie and the Clerk cleaned out the old lambing-shed, removed the rubbish, the bits of cars, the tarpaulin, the mattress, to the tip 12 miles off. They distributed the firewood and disposed of the sagging little chicken-run playpen. They worked thoroughly and quietly but found themselves shaken beyond all expectation.

The playpen and the now withered harebells in the jar brought them close to weeping.

THE OLDIES   **TONY HUSBAND**

The Hulmes were broken into last night

Scarey isn't it?

Yes, lucky we've got him

It was during the following winter that stories began. Walkers were puzzled by canned music coming from the High Greenside buildings that faded as they drew near. Fishermen down by the lake at night sometimes heard the barking of a great dog. Across the dale people saw a light like a low star on the fell-side where the empty buildings stood. After Christmas the Yorkshire farmer came back with his wife to inspect but had to turn away because the wife for no reason suddenly became very much afraid. Charlie Bainbridge was thankful that the snow came early and deep that year and stopped his weekly visit – not because of ghost talk, he had no belief in ghosts – but because the place now distressed him. When the snow melted he was in bed with chronic bronchitis brought on by the long indoor months. He grew better very slowly.

So that it was almost summer again before he got up to the meeting house once more. Rather thinner but still upright, he set off soon after his dinner at the beginning of May. He walked steadily, opening and shutting every gate as before, circling the silver shilling of the lake, through the bad village, up beyond the pigsty to the wide grass ride. It was a balmy dreamy day. He was happy to be back. The bank rising to the far side of him was rich with cowslips. Rabbits as usual. A lark in a frenzy, so high he could scarcely see it. As he came near the two pale buildings he said, 'Well now then. Very good. Swallows is back.'

He stopped and for the first time in many months looked down and across the sweep of the dale, the black and silver chain mail of the walls, the flashing sunlight. 'Grand day,' he said aloud and turned to find the Doberman standing before him across the path. Then it was gone.

He looked over at the meeting-house, but did not move. He heard a thread of music, then silence. He wondered if he heard laughter.

The silence grew around him again and he waited. He tried out some remarks to himself.

'Here's some puzzle,' was the first.

'I stand here,' was the second.

'Let's see now what it's all about,' was the third.

He walked forward to the common garth, opened the gate and looked into the derelict building. Nothing. The grass was growing again in the flagstoned floor. He walked along to the meeting-house and looked through the windows. Nothing. Not a shadow. The place seemed to have wintered well. A clear light flowed in over the bare benches. All quite empty.

But then he saw them, all three together, on one of the long seats. It was not a vision, not a moment of revelation.

There seemed nothing ghostly in it. The man had an arm along the back of the settle and the nightdressed barefoot woman had the child on her knee and had folded herself in against the man's shoulder. They looked very familiar to Charlie Bainbridge, like old friends or, as it might have been, his children. And yet changed: confident, peaceful, luminous, beyond harm. They were all gazing outward from the meeting-house, intent and blissful in the quiet afternoon.

Sir Alec Guinness

THE OCCASION was a sale by auction of rare books – mostly modern first editions and private press volumes – at Sotheby's popular Chancery Lane rooms, in the late 70s. I was officiating at the desk beside the rostrum, and after about 30 years' experience in the book trade, I knew – at least by name or face – quite nine-tenths of the 'groundlings' sitting or standing below me. Not so the auctioneer who was conducting the sale.

A private press edition of one of Shakespeare's plays came up for sale. I can't remember which one it was now. As I recall it was a handsomely printed tome, bound in green.

Bidding was brisk, and I noticed, in the far left-hand corner of the room, that one of the competitors was a rather ordinary looking gentleman, very soberly-dressed in a dark blue overcoat.

Being something of a film buff, I caught on to those features immediately, and I watched with interest as the bidding went back and forth. Finally, down came the hammer with a bang, and at a very respectable price. But to my amazement, the auctioneer called one of the well-known London booksellers as the purchaser!

I never saw a face drop so far as that of that 'ordinary' punter at the far end of the room. And it was here that I stepped in. 'Oh,' I said to the auctioneer, 'Sir Alec was bidding.'

If I'd said that Alf Bloggs had been bidding, I doubt if it would have made much difference. But the title I mentioned had made a great deal. The lot was put up again, but the dealer had reached his limit. The Shakespeare went to the chap in the far corner.

'Sir Alec Guinness,' I called loudly, since nobody else, including the man selling, seemed to be aware of who the buyer was. Naturally, there was a muttering, and a slight turning of heads, but I then forgot all about it and concentrated on the many lots to come before this auction was over.

Some short while later, a modest figure put in a quiet appearance beside me at the desk. Sir Alec nodded gratefully, and thanked me for intervening on his behalf. He paid me for his purchase, which he was obviously very happy to have made, I receipted his bill, he collected the book from the porter, and departed – blue overcoat, black bowler hat, *et al.*

O F SNELLING

NUDISM
THE NAKED

In the village of Fawkham, at the end of Scratchers Lane, lies a club called 'Eureka'. Any may enter – but those who do must be prepared to share their table tennis table with the less than entirely attired – as **Paul Pickering** *discovered*

AT THIS TIME of year, with the weather becoming goosepimple cold, one can, on the more remote beaches, observe that most contrary of creatures – the committed British nudist. What is even stranger is that the men and women with sandals on their feet and a Messianic gleam in their eyes are indisputably oldies, with breasts and botties every bit as ravaged as the headlands they adorn.

Why do they do it? Well, there is the sexual aspect, the last-chance saloon for flagging libido. But while German and French nudism have been associated with Free Love, British nudists are scandalised by any suggestion that this is what they are really up to. Adverts in *Health and Efficiency* for nudists' clubs specify Families Only.

As it is usually the man of the house who is seized by a sudden Sanatogen-induced raptus to wander naked in our icy, prickly Albion, he has to persuade the rest of his astonished relations before he is allowed behind the barbed-wire to shuffle 'sky clad' within easy reach of East Grinstead.

If his brood do not go along he has to rant and sulk, Lear-like, until they do. Being a successful male oldie nudist must thus confer a feeling of Victorian authority hardly known in our increasingly rare nuclear families.

A couple I spotted near Hastings were typical, by which I mean extremely self-conscious. They had not joined a club yet and were, as they put it, 'free range'. The obsessively private 'British' part of them was triumphing over any notion of being free spirits, at one with creation as nature intended.

Both were in their ample forties. The woman, who looked not unlike Clare Short MP, was viciously skinning what I first thought was a baby but which turned out to be a cooked chicken. Next, she disembowelled a melon with a quiet fury.

Her husband, incongruously, sported tartan socks and those leatherette sandals liberals used to swear by. 'We're not doing anything criminal,' the chap insisted with the kind of voice that makes announcements that trains are cancelled on Network SouthEast.

A little way along another couple had built a fort out of a beach umbrella, cooler bags and several blankets. They lay, scowling defensively on their stomachs. A small boy ran up, put his tongue out, and sprinted away again. There

74

T R U T H

did not seem to be a lot of point to being nude in the first place.

Next to these castle builders sat Bob and Mary, slightly trimmer adverts for middle age.

'We used to do it in Yugoslavia and one day I thought why not carry on at home,' smiled Bob. 'You do find a lot of people on this beach are reserved on account of being laughed at. And you can attract the wrong sort. Men who like men. I never encountered anything like that in Yugoslavia, which was very orderly before this present slaughter.' Bob and Mary sat with their legs wide open, spilling

the contents of crusty cheese-and-tomato rolls.

'Don't get us wrong,' added Mary. 'We're not exhibitionists. We both work in local government. I believe there is a time and place for nudism. I would never dream of stripping off at home, in Harrow on the Hill. People come from all over the country to beaches like this to make friends and have a giggle. I cannot see the harm in it. The National Trust and some councils try and stop it, but they won't. We used to go to Brighton. Do you want a scotch egg?'

For me, there is something endearing in a 30s garden suburb way about

British nudism. The movement claims to hail from an era of wild idealism and experimentation at the start of the century.

An often-naked great aunt informed me that the Far Right and the Far Left patronised the same naturist camps in Germany, not being able to tell each other apart, unless they talked. This is not common with modern British nudists, who sit cocooned in silence. Especially the solitary male.

Perhaps it's our damp heathlands that makes him shrink from extending himself. Or is it that when a pastime so obvious as taking one's trousers off becomes

In the Nineties, British naturism seems thankfully destined to remain the preserve of the dotty. The trouble is that nudism does not dovetail well with our consumer society. How on earth would a nudist accessorise? What do you buy a nudist for Christmas?

a passion, it also becomes nakedly absurd?

The isolated male lives in dread of David Attenborough creeping around a dripping elm: 'And here we have a perfect example of the solitary male nudist. Note the age and the wonderfully shrivelled penis... Note the fury at seeing an outsider because he cannot logically explain what he is doing...'

Naturism lost its popularity in the utilitarian climate after the Second World War and some also blame the decline in classical education. At my school we were forbidden to wear trunks in the swimming pool. A beaming headmaster frequently explained that Ancient Greek boys played all games in the buff.

When I ventured that school prefects were allowed to don trunks, he chuckled and muttered opaquely: 'Who guards the guardians, eh?'

In the 90s, British naturism seems thankfully destined to remain the preserve of the dotty. The trouble is that while nudists have made a Danish Bacon advert (lower-fat bacon doesn't spit on the barbecue) and poetesses promote the fad on Channel 4, nudism does not dovetail well with our consumer society.

How on earth would a nudist accessorise? What do you buy one for Christmas? 'Only something to... you know. Stop it. When you get excited...' confessed Bob on the beach.

Most British male nudists are terrified that people will make this connection between their taking their clothes off and their

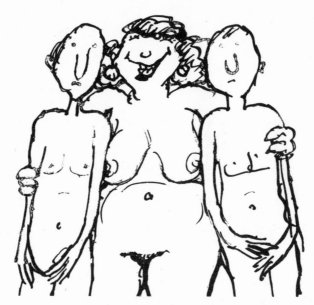

Getting into many of the older nudist camps is rather like being put up for the Garrick

propensity to have an erection. The official naturist magazine, *Health and Efficiency* (established in 1900 and incorporating *Sunbathing Review* and *Vim*), offers literary guidance on what to do in case the male member becomes priapically engorged when at the nudist beach. One correspondent recommended learning Gerard Manley Hopkins's 'The Windhover' by heart. 'I can assure you it is the only thing that works in the end.'

Whether or not your 'end' responds to Victorian lyric poetry, getting into many of the older nudist camps is rather like being put up for the Garrick. One is proposed, seconded and extensively vetted in the same way.

As well as insisting members have a family in tow, some clubs even forbid sunglasses, since they allow the naughty to leer in privacy. They also make you work for hours doing things

such as scything stinging nettles to rub out any flicker of passion or appreciation of the scenery.

Come to think of it, I don't know of any countryside view that would be improved, for me, if I took off my clothes. Yet it might greatly diminish the happiness of other innocent passers-by.

At the other end of the scale from the strict stalags of nudity is the open club. Anyone can walk in. I strolled into one called Eureka in Kent. The club just had to be at a village called Fawkham, up a road called Scratchers Lane. I kept my clothes firmly on. The place itself reminded me of a DSS version of the Last Judgement.

Tubby, bald, late-middle-aged men peered hopefully out of a building which seemed to have been partially destroyed in an air attack, though I am told things have improved. In fact, now that planning

permissions have been obtained, business is booming.

'He's a magistrate,' remarked a woman called Betty, well into her barmaid-glam fifties, pointing at the hairy bottom of a man crouched over a table tennis game, stiffly ready to serve.

'This is the sort of place you could be dancing with a doctor and not realise. There is no class with your clothes off.' Betty's breasts hung down like spaniel's ears. The milk jug for our coffee was in the shape of a naked breast. Betty said she'd be mother. Outside the window, on the grass, a washing machine was quietly rusting.

'You're not embarrassed with your clothes on?' roared Sid Leicester, also over the half century, who was a naked Lambeth Refuse Collector. In one corner sat a 35-stone man known as Fat Harry, stretching a huge pair of sweaty green underpants over his golf ball sized knuckles.

Eureka is the Arthur Daley end of nudism. Sid's other hobby was motorcross, although he had thankfully never been inspired to combine the two due to the mudguards not catching all the stones.

Several couples wore track suits. When I said this was against the spirit of the thing they said that they were nude underneath. Their children looked on the edge of panic as to why their father was punishing them in this revolting way.

This was not quite the sylvan idyll of male fantasy, peopled with the prettier members of Sunset Boulevard or perhaps a sprinkling of youthful Mitford sisters.

More sub *Stars on Sunday*. The carpet was disintegrating and there was that sour-sweet smell of excited bodies, more monkey house than musk.

Yet the club, with its extensive grounds and revealing woodland swings seems to have a definite attraction for the 'solitary male' who has given up all hope of winning a Nobel Prize for his contribution to the plastics industry.

'Sex? Occasionally things get wild,' Betty confided. 'But if a man puts his arm around me in here, Sid understands. If he did the same thing outside in the pub my husband would knock him out. It's all very civilised.'

Eureka was founded nearly 25 years ago by Mark Wilson, sixty-four, formerly a civil servant grade III in the Colonial Office.

When I rang him to ask about recent improvements, he said: 'We carry on regardless. Papers close. Governments fall. I was first written about in the *News Chronicle*, but we go on.'

Walking round the grounds on my visit he observed: 'We have everyone from vicars to witches, bankrupts to bank managers. We've had some of the most famous faces in the West End on that multiple swing.

'This is certainly not Cold Comfort Farm with a barbed-wire fence. Some are like Approved Schools. Unlike other clubs we have dances at night. The majority don't. They feel that if their members get struck by moonbeams anything could happen.'

According to Sid, it sometimes did: 'It's friendly. The women approach the men. Betty used to like dancing with a couple of black blokes. Great big chaps. We get a lot of passing trade from sales reps.'

One only hoped, for decency's sake, that they all knew 'The Windhover' by Gerard Manley Hopkins.

Agony
URSULA WYNDHAM

Q I hate the American term 'significant other' for the person with whom you are having an ongoing relationship. Can you suggest an alternative?
A I think 'concubine' and 'catamite' are beautiful words. Whether they are suitable terms in which to introduce your partner is perhaps debatable, so why not introduce significant others by their personal names and allow the company to draw what conclusions they please? For old women to introduce old men as their 'boyfriend' is pathetic.

Q I am worried about myself. I forget people's names so that they have to introduce themselves. I make a shopping list and still fail to collect all the items. I promise to take something to a friend – and turn up without it. Am I past help?
A Join the club. I and my friends are all along with you. Do not fret: it is when you have ceased to be aware that the alarm bells are ringing. One brave soul admitted, 'When I enter a room full of people I know well, the only name I can remember is Alzheimer.'

Q My husband and I have been married for more than 40 years and I'm sure he cares more for his dog than he does for me, although I do more for him than the dog does. When I've pointed this out to him, he replies that the dog doesn't argue with him. How can I make him see how much his rudeness upsets me?
A By following the dog's example. This is not an uncommon factor in a long married life. The dog gives him undiluted love and asks nothing in return. What more could an old man want! I never tried to compete with a dog during my love life. Other women were, by comparison, far less competitive. Women will make a wrong move. Dogs won't.

Q I want to know if my parents still have sex. Can I ask them?
A Yes, if you phrase it differently. You are suggesting that the old folk have never known the magic of human love and that you were born as the result of an animal exercise. There are two underlying questions: Can he still do it? Does she still enjoy it? I decided that my father lost his powers in his early sixties because of his fondness for telling of the mayor of some city warning Mr Churchill that his flies were undone, and receiving the answer: 'Have no fear, Mr Mayor, dead birds do not drop out of the nest.'

A Scholar and a Gentleman

My last letter to my publisher, written from South Africa a few weeks before his death, told the sort of true traveller's tale that delighted John Murray VI.

Arriving at sunset in the isolated hamlet of Campbell on the edge of the Great Karoo, I had some difficulty finding lodgings; the local Afrikaners spoke no English and were suspicious of a female sexagenarian bicyclist, suddenly appearing out of nowhere.

Then, in a tiny stone church built by English missionaries in 1832, I noticed a dusty glass-topped display case containing Livingstone's *Missionary Travels in South Africa* (1857). This large volume, open at the title page, gave the publisher's name and address: John Murray, 50 Albemarle Street, London. One hundred and thirty-six years later another Murray author drew from her passport that letter (To Whom It May Concern) with which Jock thoughtfully equipped 'his' travellers at the beginning of each journey. It was headed John Murray, 50 Albemarle Street, London.

Beckoning to the uneasy Afrikaner couple now dwelling in Livingstone's Campbell home, I pointed to the title page and then to my letter. At once they relaxed and smiled and invited me to stay the night. Even in the Karoo, pampered Murray authors can have occasion to feel grateful.

Jock's relish for such linkages, and his lifelong obsession with the late Lord Byron, did not prevent his seeing in which direction Murray's should turn during the post-war years – a critical period for publishers. He marvellously combined the romantic – revering the past and to an extent emotionally dependent on it – with the shrewd businessman who realised that a successful publisher must have one foot in the future.

The witty social Jock, all bonhomie and graciousness, eschewing the vulgarity of money talk, knew how to keep his own distinctive show on the road in defiance of transnational highwaymen. The House of Murray has survived since 1768 because each generation had the vision to adapt

Energetic, eccentric, frugal and generous, Jock Murray was a bookman of the old school, the sixth of his line and the father of the present incumbent at the famous publishing house. **Dervla Murphy** *recalls her long-standing friendship with the bibliophile, Byron-lover, and inspired editor who published her first book*

without compromising standards. The weight of tradition, although formidable indeed by the time Jock joined the firm in 1930, was never allowed to smother innovation.

But for a chance encounter with Penelope Betjeman I would never have met Jock Murray. Having cycled to India in 1963 I met her in Delhi and as we pedalled together through a crowded bazaar – Penelope with a load of firewood tied perilously to her carrier – I confessed to literary ambitions.

'Of course!' shrieked Penelope. 'Marvellous journey! Marvellous book! You must send it to Jock Murray.'

'To whom?' I yelled above the blare of rickshaw horns.

'To Jock Murray in Albemarle Street. You'll adore Jock. Everybody adores Jock!'

This suggestion genuinely shocked me; lèse-majesté and all that. John Murray was associated in my mind with Jane Austen, Byron, Borrow, Darwin, Livingstone, Isabella Bird, Younghusband – not to mention Freya Stark, at whose shrine I had been worshipping since early childhood when *The Valley of the Assassins* was read to me by my mother.

Back in Ireland, I ignored Penelope's preposterous advice and simultaneously sent off three copies of the *Full Tilt* typescript, not really expecting anyone to accept it. Embarrassingly, everyone accepted it.

Hastening to London to deal with this contretemps, I didn't like what I found. Not for nothing was I a county librarian's daughter who by the age of ten could tell from a distance the publisher of a given volume. (Fifty years ago imprints maintained a decent consistency.) I went on to develop some awareness of publishers' wily ways and in London I sensed heavy editorial hands all poised to turn my book into their book. ('Perhaps we could expand a little on that attempted rape…')

Telling everyone I would think about their offer I returned home and found a letter from Penelope – 'Have you sent your book to Jock Murray? If not, why not?' Thus it happened that a faint and dog-eared third carbon copy went off to No. 50 Albemarle Street.

A week later I had been summoned to The Presence by telegram and was ascending that hallowed staircase, quite unwomanned by suspense and awe. Jock's office was cramped, chaotic and almost as dusty as my own house. Typescripts, photographs, maps, manuscripts, newspaper cuttings, dust-jackets, bulging files and books old and new cluttered every surface, including the floor.

In a corner sat 'young John', as he was then known, experiencing his first week as a publisher and looking almost as nervous as I felt. (Now that neophyte is John VII – which, it suddenly strikes me, has a disconcertingly papal ring.) This was a reassuring scene, far removed from the bright, tidy, sterile offices of Those Others.

Very soon I no longer felt nervous. The legendary Jock alchemy was working; it seemed I had known this adorable person (Penelope had been right!) not for minutes but for years. Jock wanted to publish my *Full Tilt* and there was no squalid talk about baffling royalty percentages and terrifying promotion campaigns.

Then came an invitation to stay at Cannon Lodge; like many another Murray author, I had found not only a publisher but a whole family of friends.

Jock was an exhilarating mix of the conventional and the eccentric. Stacking plates was an unforgivable crime but driving through red traffic lights – given a sporting chance of getting away with it – was just good fun. (Good fun for Jock, not necessarily for his passengers.)

His famous frugality – typified by turning off lights in unoccupied rooms, wearing a slight frown as a general reprimand to whomever might have left them on – his frugality exactly accorded with my own. It could however slightly irritate some of the younger generation who found it difficult to reconcile with his equally famous generosity, overlooking the

simple mathematical fact that the frugal have more with which to be generous.

Frugality also determined Jock's advances to authors. He rightly expected a book to prove its worth before its publisher disbursed. The headline-grabbing advances with which the more notorious conglomerates wage their sordid wars caused Jock to smile one of his rather wicked small smiles and say nothing.

Now, while those conglomerates lurch from crisis to crisis in a stormy sea of their own creation, loaded with bewildered, seasick authors, the little House of Murray sails serenely on its way into the 21st century, steadily steered by John Murray VII.

Many of the Murrays' 'extended family' of author-friends who enjoyed the hospitality of Cannon Lodge will remember Jock's disingenuous habit of suggesting that 'early beds' would be a good idea. Then, having genially but firmly shepherded everyone upstairs, he would sneak away to work for two or three midnight hours on some typescript in urgent need of loving editorial care. And loving care was what those typescripts got, down to the last dash (of which he disapproved, pace Byron) and semi-colon.

As an editorial team, he and his wife Diana were inspired and inspiring. Jock's several pages of notes in tiny handwriting ('mere minutiae' he would

> **Very soon I no longer felt nervous. The legendary Jock alchemy was working; it seemed I had known this adorable person not for minutes but for years**

murmur self-deprecatingly) acted like those pinches of yeast that lighten a mass of dough. Then Diana would produce her notes, approaching the typescript's problems from quite other but equally important angles; this was yin and yang in perfect balance.

The loving care devoted to typescripts was extended to their creators, whether successful or not. So tender-hearted was Jock that even unknown would-be authors caused him many a sleepless night. How to word a kind rejection letter to someone who had plainly laboured for years on some utterly unpublishable work?

Regularly Jock was reminded that printed rejection slips are standard practice in the modern age; then he would brandish his eyebrows in his inimitable way, thus conveying that no such barbarism was acceptable to him.

At the root of Jock's celebrated charm was his respect for his fellow-beings and his awareness of their vulnerability. The effervescent, inquisitive, enthusiastic Jock, often melodramatically gesturing, usually ready with the appropriate aphorism or bon mot, was in part a cover-up for that other Jock whose own vulnerability was extreme and whose last months were darkened by the Bosnian tragedy. His caring for his authors was only one aspect of his caring for all of humanity.

Modern Life

What is... The New Man?

THE AMERICAN novelist Vanessa Drucker once told me she had always had a bit of a thing for old, old geezers. 'The trouble is,' she said sadly, 'you get fond of them, and then they die.' 'And leave you with nothing but their money?' I said. 'Not,' she said, 'as such. I find I fall for poor old geezers.'

This should put a spring in the step of all old geezers, for Miss Drucker is a statuesque, raven-haired party, rather in the mould of Elizabeth Taylor in her younger days, particularly those younger days when she was off the turps.

Alas, for younger geezers, there is less hope. It's no good just waiting to grow old, because by that time Miss Drucker will be old, too, and will either have grown tired of the whole business, or be casting her eye on sprightly centenarians.

Things are marginally better for blokes. Blokes have short hair, drink beer and watch football. If they are musicians, they play in the brass section. If they went to public school, they go into the city. Blokes carry plastic gym-bags with sporting equipment logos on the side; they use nasty personal grooming products from Boots. For a while they were desperately unfashionable, but some women are starting to fancy blokes again, and they now have their own wireless station: BBC's Radio Five Live, aka Radio Bloke.

The real losers are New Men. You will have seen New Men in the street. They wear puffy shoes like cheap pasties; dreary clothes; round gold-rimmed spectacles. They talk in whiffling, polytechnic voices and lean forward to hear your reply. Their shoulders are hunched, they are going bald in that particularly unforgivable way, and their mouths are frequently obscured by an unwholesome pubic fringe.

They are frequently to be found living in some form of marriage with a woman called Ros, who comes in two varieties.

Ros 1 is strident and unkempt. In her youth she travelled a lot, which she believes has broadened her mind. They met somewhere horrid, like a bus station or a Botswana Folk Nite at a pub on the outskirts, and are now going slowly to seed: her shin-hairs poke through her tights, he has an ear infection. She hates him, but he defers to her: 'No, let Ros have her say.'

Ros 2 is a wan, fey sopranino who is Into Things. Ley-lines, metempsychosis, Gurdjieff, crystals, all these give outward expression to her inchoate sense of guilt and shame. She may possibly erect a shrine to her ancestors, and in middle age is liable to 'remember' that her father interfered with her when she was little. The truth is that she is still little, but instead of encouraging her to grow up, the New Man gorges himself on her weaknesses like a colonial District Officer smiling upon the fuzzy-wuzzies.

New Men care. They believe the world is a phallocentric conspiracy. They treat women with deference and kindness. They change the babies' nappies, clean the lavatory, are gentle,

opposed to violence, non-competitive, home-loving and frequently vegetarian.

This, you may think, is all very nice. But it is not. New Men are ghastly. Their feminist posturings are like the public charitable donations of a rich and nasty man: a device to conceal and to win approval. They are like those horrible, shouty American men who tell you they don't give a *Goddamn* what anybody thinks of them, no *sir*, and then look anxiously to see if you approve of their staunch independent posture.

It is important to see through all this nonsense. A friend of mine was grilled by a committee of progressive film-financiers about whether a script she had written was sexist. 'But I'm a woman,' she said, 'and I wrote it.' This cut no ice with the committee – or, rather, the lone man on the committee who was the one doing the grilling.

The simple truth is that the silly arse was after a leg-over with one of the committee women. This is why New Men do it. Forty years ago, they'd have had a tattersall waistcoat, a Vauxhall with reclining seats, a chromium cigarette case with an enamel Scotty, a

comb in a leather case which said 'Comb' on it. Now they flaunt a gentle voice and feminist credentials.

But the New Man is doomed. Not by recent, and equally doomed, attempts to gain sympathy for men, puzzled, bewildered and threatened by powerful, independent women; nor by silly American ideas like the Guy Movement, where public relations executives and orthodontists pay $1000 to spend the weekend eating fried food in the woods and smelling each others' bottoms.

What dooms the New Man is evolution. The reason he is stuck with Ros 1 or 2 is that no other woman would have him. Though in theory they may admire his non-threatening, egalitarian, softly-spoken, non-judgmental, sheer bloody niceness, the primitive bit of the brain in charge of reproduction declares, quietly but firmly, that he would be useless in a tight corner, and it is simply not on.

She will trust him, confide in him, weep on his shoulder, but when, emboldened by her confidences, he finally makes his tentative, asparagus-stalk pass, she will unhesitatingly decline, and run off with a cad, a bastard, a bloke or even a middle manager.

The New Man has slouched up an evolutionary backwater. His reproductive strategy is as doomed as that of the kakapo, the flightless nocturnal parrot so winningly described in *Last Chance to See* by Douglas Adams, and not dissimilar.

Like the kakapo, he is dun-coloured, incapable in a crisis, and his mating behaviour actively repels the female. He is, in short, facing extinction. Perhaps we should set up a protected reserve where he can reproduce in safety. Then again, perhaps we shouldn't.

MICHAEL BYWATER

Olden Life

What was... Virol?

IF ONLY the mother of my friend Johnson had not had such faith in Virol, his life at my prep school in the Thirties might have been bearable. Matron had been cajoled into allowing him Virol as a substitute for the standard daily dose of cod liver oil, supplemented with stewed onions when there was a hint of a cold.

According to the pre-war advertisements, Virol was a panacea for all ills. Hoardings proclaimed its value in treating menstrual disorders, chronic fatigue, insomnia and a host of other complaints.

Johnson's undoing, responsible for the daytime bating, and the regular running of the gauntlet of knotted towels, was that proudly displayed on the platform at Oxenholme Junction, where the boys changed trains for the last lap of their journey back to school, was an enamelled hoarding which proclaimed 'Virol – anaemic schoolgirls need it'.

Johnson probably wouldn't have been a success anyway – but taking the potential prescription for anaemic schoolgirls was all that was needed to make his life hell.

Virol had huge sales; it supported a company which made nothing else. Doctors began to take notice; could it really have all the properties claimed for it? If so, how had they escaped attention in their *materia medica* classes at medical school?

The doctors were right. The recipe could have come from H G Wells; analysis showed it was a 20th-century 'Tono Bungay' composed of 59 per cent sugar (maltose) and 12.5 per cent fat. The rest was totally inert.

The BMT and Martin Olaks, the fount of all pharmacological wisdom, published this analysis, and Virol, like Tono Bungay, disappeared.

I met Johnson, by chance, a year or two ago in a pub. Now retired, his life had been worthy and mundane. Having learnt from his own experience, he sent his son to a state day school. Unfortunately, since then the young man has spent the greater part of his life in prison.

Who says that the old-fashioned prep schools are not character building?

DR THOMAS STUTTAFORD

Goodbye to all Tat

*It was the pitying glance of a superannuated starlet that finally released **Frank Barnard** from the purgatory of 'the trade'. Here, in an Oldie exclusive, he tells the full inside story of the slight rise and sudden fall of Nuffield Antiques*

THE SEX SYMBOL pauses at our stall of old toot. She picks up the grotesque ceramic figure of a drunk. Somewhere under the headscarf and behind the dark glasses is Joan Collins.

I remember seeing her with no clothes on in some late-night cobblers made in the Seventies. Behind her, poised plumply like a lackey to a Royal, is vaguely familiar Christopher Biggins. She passes him the figure, expressionless, and he reads plummily: 'Sweet Adeline'. He gives a short laugh and returns the figure to Collins who replaces it on our stall.

I sense an opportunity for a compelling spiel that will clinch the deal. All I say is: 'Fifteen pounds.' Collins and Biggins smile at me thinly, the smile you give to someone who has just told you he's a flowerpot. I have a feeling they are sorry for me, as you are for someone who thinks he's a flowerpot. As they move away, into the gloom of the dingy village hall, fifty-something women turn to fifty-something men and say: 'Do I look as old as that?' Fifty-something men say: 'Joan who?' and the dangerous moment is submerged in a litany of what she was in and when and who with and how she's never been a proper actress really has she?

We look at each other, fellow flowerpots. We look at the junk on the table in front of us. We look at the pitiful labels: 50p, £1.75, £3.00. We look at the other stall-holders as they dust off a plastic Mickey Mouse and re-position a chamber pot. We look at each other again and, without a word, the business of Nuffield Antiques draws to a merciful close.

It was meant to be fun. We'd slept through *Antiques Roadshow* for years, watched the first 10 minutes of *Lovejoy* before remembering how rotten it was, could recall Arthur Negus getting irritable with his guests and wondered where John Blye bought his suits. We even had a Volvo estate. All it took was a rummage through the attic for likely stock, some business cards saying yes, we really were Nuffield Antiques and suddenly we were trade.

We tried to cultivate a raffish, knowing demeanour. We went to sales. We looked under vases at marks that meant nothing to us. We looked inside drawers to see if they were really old and couldn't tell. We sucked our teeth

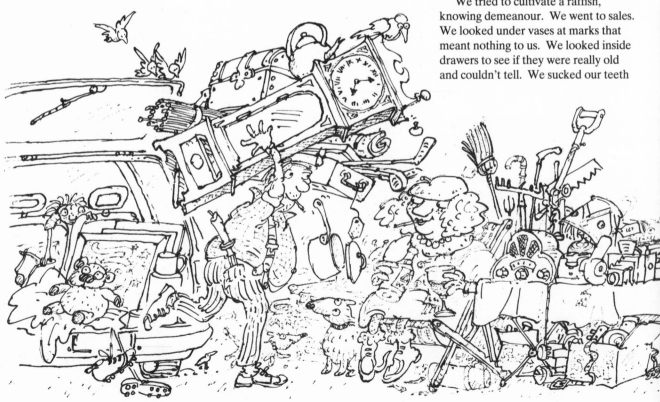

at prices and then found they'd been bargains. We snapped up some bargains of our own and found they were fakes. We were beguiled by the glitter and ignorant of the dangers, like children in a sweet factory.

At auctions, fairs and boot sales Nuffield Antiques was to be found scuffing its shoes and sucking its thumb. We always started sensible. Catalogues would be studied and items identified. Prices would be fixed and level-headed notes written in margins. Then those things would go for funny money and we would bid successfully for objects we had never noticed but looked alright from a distance of 40 feet. After the sale we would join the line to pay, holding the cardboard box containing the phoney, cracked whatever-it-was, unwilling to admit

even to each other that we'd been done… again.

'Good sale?' the woman would ask behind the cash desk; the woman with the velvet hat, the wooden beads and the bloodbright lipstick.

'Pretty good, pretty good.'

'Oh you bought that, did you? I wondered who bought that.'

There was the look again, pity mixed with mirth scudding about the face like a gnat over water. It was difficult to be dignified, to walk away with the rattling box of tat and into the usual argument.

It was always the same and fell into four stages. Stage one: 'Not very good, is it?' Stage two: 'Oh, it's all right, it's not that bad.' Stage three: 'Okay, it's ghastly, it's terrible.' Stage four: 'Well, why did you buy it?' 'Me buy it?

Come off it. You put your hand up.' 'Only because you told me to,' and so on and so on.

We hadn't got round to selling, just buying. 'There's only three things you need in this business,' a man called Blossom (Christian name) told us at a country house sale. 'That's stock, stock and stock.' We did the posh things Blossom went to, where you'd see nutcrackers for £1,500, and we checked out the booters, 15-stone country-and-western lovers who rigged up bright blue polythene sheeting to keep the rain off their collections of lacquered brass door-knobs, broken garden forks, Frank Ifield 45s and bits of coloured plastic pressed into many shapes. We heard rumours of stolen goods being passed on for rock-bottom prices but never had a chance to wrestle with our consciences.

It all seemed a long way from the smooth and cosy old-things atmosphere concocted by Hugh Scully, or the merry slippery japes of Lovejoy,

83

Lady Jane and Tinker, or the irritatingly knowledgeable Negus muttering: 'See that? Whoever made this really knew his stuff. Even carved it on the inside.' What little we learned simply showed how ignorant we were. It was a play in which, like bad actors, we were rocky on characterisation and uncertain of our lines.

We took a prompt or two from Miller's price guides and furtively consulted pocket books about silver and ceramics and collectors terms. Our performances improved. We picked up stuff in shops and said, 'Nice bit of Doulton' and it was. We'd say, 'Ah, Faience' and it would be. The aged gents in brown dustcoats at auctions gave us the nod-and-wink reserved for the trade. It was time to sell.

We decided to start with modest village hall affairs in Chiltern beauty spots. It was also where we finished but we weren't to know that.

Setting up is an art. Spot-lamps, green baize and display cabinets are swiftly conveyed from Volvos, Transits and Range Rovers through the rain – always the rain – to the pongy clatter of this week's hall. Exquisitely lettered labels are tied, not stuck, to the merchandise, nameplates set out just so, chairs arranged, thermoses opened and cigarettes, often in holders, lit up.

Our stuff was wrapped, by some quirk of our woodshed, in old copies of the *Sun*. Our display system comprised two or three picnic and card tables, all of different widths and levels, a moth-gnawed ex-Army blanket that came back from Belgium in 1945 and a shelf created from two logs and a plank discovered in the derelict greenhouse we've never got round to sorting out. Our labels were adhesive – once on, never off – and came in two colours, Dayglo red and Dayglo orange. The whole caboodle took 25 minutes to assemble. It was like building a Zeppelin…

Our display attracted a heartening amount of interest until we realised the doors weren't open yet. Our first visitor was a squirey character with a strawberry nose and a hectic jacket. He had been hired to vet the stalls to ensure it was an antiques fair, sorry fayre, and not a jumble sale. A third of our stock bit the dust. 'Fake, modern, inappropriate, take it to a boot sale, really not us, are you serious?'

Sifted, fellow stallholders rushed to study our dregs. Something was wrong. Still the doors weren't open and we'd sold half our stuff. No bargaining either. 'How much? I'll take it.' Prices we'd agonised over – 'nobody's going to pay that' – were greeted with the savage smile of Dracula glimpsing a plump white neck.

The seventy-year-old with the Hermes scarf round her head who specialised in art deco jewellery snatched the spider brooch that had been haunting the family for generations and only then observed: 'Frankly, my dears, you're giving your bits away.' Within five minutes our ex-bits had appeared on other stalls at twice the price.

There were consolations. We counted the money. There were lots of nice jangly pound coins and rustly notes. We experienced the tactile pleasure that motivates misers. We conveniently forgot the cost of getting there, the price of the stall space, the four bacon rolls from the breakfast bar and any notional rate we might care to apply to our time.

Consolations, too, in seeing our ex-bits not sell as the public finally shuffled into view. They had the aimless, empty-eyed mien of workers from Lang's *Metropolis*. They passed before us, smoking, sniffing, coughing, sucking teeth, chewing gum, picking things up, grunting derisively at prices, putting things down, shuffle, nag, sniff, sniff, nag, shuffle…

Our under-priced bargain basement did well. Two thirds of the stock went. One man even bought our logs while the vetter had his back turned. Hermes Scarf sold nothing. The spider brooch lay placidly awaiting a new exorcist. The day was toweringly boring. Bums went to sleep, knees set solid.

The *Metropolis* extras thinned and finally faded. We counted our money, jangling and rustling just to be irritating. We never did so well again. Blossom had been right. It was a question of stock. The stuff we'd had that first time had most of it been accumulated over decades; good, honest pieces, hard to find, easy to sell and everyone's after them.

Still, we persevered. But one day, just before Joan Collins, we did the calculation; petrol, space costs, refreshments, profit, not to mention time. 'You know,' said one half of Nuffield Antiques, 'we'd do better selling those bacon rolls.'

It was the pity in the famous Collins eyes that clinched it. 'My God, she thinks we need to do this. To sit all day, with deadened bums and hate in our hearts, desperate to flog a pitiful array of beads and baubles to *Metropolis* folk.'

'Anyway,' we agreed as we loaded the Volvo for the last time, 'we never wanted to sell Sweet Adeline anyway.'

What we did sell was the Volvo. At a cracking loss…

M'LUD **KATHRYN LAMB**

THIS MAN HAS SPENT HIS ENTIRE LIFE WATCHING TELEVISION…

HE HAS LOST THE ABILITY TO THINK, OR DISTINGUISH BETWEEN FACT AND FICTION!

CAN YOU TELL ME WHAT HAPPENED IN YESTERDAY'S 'NEIGHBOURS'?

PIN-UPS

Mary Whitehouse

picks her top six

1 Ernest Whitehouse
Endlessly patient – well, he has to be, doesn't he? He's a very nice man, too!

2 Lord Lew Grade
Just about the only man involved in television prepared to meet and support us in the early days of our campaigning. It was not an easy thing to do.

3 Van Gogh
A painter whose sense of abandon in colour and shape has inspired me since I first encountered his work in college more than 60 years ago!

4 Margaret Thatcher
For the kindness which lies behind her often austere exterior. I remember the occasion when we presented our Award to *Yes, Minister*. I stumbled and banged my very sensitive shin against a wooden step. Within seconds she had grabbed people to form a barrier between me and the press.

5 Malcolm Muggeridge
His courage in publicly declaring his newly found Christian faith after almost a lifetime of atheism inspired the greatest admiration.

6 John Parrott
A wonderful snooker player with an apparently unshakeable good temper.

Right: Indefatigable moral campaigner Mary Whitehouse

MANY ELDERLY people are condemned to watch television all day and all night, but it is only on my visits to a health farm in Suffolk that I become aware of being a citizen of the electronic age.

The experience, now repeated four times a year as I struggle to remain within the guidelines on fatness laid down by Mrs Bottomley, does not warm me to the rest of the human race, or to my fellow countrymen. Even the ranks of oldies marching past the Cenotaph on Armistice Day made me scowl. Fools, dupes… they allow themselves to be put on exhibition like this so that the young can laugh at them, and the politicians on parade can look fresh and purposeful by comparison.

Nearly everybody who appears on television looks untrustworthy, but Britons never look worse than when they appear as the studio audience on BBC 1's *Question Time.* I appeared on it once, many years ago, when Robin Day was the question-master. Although mildly irritated by Day, I found the audience so moronic, dishonest and unpleasant that I lost my temper with them and have never been asked back.

In the performance I watched while at Shrubland Hall, Sir Norman Fowler appeared with Gordon Brown and two stooges – a fat lady and an old man – whose names I did not catch. Brown made mincemeat of Fowler, demanding to know why the government spent £1 billion on this and not on

RAGE

Auberon
Waugh

that, in an angry, hectoring tone, full of contempt and loathing. I would not have minded this, having no particular love or admiration for Fowler, except that I thought Brown equally odious, and would have liked to see him humiliated too.

Brown gave a foretaste of what we can expect when the Tories are wiped out at the next General Election: quite quick and glib, with an impatient, thuggish manner and a brutal gleam in his glass eye, he appears the answer to every British whinger's dream – a tough, embittered proletarian, seething with resentments, who swears he knows the answer to everything. Maddened by the scent of power in his nostrils, he will stop at nothing.

It is only after one has studied the studio audience that one realises how these

two ratty little men trying to score off each other, one being rude, the other being unctuous, represent all we have by way of political debate in this country. *Question Time* may show Britain at its worst, but so far as the level of political debate is concerned, it is spot on.

Silly, unpleasant faces make carefully prepared demands for prisoners to be treated more harshly, for the government to spend more money on pensions or education or health or road safety. Other faces simply whinge about how unfair it is that anyone should earn more or own more or go to better schools or do better in exams than anyone else. Everything they say is odious and ignorant, yet this, we must accept, is the true voice of urban England.

At any rate it is the true voice of those prepared to express an opinion, which may not be the same thing, but these noises offer the only guidelines politicians

have – these and the ever-encroaching pressure groups, whether anti-smoking, anti-alcohol, anti-hunting, pro-Life or anti-Life. It is to these people that our politicians must look for approval, since nobody else is interested in them, and it is an essential part of the political sickness that sufferers must win approval and admiration even as they exert power.

The result is a general paralysis. The government can't tell us what we all know – that government spending is hopelessly out of control, health and education are kyboshed by idle or redundant employees, the police have degenerated into a gang of self-serving racketeers. Any of these admissions would allow points to be scored by Gordon Brown, in his monomaniac desire to make everything worse. There can be no debate.

It may have been a happy accident that Fowler and Brown were both nasty pieces of work. Sweep them

'This is Elfreda. She can tell your fortune from your postcode'

away and the ghastly audience remains. The audience can't face truths about our schools, our young people, our teachers, our national resources or anything else – let alone about themselves. The fact that the two politicians are prepared to play along with with these conventions may make them all the more easy to despise, but it does not offer any solution.

The answer is surely that *Question Time* shows Britain at its most unattractive for the simple reason that the English (in particular) don't really want to discuss politics. We are not a nation of intellectuals and we are not interested in politics. We will vote when elections come round but that is about it. Force an Englishman to express a political opinion, and he will make a fool of himself.

If the politicians were left to get along without public notice, briefly reported only in the posh papers, they would assuredly do a better job. Any extension of democratic debate is a mistake. Even the politicians have gained nothing from appearing on television, since they are now more despised than ever.

The general public has shown its own preferences, which are for television soap operas and the sadistic hounding of any celebrities who emerge from them. These people are quite capable of throwing out any government which causes them inconvenience. My point is that they are less likely to be inconvenienced in this way if they are not consulted too much about the government of the country.

'COME AND MEET Sam,' said Jack McGowran, who was in his dressing room taking off his make-up after playing Clov in Samuel Beckett's own production of *End Game* in Paris in 1964. Beckett came into the Closerie des Lisas about half an hour later and sat down with McGowran, myself and some intense Frenchmen.

He was very tall, over 6'3", graven-faced like an Aztec chief. His accent was distinctly Dublin, sort of lower case Shaw, but with the same sardonic whip. He had been involved in a libel case I had written about in a book, but clearly had not relished the part he had taken in it so there was no bad feeling.

Sport was what he wanted to talk about – to Jackie (who had been Irish high-jump champion) about the centre of gravity and its relation to the high jump, and to me about the potential of the new fibreglass pole in the pole vault.

Jackie McGowran, who could spin tales like Oscar Wilde or Brendan Behan, recalled a hammer-throwing schoolteacher, named McGlashan, who had taken to the drink. At a teachers' conference in Bundoran, McGlashan had complained at breakfast that a black man with a sword had emerged from the boiled egg in front of him and was about to decapitate him.

His friends had locked him in his room, feeling that he lacked the stamina for the serious drinking that such a week entailed, and were taking a bracing walk on the pier when, looking back to the hotel, they observed a wardrobe being pushed out of the window of McGlashan's room. When they rushed back to investigate they were assured by the hammer thrower that the black man was in the wardrobe and the problem had been resolved.

The high point of McGowran's story, however, was that when he had recounted it three weeks later at the Great Southern Hotel in Galway to a retired lieutenant-colonel from the Indian Army with whom he was taking a snifter at 3am, it didn't take a feather out of the military gent. He listened

I once met...

Samuel Beckett

to the narrative politely, taking it as a matter of course. 'I have a simllar problem myself!' was his only comment.

After a pause, he added confidentially: 'But fortunately just now the person concerned is up my left sleeve. By a stroke of luck he has a long beard so I can reach up and pull him down when I feel like it.' He then, according to McGowran, proceeded to put his right hand up his left sleeve, whip it down and stamp whatever he thought he had in it on the carpet, with the remark: 'That'll fix him for the night.'

During the telling of the tale Beckett's face had changed. Angst was responding to Celtic massage. He was smiling now like a poet in an Irish pub listening to similar inspired guff. Even his accent increased its Liffeyside content, as he gently urged McGowran on with encouraging comments. The locals looked on with some unease. After all Sam was a High Priest of the Absurd. Was he about to defect, relinquishing his role at the Gate of Misfortune? It was all right to roll the stone up the hill forever but you mustn't get it over the top.

Sam solved the problem by going out to get me a cab. He came back to say goodnight whlch he did wlth elaborate courtesy. When I looked up to reply, he seemed taller than ever, but I could see the Aztec mask was back.   **ULICK O'CONNOR**

'They're fine – I'll take them all'

Nevermore, Hector

*He was an orphan, an avian genius, a psychopath, and **Paul Pickering** ran four marathons to keep him and his live-in lover in rats*

Bored with bedsit tedium and The Archers, he beak-drilled his way through a plasterboard wall to proclaim 'I'm Hector' to a dozing Irish labourer who promptly ran screaming into the street

SO FAREWELL, sweet Hector. The raven I have adopted at London Zoo for more than 10 years has been put down by the Royal Zoological Society. As indeed has Doris, his companion and close confidante.

I found this out when visiting the old bird's cage, only to be confronted with a revoltingly cute black and white lemur, the sort of thing serial animal exploiters like Richard Adams and David Attenborough take to their press launches.

When I asked a keeper where Hector and his mate Doris were, the answer at least was guiltily apologetic. 'We, er, had to. He was getting on. He'd had a good innings. He was falling off his perch. Well, he couldn't stand on his perch without propping himself against the side of the cage. His mate? Yes, she's gone too, I'm afraid. They are very social birds, ravens.'

I thanked him out of some strange English politeness, trying not to cry. I do hope though that when I snuff it no one grabs hold of my lady wife with a cry that she has always been wonderfully social and attempts to throw her on the funeral pyre after me. Or that if I am spotted propping myself against a winter cherry in the grounds of an old person's home, I will not be whisked off to the vet's for my 88p's worth.

I pray that Hector did not go gently into the good night, but took a tasty extremity or two of the vet with him. 'He was not an easy bird. Not an easy bird at all. But could he talk!' said one of the other keepers, shaking his head.

Talking was how I met the bird a decade ago, as I passed a cage near the panda enclosure. 'I'm Hector,' intoned a cool, mellifluous baritone. I looked around. All I could see was a blue-black raven as big as a large domestic cat and a bright red sign noting *This Animal Is Dangerous*. It was love at first sight. 'I'm Hector,' he repeated. The voice was pure Richard Burton but with slight undertones of the Master, Noël Coward.

He could also say, 'How are you today, madam?' and then lapse into Arthur Mullard cockney with 'Give us it here, then'. This was part of a game he played with children.

He would keep a coin or a button or a shiny pebble in the back of his cage. On seeing a young, smiling face, Hector would hop up to them and proffer the button. They would take it. 'Give us it here, then,' Hector would say. As they endeavoured to hand it back to him, he would try to remove their fingers with his beak.

'There's a dark side to Hector. He was thrown out of the Tower for attacking people, and he nearly had my eye out,' said a former keeper, who had to get the bird to savage a broom just to clean his cage. The broom would be introduced into the main enclosure. Hector would seize upon the bristles. As carefully as he could the keeper would then throw the broom and Hector into a room at the back. 'If you asked me to go in with Hector or go in with the tiger, I would take the tiger any day,' he said.

The bird's route to the zoo, as the institution's only black political prisoner, was a circuitous and tragic one.

He was discovered, a furious, fluffy creature, wandering alone in the

Black Mountains of Wales, by a social worker living in south London. The raven learned to ride on the steering wheel of the social worker's mini-van and, on a diet of Pedigree Chum, quickly grew into a very powerful, but not entirely balanced bird. The social worker was prone to bouts of depression and often left Hector alone, listening to Radio Four where he picked up his faultless diction and doubtless heard Coward.

Sadly, a new home had to be found for the raven when, bored with bedsit tedium and *The Archers*, he beak-drilled his way through a plasterboard wall to proclaim 'I'm Hector' to a dozing Irish labourer who promptly ran screaming into the street. Hector was dispatched to the Tower of London and the care of the Yeoman Raven Master. At least there he could fly free.

One would have thought that the food and freedom and international fame of the Tower grounds would be an ideal solution. But just as a hand-reared mallard becomes a feathered Al Capone, so a much more intelligent crow who has lost all fear of humans (even social workers) is a flying nightmare.

Hector was soon stripping the rubber bits off windscreen wipers and neatly pecking the surface of guardsmen's boots, puncturing their legs if they went to kick him. When another raven was stabbed by a tourist, Hector began to mark Americans for air attack. He hated bright-coloured plaid jackets.

One fateful day, with his cry of 'Give us it here, then', he launched himself at the floral hat of a lady from Little Rock and tore it to pieces, stamping on the bits and laughing. He then walked up to where she had collapsed on the ground and announced 'I'm Hector'. Hysterical with shock and thinking she had become an extra in *Exorcist III*, the woman was rushed to hospital. Hector was taken to Regent's Park where he met Doris – the love of his life.

He and Doris tried to have a family but Hector would usually end up throwing the nest around the cage. 'Crows easily become paranoid. Hand-reared birds such as Hector have no fear and so when they get angry they attack. And once they start to go for people they seldom stop. We call this type of behaviour mobbing. He is a very sick bird,' said my former tutor, Dr Uli Weidmann, a distinguished animal behaviourist.

Dr Russell Coope, a specialist on birds of prey, added, 'Ravens have great memories, and in Hector's case

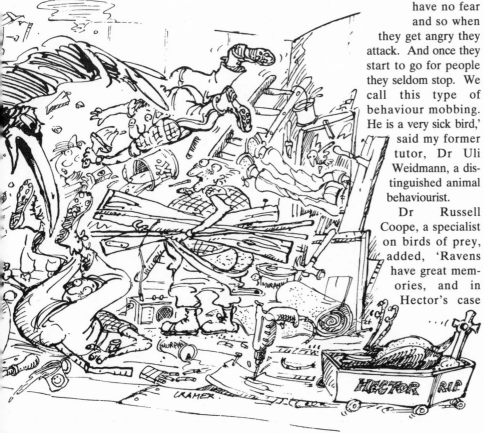

he must have been injured or insulted in some way. Ravens are the brightest of birds. Much more intelligent than parrots, and they love to tease people. A few like Hector develop bad habits. One raven I knew used to hammer at ladies' painted toe nails when it was fashionable to have shoes with open toes.'

Hector became increasingly dangerous and unapproachable. He was Keats's bird in a gilded cage and, simultaneously, all heaven in a rage. He was magnificent.

I very gladly completed four marathons (three London, one Hull) to help keep him and Doris in rats, happy in the knowledge I was the only one, among all those double glazing executives and Youth Club pederasts, running for something thoroughly bad.

And now he is gone, to the ultimate gothic horror set, hopping around in Hades with Robert Maxwell to snack on and the Queen Mother to look forward to, with his *Götterdämmerung* groupie Doris. I only hope that on windy nights, when the moon is out, the 'humane' souls who dispatched him and Doris might catch the sheen of his feathers in the darkness at the bottom of their bed. Hear his jack-knife beak tapping at their window. Tremble at his low, guttural laugh.

Sooner than they think, they will have to follow Hector, to meet up with him again. And Doris. Who no doubt will be waiting, refreshed, talons sharpened. For there is no such thing as nevermore to a raven.

A RIGHT ROYAL COCK-UP

*It fell to **Martin Locke** to provide an impromptu climax to the Royal College of Music's Royal Concert – a memory which fifty intervening years have done nothing to dim*

Shortly after the war I was a callow piano student at the Royal College of Music. War-time shortages continued. Coal strikes and power-cuts meant crippling hours pounding keyboards in unheated rooms in sub-zero weather.

Moving from one practice-room to another provided the only opportunity to restore circulation to the legs, and while doing this one cold winter's morning the Registrar approached, shot his lower plate at me in an alarming grimace and asked:

'Your name Baker?'

'No, sir. Locke, sir.'

'You'll do, then. Timpani, First Orchestra, next term.'

This was astounding. The RCM ran two orchestras, with a natural progression from Second to First as talent increased. A solo pianist had no place in either, except possibly to hit a triangle in an emergency, but even then only in the Second Orchestra. The percussion section (or 'Kitchen' as it was commonly known) of the First Orchestra was reserved specifically for those on a conducting course. That position gave them better opportunity to observe and learn from their professor in action.

Weeks of intensive training by one of London's leading timpanists were necessary before I could with anything less than terror join the 'Kitchen' as its principal, surrounded as I was by others often older and certainly more experienced in this group activity.

And then I found that the rehearsals were leading to the principal 'event' in the RCM calendar – the Royal Concert. This was the academic and social climax of the year, at which the First Orchestra would perform demanding works, star soloists would play excerpts from concertos, and the annual prizes would be announced. These, if the demanding workload of the Royal Family permitted, might be presented personally by the College's patron, Her Majesty the Queen.

There came a day in June, I think. The routine was well-established and rehearsed. The orchestra would take their places first, to tune-up, scratch, blow and thump their own particular 'difficult bits' as normal. The audience would filter in and sit down to study programmes and hats. An anticipatory silence would then descend. Following a discreet signal, we would all, orchestra and audience, rise to our feet as the Royal Party took their seats in the balcony. Then everybody would sit down again to await the drum-roll by me, timpanist of the First Orchestra, heralding the National Anthem. Then the audience would rise and we could launch into a stirring performance of 'God Save the King'.

All went well until the Royal Party entered – Her Majesty the Queen, as expected, and, as a bonus, Their Royal Highnesses the

'Remind me – am I getting up or going to bed?'

Princesses Elizabeth and Margaret Rose. The Princesses themselves were not entirely unknown to the students. They frequently came to College for their own tuition and, from those who had discreetly leant an ear against the door, were quite a match for some of us. Furthermore, extremely privileged students might be summoned to the Palace to provide suitable accompaniment to the delicate tinkle of teacup in saucer. Dvorak's *Humoresque* and cucumber sandwiches. It was even rumoured that their Majesties sometimes retired, leaving the Princesses to have half an hour's conversation with people of their own age.

So as the Royal Party took their places, I'm afraid my concentration was on a very smartly-dressed Princess Elizabeth. A good, fashionable top-coat, plain but well-shaped in a sort of pinky-mushroomy-beige. A discreet handbag in another shade of pinky-beige. A champignon-shaped hat, very simple and neat, but in another mushroomy-beige.

Shortages applied to everyone, of course, no-one had matching accessories in those days, but I was dreamily fascinated by the slight variations in tones. Until someone kicked me. The conductor had been shaking his fist at me for some time to encourage me to start the drum-roll in G which would open the proceedings. Not a good omen…

The grand finale to the concert was to be Rimsky-Korsakov's *Scheherezade*.

The conductor had been shaking his fist at me for some time to encourage me to start

Possibly a little taxing for a student orchestra, but with lots of enthusiasm we got through most of it. However, near the end there is, in the timpani part, a long slow murmur in F natural on the lowest-pitched and largest drum, *ppp*, which is followed in due course by a sudden *ffff* (yes, four of them) in F sharp on the smallest drum.

Just before the previous Christmas, the orchestra had accompanied a performance in the Opera Theatre in the basement. It was agreed that the timpani could stay there over the holidays, providing I came back a day early to restore them upstairs to the Concert Hall.

A dreadful winter, burst pipes, and the timpani were floating in the Opera pit. Total despair, as proper skins were impossible to obtain and we had to nurture what we had with the greatest care.

This is why I had never dared to rehearse that top F sharp – ever – and by agreement. The skin had never been tuned so high, nor attacked by anything over a single *f*. The risk was too great.

My performance began. During the long, slow F natural on the largest drum on my left, I leant across the two intermediate drums to the smallest drum on my far right, tentatively winding it up – fearing a split in the process – listening to the squeaks as the skin stretched to an unaccustomed pitch.

One of the essential techniques with the drum is that you do not ever 'hit' it. You pluck the note out, aiming to retract the stick from a point only just below the surface of the skin, and nearer the rim than the centre. Rather like a karate blow. However, I am left-handed. Came the moment, crouched to my left in readiness for the climax as the conductor assured himself the Kitchen was ready…

Overarm I went, all finesse forgotten, across the intervening timpani, straight through the centre of the skin and up to the shoulder in the smallest and tightest drum in London. Luckily for me, others continued to create just as much pandemonium.

The student in charge of the cymbals was South African, simian of features with a grey-green complexion. A cymbalist's wrists go through leather straps, to which each cymbal is secured by a Turk's-head knot on the inside. Someone – we never found out who or when – had with a razor-blade cut halfway through the knot on the right cymbal.

Not at the moment of my disaster, but when Rimsky-Korsakov next called for maximum effort, Geoffrey's right cymbal, having effectively clouted his left, went on upwards high into the air. It was a miracle that no-one was killed, as all were so busy puffing and banging and scraping that none of us were aware of the un-suspended Sword of Damocles on its way down.

The cymbal thus arrived unexpectedly for both orchestra and Rimsky-Korsakov. On edge it landed, on the top rostrum of the orchestra, whence it rolled down, a step at a time with entirely its own rhythm, ending up at the conductor's pedestal going round and round like a plate. *Boing-boing-boingggg*, hypnotising the first violins, who could at least have put a foot on it.

All was not yet over. Mortified by his calamity and duly aware of the occasion, Geoffrey fainted. Through the tubular bells. Gracefully but not silently he carried them with him amongst the double-basses.

As in a car-crash, Nature has thankfully wiped out any memories after the disasters during the Royal Concert in the Kitchen.

La Dolce Vita

*When **Nick Baker** got his first view of the
Eternal City, he found it pretty much as it has
always been – gracious, opulent and brash*

I had never been to Rome before. It was
hot. I had booked four nights in an old
hotel up a side street. My room was on
the ground floor. I opened the double
windows inwards, revealing shutters
chained and padlocked against thieves.
Someone was tuning up a Suzuki directly
outside, breaking off occasionally to shout
football opinions to his friend. Oh, well, I had
wanted to hear Italian spoken. Peering down-
ward between the slats my view was chrome
tubing and feet on pavement.

That evening I had two suppers: a pizza
from the Brothers Filli, then, at a café near the
Piazza Ancona at 3.00 am, soup, red wine and
tagliatelle. The women near me were dressed
as for the theatre and the men appeared to have
been doing deals since lunchtime.

Next day I took a conducted coach tour
of the ruins including a crushingly boring 19th

*Piazza San Bernado:
'At the Moses Fountain
he intoned, "Restor-éd
two years ago, one
million dollars, can
you imagine"'*

century church; even the ante-rooms had ante-rooms. The guide strode up and down the bus giving us the lowdown in Italian, French, German and finally, English. At the Moses Fountain he intoned 'Restor-éd two years ago, one million dollars, can you imagine.' By the Capitoline Hill we got 'This was-a Roman Supermarket, here was parking for five-a-hundred Chariots two-a-thousand year ago, horses' pollution some problem, can you imagine.'

We swung through the Piazza Barberini. A man of about forty wove at speed through the traffic on a Vespa; his right leg flung casually over his left, left hand on the left handlebar, right hand on his right hip. No crash helmet, can you imagine.

One evening I went to the Via Vittorio Veneto and sat drawing outside the expensive cafés. Up near the Café de Paris a photocall for a fashion show attracted a big crowd and a lot of police. Under floodlights tall girls sweated and posed in fur coats, fur hats, grey fur, white fur, fox fur. I found my way inside and could have sat on one of the gilt chairs and waited for the show to start. Instead I discovered a 'piano bar' below ground in the same block.

A middle-aged man in a white jacket played a white grand piano and a synthesiser and sang. The scene was bathed in pink light and mirrors. A painting behind the pianist, by Bernard Buffet out of Modigliani, showed the back view of a beautiful girl peeling down her knickers. 'Roman' statuary stood on pedestals, mainly women undressing. I ordered a Ricard and sat on one of the plush banquettes. Five girls sat across the room with their shoes off, feet up, doing their nails and chatting. When I started to draw, the two heavies in DJs came over, looked, smiled and went back to their posts.

One of the girls was called Carmen. She had on an olive-coloured wool dress and shoes, that was all. I gave her a drawing of herself and she told me her family were in Rio de Janeiro; would I like to go upstairs with her? I assumed she didn't mean to the fashion show.

'You are a very beautiful girl, but no thank you' I said, realising how ghastly this sounded. I felt the girls and their minders had accepted me and allowed me to draw. I didn't think they saw me as a punter but the offer was made just in case. Anyway I didn't want to. I had seen the three men who had 'gone upstairs' since I had arrived.

I offered to buy the girls a drink but the bigger minder very kindly restrained me. At £11.50 each, he did so fairly easily. I dropped all

Main picture: Via del Nazareno, the Way of the Nazarene

Left: Putting on the style in the Via Veneto, outside the Cafe Doney

Five girls sat across the room with their shoes off, feet up, doing their nails and chatting. When I started to draw, the two heavies in DJs came over, looked, smiled and went back to their posts

Above: The Piano Bar, Via Veneto

Left: Via Ancona, 3.00 am – 'The men appeared to have been doing deals since lunchtime'

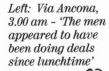

my small change on the marble floor. It was
carefully gathered up and courteously returned.

On my last day I found myself near the
Trevi Fountain in the late afternoon. It had
been drained of water and surrounded with
wire fencing to tart it up for the World Cup
football fans to frolic in the following summer.

To make a wish, or for good luck, you stand
with your back to the fountain and throw
three coins over your shoulder, hoping they
go in. I felt strangely self-conscious about
doing this on my own. A pretty girl was
being photographed about to throw in
her three coins, so I sidled up near to
her and when she threw her coins
over her shoulder I threw mine.
Her family are probably still
wondering who that prat
next to her is.

*'St Peter's Square –
how many acres
of Kodak that
piece of ground
must have seduced!
I asked two
Americans to take
a photo of me
using my camera.
Il Papa wasn't
in Rome and the
Sistine Chapel
was closed, the
priest said. For
re-decorating the
ceiling? Ha-ha!'*

IS JOAN LITTLEWOOD still with us? My God is she!

When having Joan as a house-guest means talking into the night – perhaps on the recent spate of books on Christopher Marlowe and her theories on his murder – and the very next morning over breakfast she takes up the conversation where she left off – then – then you know for sure that she is most certainly still with us.

Joan is a brilliant conversationalist and one of the most attentive and en-couraging listeners I have ever known. Her voice still has those warm notes that made her talks, early in her career for the BBC in Manchester, so successful.

She sometimes signs her postcards Madame Hell – always postcards, for as she says, 'It is possible to put every-thing you want to say on a postcard'.

I worked with her at the Theatre Royal, in Stratford, east London for six years, when each show triumph-antly transferred into the West End, making it possible for her partner and manager Gerry Raffles to keep 'the home fires burning' at Stratford. She was and is my university.

When she left the theatre because of her beloved Gerry's death, coun-tries – not just theatrical manage-ments, but countries – Germany, France, a continent even – Australia – offered her anything to come and run whatever she wanted, a 'fun palace' or a National Theatre.

Her rehearsals were not just about the play but involved discussions about poetry, the latest trends in architecture, or even the (then very new) science of cybernetics. Books were always scattered about the green room and we'd better have read them.

Delicate is how I would describe her and her methods of work. The work that went into the preparation of even the simplest scenes was ex-tremely delicate and painstaking. Her rehearsals were usually conducted in a circle of light on-stage in the otherwise darkened theatre.

In that circle the concentration would be intense but easy, the kind of concentration one remembers as a kid, modelling something in plasticine, not wanting to draw up the spittle at the

Still With Us
Joan Littlewood

corners of your mouth in case the sound of that drawing up would disturb the act of creation. Deep, wonderful, natural unstrained con-centration that all of us are born with and then forget. Joan – circling the circle of light, listening, watching, occasionally making quiet remarks – reminded us of that gift, that power of concentration we were all given at birth and knew as children.

'Our work,' she said, 'must never look like work. We must be human on that stage, not seem as though we are acting.' The hours of delicate work that made it not look like acting were endless.

Joan is a seducer in the theatre. 'Our job is to seduce. Bloody Brecht and all that alienation. Extend your arms, you only have to love 'em.'

Not to be called to rehearsals gave me a sense of loss. One day I wasn't called until late afternoon. I went in any case during the morning's session, just to sit in the stalls and watch. I gradually became aware that there were other white faces – people sitting, quietly watching. I am enslaved, I thought, and left and went to the cinema.

Coming out, I realised I was going to be late and as I dashed into the theatre faced a furious Joan. One did not keep Joan waiting. She herself tried never to keep us hanging about. 'I'm sorry, Joan,' I said. 'Where have you been?' she demanded angrily.

'I was here this morning, in the stalls watching, hanging on to your every word and thought, bugger this, I'm going to the pictures.' Her face broke into that marvellous grin of hers and she said, 'Ah, you are learning.'

She had a temper that had to be seen to be believed, but often after one of her outbursts she would run outside to laugh. 'That was a good murder I just committed,' she would say. If you could withstand her onslaught, the resurrection would surely follow. If you couldn't with-stand it, you had to move on.

Her fingers are long and artistic, her hands soft, there are flowers on the table at breakfast, she is a romantic in the true sense of the word. The story of her man Gerry and her love for him is one of the great love stories, as yet never told.

She is tough, no denying, but tough in a naturally maternal way, certainly not the clinging kind. ('Get out of the nest, learn to fly, you don't need me.') She loves good wine, good food, good gossip. (I must be careful about the wine. 'Good' does not mean expensive. Her favourite 'plonk' is Côtes du Rhône for the everyday enjoyment of drinking.)

Her betrayals were legion (in work that is) but only because at that time she felt that someone needed a shock to the system. There were those who said that they would never work for her again. But their mistake was in saying 'work *for* her'. You worked *with* Joan, and not understanding that led to many a downfall.

It is good that her laughter is still with us, the kind of laughter that is full-throated and generous. Her anger is also still with us: get her on today's politicians, or on the state of the country which, of course, she loves – well not the country exactly, but the spirit that was once Elizabethan England.

She still despises bullshit but can admire good sleight-of-hand and fakery. She defends to the death those she loves or approves of.

She is full, still, of a human spirit that is truly blessed, the kind of spirit that when found makes one proud of the human race.   **VICTOR SPINETTI**

WHEN I SAW that shares in Kleeneze Holdings had soared on news of an invention that claims to bring old batteries back to life, my mind immediately flew back to schoolboy summers more than 30 years ago.

The word Kleeneze didn't mean batteries then. It meant brushes. Brushes of all kinds – hair brushes, yard brushes, pipe brushes, lavatory brushes – and real ones they were, too, with luxuriant natural growths, none of your modern plastic rubbish.

But when my headmaster used the word about me, it wasn't intended as a compliment. It was the first morning of my last term. He looked grave – he modelled his demeanour on the great Dr Arnold of Rugby, whom he thought he resembled.

'Trelford,' he said finally, with evident reluctance, 'it appears that I have no choice but to make you head of the school. You are the choice of the senior common room. You are captain of cricket and you have your colours for rugby and athletics. You had the highest marks in the public examinations. But,' – and here he adopted a deeply pained expression – 'it concerns me greatly that the head boy of this school should look like an advertisement for the Kleeneze brush company. Will you please promise me faithfully, for the sake of the school, that you will keep your hair decently cut?'

By sheer coincidence, when I left school at the end of that summer term, I picked up a copy of the local newspaper and the magic word sprang out at me from the page: Kleeneze! They were looking for door-to-salesmen. I said to my mother: 'If I look like an advertisement for the Kleeneze brush company, maybe I should answer it. It must be predestined.'

I was looking for casual summer work, so I applied. Much to my surprise, I landed the job. No wage, but 40 per cent commission. I was given my suitcase of brushes and for several weeks carted it round the doorsteps of Coventry housing estates. It proved to be more of an education than I'd ever had at school.

my first job

Donald Trelford

When I pressed the bell on some unsuspecting family, the vital thing was to speak to the housewife. If a man appeared, the chance of a sale receded almost to vanishing point. The trick was to say quickly, 'May I speak to the lady of the house,' before the door could be slammed in your face. Even then, I was often pursued to the garden gate by a cascade of ingenious oaths.

The first important lesson I was given on the techniques of door-to-door salesmanship was a very simple one: GET THE POLISH ON THE DOOR! I quickly discovered the wisdom of this advice.

As soon as I caught a glimpse of a housewife's apron, the tin was out and the polish was on the door – a halo of gleaming purity, making the rest look grubby and squalid. It worked: she had to buy the polish now, to clean the rest of her filthy door.

That was the breakthrough. The rest was just mopping up. Not that I asked for an order straightaway. That was the next lesson I learned: KEEP THE PUNTER TALKING. It could be about anything – the weather, the garden, the children, her holidays, anything. In the end she was glad to place an order, just to shut the door and get on with her day.

All you had to do was outlast her. It was a matter of psychology really: the post-Freudian gladiatorial contest of the suburbs. Just you and her, and nothing to help you but your wits and the thought of a bite at that 40 per cent carrot.

You soon learned who to look out for. The lonely and the unloved: they'd buy the lot. Old spinsters, too: you could squeeze out what was left of a maternal instinct. Goggle-eyed newly-weds: I (almost) wept to take their money.

The ones to beware of were those who wanted only a chat and some cheap entertainment. Consuming interest all over their faces, inspecting every item with painstaking care – then they would shut the door without so much as a spout brush.

Then there was the weather. Pity for a poor rain-sodden figure sold no end of brushes. One black cloud and I'd make for the nearest lace curtains and aspidistra.

Soon I was earning about twice as much every week as the city's car workers. But I gave it up in the end: I'm not sure if it was my conscience or my feet that gave up first.

But I look back on that period of my life with a special affection. In fact, I think I'll buy some of those hot shares in Kleeneze, just for old time's sake. I might even get a hair-cut.

What could be more mind-broadening than a cruise around the classical world, stopping off at selected sites to absorb the lessons of the ancients as it were by osmosis? **Peter Black** *clambered aboard a touring steamer, slipped on his deck shoes and prepared to be culturally enriched*

A Tourist in the Ancient World

THE VIEW OF ATHENS through the porthole is not pretty but, as dear Carrie remarked, it will be a different view tomorrow. Our steward said his name was Danny, and his purpose was to convert our smallest wish into immediate satisfaction. He added that he had had only two hours off duty that day, and people who envied his life at sea should consider the unsocial hours and his dependence on passengers' kindness for tips.

Companions at dinner were a mother and daughter and a fat youngish woman. Conversation lagged until the first course arrived.

'Why, it's almost a meal in itself, isn't it?'

'They certainly don't mean to starve us.'

'What I like is, it isn't smothered in sauce.'

'A good appetite is the best sauce.'

'There's only one meat I can't eat, and that's veal.'

'With me, it's pork.'

'With pork, you've to know the butcher and you've to know the cook.'

'My husband says if he had this way he'd be a vegetarian.'

'Being a vegetarian, that's all in the mind.'

'Like the Arabs,' the old lady said mysteriously. 'We had some done for shoplifting in our town. Thousands of pounds in their pockets, they had.'

'For myself, I've got nothing against the Arabs.'

'Or gays.'

'I say, if it wasn't for the gays, there wouldn't be half as much fun in the world.'

Carrie and I agreed as we got into bed that there was nothing like good conversation to pass an evening quickly.

THE PARTHENON. In the coach I sat next to a big man with a strong and rumbling Yorkshire accent. The guide also talked incessantly, finally glaring at me and saying, 'If people speak, I must stop.' 'Good idea,' boomed the Yorkshireman, but he was shushed into silence.

'Now I resume my historical remarks. Now I tell you things about the coming of theatre. Before Greece, is no theatre. The followers of Dionysus, who is the Greek god of wine, like to drink and after to jump and say jokes, so the people who like to listen to them stand round them in a circle and this is how the theatre begins.'

I said afterwards to Carrie: 'I am a man more guided against than guiding.' We agreed that this is one of the funniest things I have said.

AT SEA. The waiter in the bar before dinner overcharged me by 4p. We were entertained by an Egyptian conjuror. A passenger in a blue blazer with stiff white hair and a Navy tie guffawed, 'Oh, yes, the old gulley-gulley man,' and claimed he had seen through all the tricks when he was ten. But the conjuror filled the inside of his shirt with live chicks and obliged him to tear it open to get rid of them.

OFF SANTORINI. We decided to take the buffet lunch on deck, in order to eat less and meet more fellow passengers. We took our plates to a table occupied by a smartly dressed, handsome couple. The man said as soon as we sat down, 'I'm in fish. I drive a van round Beckton, selling fish. I always tell everyone, then they don't get wrong ideas. You know the best fish there is? Skateknobs. Ask for skateknobs, fry them in deep fat.'

ON SHORE. A ridiculous mishap in a souvenir shop. It was crammed with lewd statues of a god named Priapus. When I tried to buy a pair of sandals a girl tried to sell me one of these objects. 'All copied from men of Santorini,' she giggled. I pretended not to understand her, but in turning away I must have brushed against one and knocked it over,

'Whilst welcoming all foreign investment, we oppose your road-building programme on the grounds that it will increase traffic and destroy the essential nature of the English countryside'

breaking off the part. The girl said, 'Now you must buy; is 200 drachmas.'

OFF NAPLES. The Ladies' Night Ball. The ladies were supposed to be the hostesses to their partners. I let Carrie take me to the bar and, as the ship's programme put it, 'ply her man with the drink of her choice'. The waiter short-changed her by 8p.

Dinner offered the usual choice of some 60 dishes. The waiter said, 'You've got a healthy appetite, old boy,' and to Carrie, 'He must take some feeding at home, dear lady.' His familiarity continued when he poured the coffee. He said it was a funny thing, he couldn't drink coffee himself, or tea. He took buckets of water – buckets of it. 'My wife likes tea, herself. Two of our four, the baby's too young to count, like coffee. The others take after me. Buckets of water. Remind me tomorrow, I'll bring some snaps. Funny old world, isn't it?' I replied, with a hint of reproof, that it certainly was.

POMPEII. A vexing and fatiguing tour, dogged by Priapus. The guide said, 'Now we come to the house of Priapus where is famous indecent painting. Until three four years was not visible by ladies for its indecency.'

Back on the ship I found an envelope slipped under our cabin door. It contained an invitation to the Captain's cocktail party in the grand lounge tomorrow evening! I wished Danny to take a note of acceptance at once. He replied there was no need, as the Captain took it for granted. He added that he welcomed these functions, as they gave him a quiet hour to rest his leg, which was playing him up.

The following evening, at sea off Alexandria, a crowd of passengers was milling about outside the great lounge for the Captain's bash. I supposed they were waiting to see the distinguished guests arrive and was embarrassed, as I tried to steer Carrie and myself through them with what I hoped was a courteous smile, to hear the big York-shireman call out: 'Nay, lad, get in line. We're all wettin' same as you!'

At the door an officer announced us in ringing tones. The Captain took my hand in a manly sea dog's grip. I thought he was about to speak, but we were guided on, and that was it. The Yorkshireman invited us to join him in a drink before dinner. The waiter overcharged him by 14p.

ALEXANDRIA. Carrie and I attended morning service. The congregation, mostly elderly, did not sing confidently, the loudest sound being the 'esses'. The officer deputising for the Captain must have been unused to the job. He made us sing all seven verses of 'Oh valiant hearts' and all four verses of Kipling's 'Recessional'. There was more awkwardness when, just as we had all begun to sit, he told us to rise. My knee-caps sounded two frightful reports; I would have been deeply embarrassed had there not been a perfect volley of cracking knee-caps from all over.

AT SEA. A quiet morning. Interesting talk with a stout gentleman, much too old for the costume he was wearing – a gold necklace and bangle, and a very tight pair of bathing drawers. He said, referring to other sunbathers: 'Funny-looking lot, aren't we? Did it ever strike you that man made the wrong choice by electing to walk upright? Once you're past fifty everything – chins, stomach, backbone – begins to sag. If we'd stayed on all fours we'd all keep nice flat stomachs.' I copied this thought into my diary as I consider it a profound one. Carrie only said: 'He may be right, but it's too late to think about it now.'

VENICE. Our last day. Packed and gave Danny what I hoped he would consider an adequate tip. He smiled wistfully as he thanked me, saying that because of an unusually fast turn-around due to striking dockers he would have to prepare his cabins for their new occupants in three hours' time. 'There goes my chance to see the Accademia.'

THE OLDIES   **TONY HUSBAND**

Dorothy Tutin

picks her top six

1 Les Dawson
Made me laugh – and I
thought him sexy.

2 Kathleen Ferrier
She was as lovely and warm
as her voice.

3 Dinu Lippatti
Inspired and inspiring
– a perfect pianist.

4 Buster Keaton
Brilliant, beautiful,
intense, daring and
funny.

**5 The entire cast of
Cheers – or is that
cheating? Otherwise
Shakespeare**
Thank God no press
could expose him
or his life – so
he remains as
mysterious as the
greatness of his writing.

6 John Keats
He kept me sane at school –
I don't know why – I loved
all his poems, even the
bad ones.

Right: actress Dorothy Tutin

Keeping it in the

Mrs Betty Gathergood, now seventy-seven, first came to Dr Johnson's House off Fleet Street in 1919 when she went to live with her grandmother, Isabella Dyble. For three generations Isabella's family loyally kept the house open to the public against all odds, including the Luftwaffe. Mrs Gathergood talked to **Madeleine Harmsworth** *about her memories of the last remaining home of the great lexicographer - or 'humble drudge', as he would have it*

Illustrations by Peter Bailey
Definitions taken from
Dr Johnson's Dictionary

As a young child I had a unique playground. It was Dr Johnson's House, his only surviving residence in London, tucked away behind Fleet Street in Gough Square. I used to play in the small yard at the side of the house, or in the sizeable powder closet (where the ladies and gentlemen of the time had their wigs powdered) on the ground floor, in which I kept my doll's house.

Dr Johnson's House had been bought in 1911 by Cecil Harmsworth MP (later Baron Harmsworth). As a young man he used to walk regularly through Gough Square and, later, was horrified to learn that No 17 was to be demolished. Clearly, it was very dilapidated but it was the house where Samuel Johnson compiled his great English dictionary, and where his beloved wife Tetty had died.

Although his brothers, the press barons Lords Northcliffe and Rothermere, advised him against it, Cecil Harmsworth bought the freehold and engaged Arthur Burr, FRIBA, to supervise the restoration.

The history of the house after Johnson left is somewhat obscure. It is known to have been used as a boarding house, offices, and finally as a storage place for waste paper. During the restoration it was discovered

that much of the panelling had been preserved by layer upon layer of wallpaper and paint. When this was removed some interesting features were revealed, including a cellarette cupboard – comprising six small cupboards large enough to take several bottles lying lengthwise – inside another, larger cupboard built into the thickness of a wall; the powder closet where I used to play; a candlestick cupboard, on the stairway to the first floor, where you could pick up a candlestick on your way to bed; and log cupboards, one in a room on the first floor, the other in the garret where the dictionary was compiled.

When the work was nearing completion Harmsworth was worried about finding someone to take charge of the house. Mr Burr knew my grandfather and suggested that my grandmother, Isabella Dyble, might be a suitable candidate. She moved into the quaint little curator's cottage, alongside Johnson's House, which had been specially built for the purpose, and the house itself was opened to the public in 1912.

During the 1914–18 war my grandmother looked after the house with great care, cleaning the windows when she could not get help, even stoking the old coke boiler in the basement to

keep the radiators going. Personally, it was a difficult time for her. Her husband was in the army in France, her dearly loved daughter and her young son-in-law, who was dying of leukemia, were in the USA, and her old mother was living with her and in need of a good deal of attention.

Her great solace, she told me, was the Doctor. She had always been fond of reading, and when she was appointed curator of the house, she started to devote herself to Johnson's work, becoming ever more involved and impressed. During the war she spent hours reading him, and whenever she had problems she would turn to his prayers or his dictionary. 'My old man', as she called Johnson, 'would always solve them for me'.

My mother, Phyllis Rowell, by then a widow, arrived back in England in 1919 when I was three, and we went to live with my grandmother. In America we had lived in a large house with every conceivable comfort – central heating, an icebox, a motor car. Now suddenly we were in this tiny cottage, with no mod cons of any kind, and with gas lighting outside in the square.

But it was in fact this gas lighting, or rather the gas-lighter, who was to provide my greatest joy. When

Family

Tea for the firemen . . . .

I first saw him I rushed to my grandmother in great excitement and said: 'Ooh, there's a Mr Leary! There really is a Mr Leary!' (You see, I'd been brought up on Robert Louis Stevenson, and was thinking of his poem about Mr Leary, the lamplighter, in his *A Child's Garden of Verses*.) We went out into the square and, do you know, the old fellow knew who I was talking about. He loved Stevenson's books. He asked if I would like to help him light the lights, and let me squeeze the bulb at the end of his pole.

a'necdote. Something yet unpublished; secret history.

I think and hope Johnson would have approved of the many cats and dogs, and one rabbit, that we kept in the curator's cottage throughout the years. They certainly added their share of colour to the area. Wilfred, the large black-and-white rabbit I had when I was small, was the original model for the rabbit in the *Daily Mirror*'s 'Pip, Squeak and Wilfred' cartoon strip. Amongst our feline family was Mickey Joe, a beautiful silver-tipped tabby given to me by the publisher Michael Joseph. Mickey Joe was a great ratter and would disappear night after night to catch the rats which abounded in the newspaper world.

One day a small office-boy rang our bell and said: 'Missus, I fink your cat's got its froat cut,' and there was Mickey Joe with what appeared to be blood all down his white shirt front

and on the white tips of his paws. It was not blood but red printer's ink from a nearby printing factory.

The dye took ages to wear off and once we over-heard two American women outside in the square. One said to the other, 'Darling, do you see what I see?' and her companion replied rather hesitantly, 'I think I do, dear, a pink cat.' They had come from the Cheshire Cheese, and were wondering, I am sure, whether in England one saw pink cats rather than pink elephants.

fi'reman. A man of violent passions.

During World War II Lord Harmsworth gave us permission to use Johnson's House as a club for the London firemen, because they were not allowed in service clubs or canteens like the other forces.

Our association with the London firemen began the day war was declared. My mother and I were walking along Pemberton Row, on the north side of Johnson's House, when we noticed several members of the newly formed Auxiliary Fire Service (all volunteers) standing rather disconsolately on the steps of a large office building. Thinking they looked forlorn, my mother asked if they would care for a jug of coffee. They said they would be grateful as there was nowhere in the building they could make even a hot drink, and the local cafés were closed.

When we took them the coffee and some homemade

scones, we discovered there were 12 men detailed to this sub-station, and that they had no food of any kind, no beds, and only a blanket or two which they had pro-vided themselves. They had to sleep in a corridor on a concrete floor.

My mother obtained permission to buy and cook their food, and for them to eat it in Johnson's House. We bought some comfort-able chairs and couches. We had a piano given to us, and also several beds and mattresses so that men on leave for a day and night, whose families were evac-uated, and who often had no homes, having lost every-thing in a raid, could spend a comfortable rest period away from their station.

Then began our evenings of music. A number of the firemen were members of

At about 6.15pm all hell was let loose and incendiaries rained down. Our little cottage took the first shock. Just as we were sitting down to dinner we heard the sirens and felt terrific thuds on the roof

The Blitz....

the London Symphony Orchestra and they used to come to the house to practise. They asked if we would allow musical evenings twice a month, so Johnson's House resounded to Mozart, Handel, Bach and Scarlatti. William Read, the harpist Goossen sisters and the horn player Dennis Brain all gave recitals.

During this time we removed all the pictures in the House and packed them in large teachests. We put Johnson's letters and precious china, which included Mrs Thrale's tea equipage, and a mug, cup and saucer with Sir Joshua Reynolds's cipher, into two suitcases which we kept under the stairs.

je′opardy. Hazard; peril; danger. A word not now in use.

No bombs fell near Gough Square until September 1940, when the big raids started. We were fortunate enough to escape any direct damage until the great fire raid on London on the night of December 29th.

At about 6.15pm all hell was let loose and incendiaries rained down. Our little cottage took the first shock. Just as we were sitting down to dinner we heard the sirens, and felt terrific thuds on the roof and the sound of many planes overhead. We rushed out of the house and found hundreds of incendiaries burning all around and our roof beginning to blaze.

Within a few minutes the firemen had arrived and were tackling the flames.

Johnson's House was so far untouched, but most of the buildings in Gough Square were blazing, and the fires were spreading rapidly. We were kept busy supplying the firemen with refreshments until about 8.30pm when a water main was struck and the water supply failed. Several of the men were hurt and two were killed by a falling wall.

By this time the fires were so severe we were ordered to go shelter in the basement of the *Daily Mirror* building in Fetter Lane. My mother collected the suitcases with the letters, and rugs and cushions for my grandmother, who was then eighty-five, and with our dachshund Tuppence we set out through the burning streets, arriving safely at the shelter wet through and with our clothes singed from falling sparks.

About 9.30pm someone came into the shelter and said 'Dr Johnson's house is in flames'. My mother and I were anxious to return but were told we must stay where we were. The raid finished around 11.30pm and we rushed off to see if anything had been saved. We found the firemen had worked tremendously hard to save the House, and only the roof and part of the front wall of the garret had been burnt. But the water damage was very bad and the basement flooded.

Some of the pictures and books were damp, but only a few chairs and two tables were destroyed. We had had a wonderful escape.

hu′sband. (2) The male of animals.

In 1942 we acquired our own resident fireman. I fell in love with Edward Gathergood, one of the young firemen who came to the House. We were married in April in the oldest church in London, St Bartholomew the Great in Smithfield, and afterwards, despite wartime restrictions, had a wonderful reception for about a hundred friends at Johnson's House.

Then came Hitler's V-1 raids. They were really frightening. Day and night they tore across the sky, suddenly dropping and exploding, wrecking everything. One night in June 1944, when the V-1s were coming over rapidly, we heard one cut out and Edward said, 'This is it! Relax as much as possible.' We heard it roar lower and lower, and when it hit the shock was so great it was as though an express train had run into the building. In fact the V-1 landed a short distance away, but we took the full blast on one side of the house. The interior looked a wreck.

The shock affected my mother badly, so we three went away to the coast for a week's rest. While we were away another V-1 fell nearby and blasted part of the top wall of Johnson's House.

When it was all over and we surveyed the surrounding damage from the upper windows of the House, the realisation came upon us of our great good fortune in saving this wonderful old building – with the exception of the Dean and Canon's houses and a few in the Temple, one of the only 18th-century houses left in the City of London.

Music

Richard Osborne

NO DICTIONARY is infallible, no editor immune from minor embarrassment. Stanley Sadie's epic *New Grove Dictionary of Music and Musicians* (Macmillan) is famous, among other things, for its entry on the distinguished Danish composer, conductor, and court flautist Dag Henrik Esrum-Hellerup.

Born in Arhus on 19th July 1803, Esrum-Hellerup's rise to fame in the 1850s was, we are told, as rapid as his decline into obscurity. Some flute quartets survive (the influence of his teacher Kuhlau readily detectable) but other important works are lost, including Esrum-Hellerup's opera *Alys og Elvertoj* (much admired by Smetana).

The problem with this entry is that it is a spoof (Esrum and Hellerup are ferry terminals) dreamed up by Robert Layton, our leading expert on Scandinavian music, author of the superb (and recently revised) Master Musicians study of Sibelius, and as good a judge of a gramophone recording as you will find in five continents.

He says he didn't believe *Grove* would fall for the ruse. But they did. I've always thought it a small jewel in *Grove*'s crown – though understandably it was some time before Dr Sadie got round to taking a similarly relaxed view.

LORD FOR A NIGHT

Although in his waking life **James Pembroke** *is but a humble business manager for a certain monthly magazine, in his dreams he wears the ermine, and one night those dreams became reality – or a waking nightmare*

AS AUBERON WAUGH once wrote in *The Oldie*, an Englishman's ambition is to own a large country house. If that is an Englishman's ambition, his fantasy is to be an English lord. Oh, it will never be admitted, except by those who are honest enough to purchase a title, but on those long solitary train journeys, when minds wander, an Englishman's head is often adorned with a coronet. Hence, our belief that Tony Benn, who reversed the situation, must be mad.

I spend most of my train journeys being interviewed on television about my deeds of valour, feats of ingenuity and ground-breaking plays. But it was an alarming experience actually to enact one of these dreams of glory.

'All we have to do,' said my wife, as she then was not, 'is pretend to be Lord and Lady Brocket for an evening. Five hundred Americans have paid a fortune to have "a gala evening with the British aristocracy, at charming Brocket Hall". Chance Entertainment want me to hire four other people to make up the family. Are you on?'

'But, Josephine,' I wailed, 'who in their right mind would pay a fortune to have dinner with impostors. Why can't the real Lord Brocket do it?'

'Oh, he's turning up later.'

'But then they'll know that they've been conned… they'll be livid!'

'Rubbish. They'll know we're fakes and will just find us amusing. Look, when were you last paid a hundred pounds to go to a party?'

Three more would-be aristos were soon rounded up: Penny, a Welsh girl; Matt, an Australian; and Sara, who works for Andrew Lloyd Webber. It was decided, in the tradition of school plays, that since Matt was the tallest, he should be Lord Brocket. Sara, the second tallest, would be his wife, Josephine would be his sister, I would be his errant younger brother and Penny would be my even more errant girlfriend.

We met at St. Pancras and jumped on the train to Welwyn Garden City. It was a rather depressing entrée to the pages of Debrett's. Matt, the only real thesp, spent the journey practising his accent. We complained to Josephine that he was being over-zealous. 'Oh, it's in his blood,' she explained. 'He's from a major Australian theatrical dynasty.'

Matt's moment to outrank us amateurs had arrived. 'My father was Matt Hammond, the Chief Ranger, in *Skippy, the Bush Kangaroo*.'

The Redgraves have no cause to look to their laurels. Matt went on to tell us all about Skippy. Apparently, there were three Skippys: one for jumping and action shots, a good-looking one for close-ups and an understudy Skippy, who stepped in when the other two were resting, and who earned most of his money in commercials.

We arrived at Brocket Hall and introduced ourselves to Chance Entertainment, in the most extravagant marquee to hit English shores. There was a table in the middle of the dance-floor, where we Brockets were to sit so that everyone could get a good view of us at play. The woman from Chance

ILLUSTRATION BY SIMON COOPER

Entertainment didn't look too impressed by this troupe of bedraggled actors. We assured her that we all had black tie. Suddenly, the whole idea seemed distinctly dodgy.

At that moment a tall, confident man and woman strode in, with attendant lackeys. 'Don't worry,' said Lord Brocket (for it was he) in front of his Long Island-born wife. 'Americans will believe anything.'

It was agreed that he would kick Matt out of the marquee after dinner, and then make a speech. He left, with the fawners at his heels. It wasn't his problem.

Sara asked who were these 500 guests. 'Mostly Americans,' said the

They had paid for a night with the aristocracy and nothing we could do would convince them they were getting anything less

lady from Chance. 'They're members of the Young Presidents' Club and have paid about £40,000 a head for a week of entertainment in England. This is their last night and they want to have a good time.'

It was simple. These people had paid for a night with the aristocracy and nothing we could do would con-

vince them they were getting anything less. As for the unmasking, it would be taken in good humour – they'd all love it.

It was five o'clock and our guests were due at 6.30. Matt and I were putting on our dinner jackets, when I discovered that I had mistakenly brought my flatmate's trousers, which were three inches short. We went to the main hall and met up with the others, to compare sartorial notes. Josephine was wearing a see-through lace body-suit, which she wore in her cabaret act, Pussies Galore. Penny, another of the Pussies, was in a mini-dress. Only Sara and Matt would have been allowed into Annabel's.

We took a quick look round the house, which was all that the Young Presidents could have wished for – huge oil paintings, and sufficient grandeur to make Jack Cade leap from his grave and start all over again.

The coaches were coming down the drive. From now on I was to be the Honourable James Nall-Cain. The five of us stood in a reception line at the front door, while the guests tumbled out of their charabancs.

They were all wearing plastic boaters and had 18-inch cigarette-holders with fake cigarettes. However, the moment they saw us, they fell into an awed silence and an orderly queue. The curtseys and bows began. We were five popes, granting absolution. After an age of 'welcome to our pied-à-terre', we mingled with the throng.

They all had name badges, but the only one I could remember from the formal introductions was Beverley Whipple from Wisconsin, so I bestowed my graces upon her.

'And you know who I am, don't you?' she said coyly.

'Yes, you're Beverley Whipple, from Wisconsin.'

'And?' she demanded, hinting at greater distinction than just a curious surname. I hesitated. 'Haven't you read my book? John!' she cried to her husband, 'It's Lord Brocket!' The room turned. Beverley had bagged her tiger. In seconds, I was surrounded by outstretched hands. But I was Beverley's and not up for auction. She dragged off her prize.

'You don't know my book about the G-spot?' If I'd been told she was an author, I would have expected her to have penned a sequel to *Uncle Tom's Cabin*. She was five foot two, elderly, and apple-pie wholesome. 'I'm Beverley Whipple, who found the G-spot. You know about it, don't you?' Well, she certainly did. And two minutes of trigonometric finger-bending instruction ensured that I should henceforth be able to land right on top of it, blindfolded, from a standing jump at a distance of five feet.

Beverley also explained the mysteries of the Young Presidents. They

107

YOU HAVE BEEN FOUND GUILTY OF DOING UNMENTIONABLE THINGS WITH SHEEP...

THERE CAN BE ONLY ONE POSSIBLE PUNISHMENT...

LIFE BEHIND BAAS..!

met with their wives about six times a year for a week's 'mind-broadening and education'.

Beverley had been invited along with her husband to give one of the lectures. And what did they all have in common? They had all become presidents and chairmen of vast companies before the age of fifty. They were from all boulevards of the globe. It was quite obviously a way of making extremely useful business contacts but every time I mentioned this possibilty, they shouted me down, albeit sycophantically.

Oh yes, a title has tremendous power. Suddenly, hugely successful men and women wanted my advice on everything from their children's education to the best type of grass to import for their lawns in Buenos Aires or Tokyo.

Beverley, who seemed something of a joke to the YPs, was suddenly a star because she had me. I desperately wanted to confess to my deception. I knew she'd be crippled when she found out after dinner. Meanwhile she was feeling even sorrier for me, being the younger brother.

Occasionally, I would look over my shoulder to see Josephine's knickers peeking through her outfit. But nothing would shake their belief. During dinner, we wandered around the room to see if our guests were all right. Daughters were hurled at us for dances. All of us were dreading the moment when Brocket arrived. We clung to the doorway.

Matt got up to deliver his speech. Our peer *in absentia* arrived and literally kicked Matt off the stage.

'Some of you may be concerned that my wife is wandering around in a see-through dress,' he boomed. 'Well, here she is.' And there she was, in a long Catherine Walker dress, glowing with Long Island breeding and charm.

Some of them tried to laugh, others were livid. As I bolted for the service tent, I caught a glimpse of Beverley's tears. It was the most cruel trick.

Though £100 came in handy, fantasies on train journeys have never been the same since. Admittedly, this is partly due to the fact that I'm now married to Josephine, and silences are few and far between.

VOICE from the GRAVE

'I see no hope for our people if they are dependent on the frivolous youth of today, for certainly all youth are reckless beyond words... When I was young we were taught to be discreet and respectful of elders, but the present youth are exceedingly impatient of restraint.'

Hesiod, the Greek poet, circa 750 BC

Contributed by M S Orrock

A CHANCE TO RAGE – but what at? There's a dizzying choice. At the nanas who have decided to tear up one of the loveliest gardens in England at Hampton Court, to re-create one in the same period as the house?

At faulty appliances? I could go back to the great washing-machine row I had with Ariston, which, as its ad promises, went on and on and Ariston and on and on…

Or against the usual incumbent of this space, who declared that the country's worst current problem was, not homelessness or industrial decline or crack, but the fact that British women didn't seem keen on cooking any more – I ask you!

But I must choose, or my whole space will be taken up with *omitto ut* (I am assuming that all *Oldie* readers had Latin drummed into them once, and even know who Cicero was – what luxury, to write for such people!). So let's concentrate on the blight that has affected every aspect of our lives this past decade and more: the insistence of our masters, and those who ape them, on reducing everything to terms of money.

Was a department once a centre of excellence? Now it's a profit centre. Did people use to have a vision, a strategy? Now they have a business plan.

Britain, since the war known the world over to be hopeless at business, but still quite good at everything else – best broadcasting system in the world, a health service bettered only by the Scandinavians, a system of justice copied across half the globe – has decided that every branch of public and professional life shall conform to the norms and language of what it does worst: business.

There has grown up this quaint conviction, not only that business efficiency is the only sort there is, but that you get better performance out of everyone by relating everything to their pay (never mind that the Institute of Manpower Studies glumly

RAGE

Katharine Whitehorn

concluded that it doesn't actually work, even in the world of commerce). It's just possible that at the level of the lads who haul the supermarket trolleys around, money is the only useful inducement; but for most of the jobs that have any meaning or value, the question of short-term money is simply a distraction.

Teachers don't try harder to keep a class quiet for the sake of a few extra quid in the pay-packet; even the government would concede that if they really cared about money, they'd never have chosen teaching in the first place.

It has been suggested that justices' clerks would be motivated by performance-related pay. Motivated to what, for heaven's sake? More bail? Less bail? Less time on each case? It's an absurdity.

An athlete or an astronaut doesn't train till the muscles pop for the sake of

the cash they may make; even in the 16th century, the great Ambroise Paré knew that 'he who became a surgeon for the sake of money will accomplish nothing'. Johnson may have said that no man but a blockhead ever wrote but for money, but that wasn't how he behaved – and if no-one wrote but for money, darned few would ever write for *The Oldie*.

To suggest that some public outfits would do their accounting a bit better makes more sense (though it was after the money men moved in that Wessex lost millions on the wrong computer, the BBC couldn't seem to lay its hands on £60 million that had gone missing, and the Church Commissioners lost £800 million, so now they're selling off the allotments of the poor for property development).

But to make everyone deal in terms of money is completely to misunderstand the springs of human action. What people strive for is approval. For the approval of the crowd, if you're a film star or a footballer; of half a dozen of your own cronies if you're a senior journalist; it may be the spectre of Mother in the sky, or your boss; most usually it is your peers in the field. If they think you're trash, no amount of money will make up for it; have you ever heard anyone say: 'Well, Professor Jones got the Nobel, of course, but Smith's got a house in the Bahamas!'

The only people who do rate themselves on what they make are those for whom money is how you keep score, which used to be only stock-brokers and financial men and tycoons and so on, but is now supposed to be everybody.

In one of Patrick O'Brian's books, Captain Aubrey has spent a boring afternoon with a comptroller of excise or some such (his mistress's husband): 'But what can you expect of a man who sits and thinks of nothing but money all day!' And in Ruskin's *The Roots of Honour*, he draws a distinction

between those who have it – professionals, public servants – and the money men. He says traders care only for money because that's the role we've given them; re-define their occupation as being not so much making money from trains and tracks as being responsible for transport, for example, and they will be better men. We have tried to do the exact opposite.

The wonderful irony is that there was another set of people who thought everything, but everything, came back to economics: that art and culture and fashions and handsome houses and churches were all just a way of showing off financial clout. They were called Marxists.

We might remind our hard-headed capitalists of that, next time it's suggested that Mother Teresa would have done more on performance-related pay; that it would be more cost-effective to chop up the Three Graces and sell off the ladies separately; or that the monetary value of a Stradivarius should never be put at risk by anyone actually playing it.

'Not in the Directors' car park thank you, Nesbit!'

PRESS

Roy Greenslade

IT WAS 1968 at the *Daily Mail* in Manchester when the world changed: a woman started work as a news sub-editor! It was, in the words of one disbelieving man, the end.

From this distance, it seems almost laughable to recall the shock-waves her appointment caused. Old hands shook their heads, aghast. How could a girl do this job – their job, for God's sake – properly? The work was so demanding. The hours were so unsocial. The office was so, well, manly. Then there was the language. It was no place for a mere girl.

Younger men nodded in agreement with the veterans. While some nurtured lustful fantasies, most considered it a worrying development. But we consoled ourselves with the thought that it was just an experiment which was bound to fail.

She would never stand the relentless pace, the intolerable pressure... oh yes, and she wouldn't be able to handle compositors, those foul-mouthed printers who were known to make male editors weep.

It is impossible now to portray the reaction to her appointment without a sense of embarrassment. She was subjected to the sort of male assault course she could never hope to win. Would she accept the continuous swearing and sexual taunts that formed our discourse? Would she swear herself? Could she drink (a euphemism for get drunk)?

If the answers were no, then she was derided for not being 'one of the boys'. If yes, then she was the kind of woman we wouldn't want to know anyway.

Her difference guaranteed that she would be carefully watched lest she gain any advantages over us. Would she get preferential treatment, such as 'easy' stories to sub or the coveted early shifts? Would she escape from the public bollockings which were then the norm?

In the male-only Manchester Press Club in Albert Square (drink, snooker, drink, cards, drink and brawling, followed by one for the road at 6am) some even whispered of heresy ahead: maybe she would be promoted. Impossible, members concluded, because men would die before taking orders from a woman.

There was even concern about whether she would be paid the same as us. This was resolved in a Solomonic judgement by a union representative: 'I understand your concern, brothers, but if management gets away with paying her less than us they'll hire loads of women to replace us, no matter how hopeless

Old hands shook their heads. The work was so demanding. The hours were so unsocial. The office was so, well, manly. Then there was the language. It was no place for a mere girl

they are.' So she was granted the right to equal pay.

At this point I must absolve the chief sub-editor, one Mike Taylor, who is now editor of the *Methodist Recorder*. I recall him being particularly understanding towards the woman. Aware of his colleagues' hostility, he successfully trod the delicate line between positive discrimination and favouritism.

Underlying the prejudice was a sinister sub-text, never articulated, always present. What affronted men most about women's intrusion into their domain was the realisation that females could perform the same task as them after all. They had cloaked their intellectual work in the guise of rough trade to prevent women taking part. Now the secret was out.

Fair enough, you might say, but that was then, in the bad old days. We have come a long way in 25 years, with lots of women holding the most senior journalistic positions.

Consider Eve Pollard, Patsy Chapman, Bridget Rowe... Before them, Wendy Henry was editor of two Sunday papers in succession. And there are many more just a step away from the editor's chair. Is this not a mark that times have changed?

Up to a point, Lady Copper, up to a point. Sadly, bigots continue to deride women, especially those who have made it to the top, by asserting that it is not talent, energy and commitment that has taken them there, but only their gender. The phrase 'women journalists' seeks to attribute some kind of universal personality applicable to all of them. They are stereotyped as a race apart from normal journalists (i.e. men).

Women are deemed to have succeeded in a man's world by taking one of two routes: by being tougher than men or by cosying up to men. They are characterised, respectively, as The Bitches and The Handmaidens.

The former are accused of militant feminism and the latter of rampant femininity. It matters not that men have traditionally been promoted for equivalent endowments, being either bastards or crawlers. When men succeed by playing such roles, it is understandable, even laudable. When women do so, it is unjust and unnatural.

So deep is this prejudice that even women fall into the trap of undermining their own sex. One envious woman journalist told me, and anyone else who would listen, that another woman had been promoted over her only 'because she walks the corridors of power with her knickers in her hand'. It was an appalling libel.

Then again, the critic had once been 'Woman' Journalist of the Year. Even that title seems quaint now, so perhaps things are improving. Very slowly.

Bill Waddington

picks his top six

1 Frankie Laine
A great singer and a gentleman who is now in his eighties, but still writes to me from America.

2 Big John Wayne
Always great entertainment for me, and got me out into the wide open spaces and away from the everyday trials of this world.

3 Lord Mason of Barnsley
Came from being a coal miner to his present title. He's held a great number of government posts and is a proud but modest man. He'll talk to anyone, even me.

4 Tony Warren
The man who is responsible for *Coronation Street* which many, many millions enjoy and also all the work for hundreds of artists over the past 33 years.

5 Princess Diana
She's got a great sense of humour and understanding and leaves a ray of sunshine everywhere she goes. She also watches 'The Street' and talked to me about it.

6 Lester Piggott
The world's greatest horseman and jockey, he gets the best out of his mounts and treats them with respect.

Right: actor Bill Waddington, best known as Coronation Street's Percy Sugden

QUENTIN CRISP

A lifetime of kicking against the pricks has left the wits of Mr Crisp undulled. A self-confessed chatterer and exhibitionist, he talked with unstinting frankness to **Naim Attallah**

Portrait by **Jane Bown**

From an early age you were aware of what you call your predicament. Do you think your predicament was largely genetic or do you think there were other factors involved?

There must have been something genetic because so many people have such absolutely conventional upbringings and they still are peculiar in some way or another, including sexually peculiar. But there may have been other factors involved. For example, you could say that I lacked anyone to tell me how to be a grown-up person. My mother alternately protected me from the world and threatened me with it; my father took absolutely no notice of any of us, he hardly ever spoke to us.

As a child, your unhappiness, or sense of being different, manifested itself in all kinds of attention-seeking behaviour. Were you sure of what you were doing at the time, was it a means to an end, or did you become aware of what it was only retrospectively?

I certainly did draw attention to myself, and I think I knew that I was, but I would have denied it, I imagine.

Do you look back on that period when you were wetting your trousers and soiling yourself with a kind of revulsion?

Well, I suppose I should. I really don't look back on it at all, but certainly I was a disgusting child, there is no doubt about it. But I don't remember being ashamed.

You hated boarding school, but you describe it as a dress rehearsal for the treatment you were soon to receive in the streets of London. Would you say in that sense it was a good preparation?

Yes. I think if I had left straight from home and gone out into the world, it would have been like falling over a cliff. I had a doll's house view of the world when I was at public school. I had to learn that everybody was my enemy, and that I would have to find ways of dealing with this if I was going to go on living.

You also wrote of that period: 'What I wanted most of all was to use sex as a weapon to allure, subjugate, and if possible to destroy the personality of others.' That seems a remarkably well-formulated analysis for a boy of fourteen or fifteen. Did you actually think of it in that way at the time?

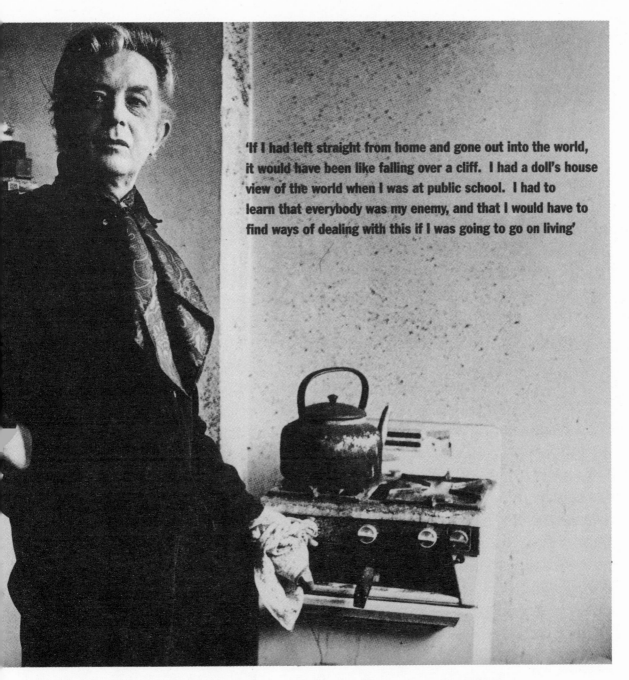

'If I had left straight from home and gone out into the world, it would have been like falling over a cliff. I had a doll's house view of the world when I was at public school. I had to learn that everybody was my enemy, and that I would have to find ways of dealing with this if I was going to go on living'

I think I did. I thought I could meet someone who would be sufficiently interested in me to do as I told him, but of course no such person existed. At the age of about eighteen, that would have been in 1927, I was much influenced by what I saw in the movies. Gloria Swanson, Greta Garbo and Marlene Dietrich were all icons of power, and the great German films were all about vamps – the word has all but disappeared from the language. The women were vamps, and they destroyed men.

In one film Miss Helm, the most beautiful woman who ever lived, sits in a tent while the men struggle across the desert, their lips blistered with thirst. She orders some champagne, drinks it, then breaks the glass on the edge of her throne and cuts the throat of one of the men for no reason whatsoever.

At some point in your youth, you managed to shift homosexuality from being a burden to being a cause. Presumably in some

The Oldie Interview

My genius is for the smiling and nodding racket which I can now practically live on. If you can get by on peanuts and champagne in America you need never buy food again

ways, far from making your life easier, it must have been made more difficult?

Of course I know now that it was nonsense to think of it as a cause, but at the time I spent my life in cafés where I sat with other gay boys, most of whom were on the game, and we pooled our tears. They were miserable and for no justifiable reason, and I therefore decided that somebody had to like the homosexual life – it was no good writing books about it, because they would only be read by homosexuals. The important thing was to live it so that people would get used to the idea.

The great weapon in the hands of integration is boredom. When you say to somebody, I'm gay, and they say, and then? – then you're in the clear. It's while you have to explain yourself and justify yourself, and they happen to be tolerant of you, that the problem still exists.

At what point did you realise that it was pointless to expect people to be tolerant or understanding towards you?

Very early on. By the time I was thirty I didn't really expect anything.

You turned your hand to writing - poems, libretti, stories - but you describe the problem as being one of having a genius but no talent. What did you mean by that exactly?

My genius is for the smiling and nodding racket which I can now practically live on. If you can get by on peanuts and champagne in America you need never buy food again, but in England you can't do that; you need to be able

to do something and do it well, and possibly even study it. I've never studied anything in my life.

At one point in 'The Naked Civil Servant' you liken homosexuality to an illness. That implies that it cannot be helped but in some cases it might be cured. Was that your view?

I suppose it still is my view. I don't remember what I thought at the time, but I have known homosexuals who have got married because they thought it might help. I didn't ever say, 'Help whom?', and indeed since they remain married and they have children, it obviously did help. The idea that people are either heterosexual or homosexual is nonsense; they will sometimes drift backwards and forwards for an hour or a week or for years, it depends.

The more the gay people now insist on their rights, the greater the distance becomes between the gay world and the straight world, and this is such a pity. I suppose I have to be careful about calling it an illness, but homosexuals seem to me to be people standing on the bank watching other people swim. In some way it takes you away from real life, away from the main stream, so if it isn't an illness, it's certainly like having an illness.

Did you ever sleep with a woman?

Never. I don't think it could ever have worked. Sexually I have no interest in women at all. I don't shun them, I simply have no interest in them.

You say at one point in the book that you regarded all heterosexuals, however low, as superior to all homosexuals, however noble. What did you mean by that?

The world belongs to straight people, and they must be regarded as superior. The superiority of numbers, of power, of know-how, of worldliness is all with straight people – that's the sense in which they are superior.

During the 1930s you began to meet a greater number and variety of homosexuals, but because you did not conform to their rules you were ostracised by them too. It must surely have been much harder to bear the hostility of homosexuals.

Yes, I was very disappointed when I first found that the homosexual community distrusted, disliked, even despised me. I got used to it and I suppose in England most of my friends were straight women, because they expected nothing of me, and in any case these were women in happier times, before they decided they had to be people. When women were women, one of the things they liked to do was chatter, and I'm a born chatterer, so that I could sit with them, and entertain them and they could be nice to me. I didn't really ever get on with men because they only ever speak about money and politics and sport, about which I know nothing.

What were your feelings about the war?

It was very nice when it came. First of all, there was a whole year in which you never saw any war whatsoever, and you could only read about it in the papers. But then the war came to London and the sky was pink with doom, the ground shook with the anti-aircraft fire, and you could hear the shrapnel falling. And that was very exciting. I decided I wouldn't accommodate the war at all, so if I was invited out I went out, whether there had been an air raid warning or not – it was all a lottery in any case.

The war seems scarcely to have impinged on you – at least it hardly figures in your account of those years. How did you manage to avoid thinking about it, worrying about it?

I just didn't alter my life, I went on exactly as though there were no war. The only wonderful aspect of the war was the American soldiers. Americans listen to what you say, Englishmen never do. It was very nice; it felt you were being courted to some extent.

You criticise the advertising industry for spreading the idea, against all evidence to the contrary, that sex leads to happiness. Would you at least concede that it leads to pleasure, perhaps the greatest pleasure of all?

Yes, it leads to pleasure, but with penalties. Homosexual intercourse is often actually painful, sometimes uncomfortable, sometimes nasty, so you have to think, do I really want this? There was once a programme about hepatitis, and a woman interviewed a young man and asked how many times on average he had sexual relations with anybody. He replied 'six', and she said, six times a week? He replied, 'No, six times a night.' Now at that rate, it can't go on being a pleasure – it must simply be a score. I think it's a form of pleasure which some people cannot do without, but I don't believe it is a form of happiness.

Could you yourself do without it?

I can do without it now, and have done for the last 20 years or so. In the past if I felt sexual urges I usually masturbated, which is less trouble. And so much cheaper.

Why is the homosexual male generally more promiscuous than the heterosexual?

I secretly think, though I have been shouted down on this, that it is because it is not very satisfactory. Just as if you eat food that doesn't nourish you, you eat more food, so people who indulge in unsatisfactory sex are often extraordinarily promiscuous.

For many years you were able to live without sexual encounters at all. Was this primarily lack of opportunity or lack of desire?

I never really desired much sex. My appetites are in general much weaker than other people's – I've never been drunk, I never over-eat, I have never done anything to excess. Even at my worst I was never as promiscuous as most homosexual men are.

Your first major writing success was 'The Naked Civil Servant' which was soon made into a TV movie. Was that the first real flush of success for you?

Yes, but it was only a mini-success. It did not lead to any work, I wasn't invited to review other people's books and say they were worse than mine, and no one asked me to write

In England if you told your friends you were getting up a cabaret act, they would say, for God's sake, don't make a fool of yourself... I didn't know there was any happiness in the world, till I got here

The Oldie Interview

anything else. It wasn't until it was made into a television play that my whole life changed. That was in 1975, and the book came out in 1968, so there were seven long dark years in between.

John Hurt's portrayal of you in the TV film of 'The Naked Civil Servant' was widely acclaimed. Were you yourself happy with it?

I was indeed. It was a marvellous reproduction of my voice for one thing. He was slightly more defiant than I ever was, but only minimally. He's born to play victims. After he played me he went on to play Claudius, which is really only me in a sheet, and then he was the Elephant Man. People sometimes ask me if I feel like an Elephant Man, and I do, I do.

Your success in England was readily exported to America. You say you have always felt your natural milieu to be American. It must have seemed like a dream come true...

It did indeed. To come here was quite, quite wonderful. Happiness rains down from the sky in America. I agree with Millicent Martin, who is now an American by marriage. She said the difference between America and England is that in America everyone is always in favour of whatever you propose to do, and this is absolutely true. If you stand up in a bar and announce that you're getting up a cabaret act, everybody will ask, where are you gonna appear? what are you gonna wear?

In England if you told your friends you were getting up a cabaret act, they would say, for God's sake, don't make a fool of yourself. Everything is a warning in England. I didn't know there was any happiness in the world, till I got here.

Your performance in 'Orlando', as Elizabeth I, has been widely praised. Was that something you enjoyed?

It was absolute hell, but being in a movie is always absolute hell. I wore two rolls of fabric round my middle tied with tapes, and then a hooped skirt tied with tape, and then a quilted petticoat and then an ordinary petticoat and

then a dress, and I had a bodice so tight that it blistered my stomach. No wonder Queen Elizabeth was always chopping off people's heads – she must have been in a permanent rage from having to wear these clothes.

You have described yourself as doing deliberately what you used to do by mistake, a way of getting the joke on your own terms. Have you arrived at a kind of contentment now, would you say?

Yes. Now I can behave in a way that is perfectly natural for me, and other people accept it, or appear to accept it. Perhaps it's all an illusion, because in America if they don't like you, they don't say so, whereas if they do like you, they tell you. It's completely the other way round in England – there you feel terribly disliked, but here in America it's easy to get the impression that everybody adores you. But I would say that I'm happier than I ever expected to be.

You were a martyr, weren't you, but your martyrdom was partly self-inflicted. You got used to living in a world which scorned and hated you. Did you become a willing martyr in the end?

I suppose I expected the world in general not to accept me, not to like me, and to throw things at me and shout at me, so yes, I suppose I was a willing martyr.

Would you have had the sex operation if it had been available at the time?

If it had been available when I was in my late teens, and I had had the money, I would certainly have had the operation. Then I could have gone away to a provincial town and run a knitting wool shop, and nobody would ever have known my terrible secret. I would have been free.

You have been much preoccupied with the business of death, and have been predicting your own for some time now. Do you look forward to it?

Yes, it's the next big event in my life. Like most people, I imagine, what one is preoccupied with is behaving nicely while you're dying. A lot of people think it terrible to die alone, but if you die in the presence of other people you have to be polite while you die, which must be very difficult. So that is one of my chief preoccupations: how to behave nicely while dying.

What is your attitude to religion... has it changed at all over the years?

No, I think it's always been the same. I don't want to say anything that might give offence, but I can't believe in a God susceptible to prayer. If God is the universe that encloses the universe, or if God is the cell inside the cell, or if God is the cause behind the cause, this I can accept.

But I think it is actually wrong to teach children to bargain with whatever they think is God: for example, if you don't eat sweets in Lent he will give you a bicycle with 10 speeds. This is undignified. If there is a force that keeps the spheres moving in the heavens, why would it be preoccupied with us, and why would it be endowed with such wretched human characteristics? Why is it angry, why is it jealous, why is it forgiving? No, I don't believe in that sort of God.

But do you expect any life after death?

I can't afford to. What little I can do and say and be is complete, so it would be very dreary to have to come back. I can't really imagine what life after death would entail; I can only imagine more of the life that I've already led, and that has been long enough.

Your life has been extraordinary by any standards, but it strikes the outside observer as having been a tragic one in some measure. Would you agree?

Yes. I don't know how it could have been changed to make it less tragic. Other people grow up with their brothers and sisters, and they get on fine for the most part with them, and then they go to school and make friends, and then they go out into the world and acquire workmates, and they get on fine with them. None of that happened to me. I was alone, and I had to invent happiness.

Olden Life

What was . . . Brown Windsor Soup?

WHEN IT COMES to food and drink, brown is not an auspicious colour. Brown ale and brown sauce, for example, were never likely to increase the culinary reputation of these islands. Brown Windsor soup, the genteel forebear of the ubiquitous 'brown soup' which enjoyed pre-eminence in every hotel and self-respecting boarding-house before – and, regrettably, after – the war, was perhaps the most gastronomically-challenged of all.

The ingredients were harmless enough – beef, carrots, flour and stock – but the whole was infinitely more disgusting than the sum of its parts. Maybe it was the third-rate, post-war flour which made it thick and lumpy, the cheap cut of beef which produced a film of grease upon the surface, or the boiling and re-

The ingredients were harmless enough – beef, carrots, stock – but the whole was infinitely more disgusting than the sum of its parts

boiling which gave it an acrid twinge. At best, which is perhaps a contradiction in terms, it was a liquid stew; at worst, it tasted of old underpants (I imagine), and made you gag.

There was a time when the railways were very fond of serving it. I remember my parents taking me to my new boarding school on what I suppose was the GWR. It seems so long ago, Brunel was probably still working on the line.

In the dining car, the chief steward, a dapper, snake-mad English eccentric called Mr Smart addressed me as Corporal and proceeded to pour Brown Windsor soup into all of our laps. Returning to school every subsequent term, Mr Smart promoted me – Sergeant, Lieutenant, Major, Colonel, etc – his hands growing ever unsteadier and less and less of the soup ever making it from tureen to bowl.

By the time I left school I would undoubtedly have been a Field Marshall but, by then, Mr Smart had moved on to that soup kitchen in the sky where even Brown Windsor tasted of ambrosia, and the newly-formed British Rail had replaced soup as the obligatory starter with something called Grapefruit and Mandarin Cocktail.

There is no case to be made for Brown Windsor. It was unspeakably nasty and its demise is a cause for celebration. And yet... And yet... When confronted with the aberrations, the unmitigated horror of some modern soups – avocado soup, melon and passion fruit soup, Stilton soup – Stilton, I ask you! It's a cheese, not a bloody soup – who among us could be as soulless as not occasionally to yearn for a bowl of rank, curdled, glutinous, greasy, steaming Brown Windsor soup? **JEREMY WAYNE**

The Parts Other Religions Cannot Reach

How to floss your brain and other aspects of Yoga explained

by **Hugh Burnett**

The ultimate aim of Hatha Yoga is union with God – escape from this mortal coil. When the breath moves the mind moves. Ergo, control the breath and you can control the mind. All the details are contained in three ancient Sanskrit books.

Yoga when brought to the West had been sanitised, so I went to India to film the Facts, first to an Ashram in Delhi sponsored by India's Ministry of Education. The Swami in charge instructed Mrs Gandhi and her family in yoga practices and appeared on Indian television. We filmed his patients being treated with yoga exercises for a variety of complaints, including diabetics who had been taken off insulin. The Swami explained the basic cleansing procedures.

'They are sucking the water through the rectum. They are going into the pond or into the tubs. Use a vacuum, suck the air and it is easy to suck the water. You can suck the air through the penis. First you put some catheter and some metals and it's required practise long time. So without any instrument you can suck the air and then water and then honey and then after mercury also. It is not dangerous. We are sucking the oil and honey and milk and after sometime you are throwing it out like urine. So no danger. Without teacher it is harmful.' (Arthur Koestler reported this as a method of birth control being recommended in Bombay, the life-giving *bindu* to be reclaimed by vacuum.)

Then the Swami explained how to clean the brain. 'We have to practise through the cleansing process first. A piece of thread in the nostrils will come through the mouth, so sometime there is adenoid. And then cough and cold will go out. This is very good for the eyes also, for hair, for throat and for teeth. Its effect is going from neck upper portion – it is good for every part of your neck. Eyesight. And sometimes you have no smelling power so it also sometimes in the ear so it will give healing power also so.

'Many diseases you can remove through the *sutermati* – that is thread, and *jalnati* – through saline water from one nostril to another nostril. And there is one cleansing process, 24ft long and very thin cloth. This is acquired practice, then after three, four days one foot will go inside. Then it is easy to swallow all after 10, 15 days.'

Awakening the serpent in the pelvis – *kundalini* rejuvenates the entire system. Heavy breathing stirs the snake force, causing it to ascend through the backbone into the head, causing ecstasy.

I met a man sitting in the lotus position in a spot picked out according to the precepts of the sacred texts: a solitary place, free from disturbances of all kinds (apart from the film crew and equipment), in a country where justice is properly administered, where good people live, and food is obtained easily;

in a place well plastered with cow dung and free from filth and insects. Clear of all anxieties, not overeating, being brave, having perseverance, preserving his vital fluids by continence and keeping only the company of men, he would not injure any living thing, would not steal, would show forgiveness, have compassion, be meek and adore God.

In Benares, Professor Misra exhibited remarkable yogic prowess. 'He is going to take a bayonet and a rod fixed to the top of it and with his eye-lid he is getting it bent. Not on the bone, but eyelid. By breath control he packs up his eyelid with air and makes it hard as stone.' Professor Misra placed the rod against his eye and bent it against a plank.

Next, fragments of broken bottles were scattered on a sheet of metal. The Professor lay on them and a mattress was placed on top of him, then another metal sheet. A heavy roller was pulled over the sandwich containing the professor.

He rose, brushed the shards of glass from his back and prepared for the elephant. He claimed he could stop his heartbeat at will and hold back a steam locomotive with his feet. The five-ton elephant failed to move the professor, braced against the plank.

Yoga also encompasses the divine art of music – *Taan*. The seventy-eight year old principal of a music college in Rishikesh explained: 'Glorifying and praising the Lord with melodious songs and chanting his Divine Name, sweet and musical tones have come to be part and parcel of the spiritual exercise of the devotee of the Lord.' He used to carry a harmonium on his head. We saw a photograph of him singing out of his ear.

His greatest feat was to play an instrument for half an hour without breathing or blinking, a coin balanced on his head. The procedure involved 'bringing the rectus abdominal muscles into vigorous play' and vibration of the stomach wall. Sounds also came out of the base of his spine.

Mastery of Hatha Yoga opens the doors to all the higher forms of yoga. All the postures – *asanas* – have a specific purpose. They remove stomach disorders, phlegm, bile, wind, digest bad food, increase the appetite and destroy the most deadly poisons. One *asana* carries the air from the front of the body to the back, kindling the gastric fires, reducing fatness and curing all diseases. Another opens the door to salvation. The breath held in the body, the mind undisturbed, the eyes gazing between the eyebrows, there is no fear of death. There is even a posture to make one intelligent, although it is difficult to do.

Nauli, control of the stomach muscles, removes dyspepsia, increases the appetite and digestion, brings happiness and assists with vital functions. One can also shrink to the size of an atom, expand in space, levitate, reach out anywhere, even to the moon, and become invisible.

In Poona, at another institute recognised by the Indian government, a Yogi had carried out a more unusual practice. The ancient books teach that in order to levitate, all the orifices of the body must be closed, including two inside the back of the mouth, near the nose. To cover these the tongue needs to be extended. With the edge of a lotus leaf the tendons under the tongue are gently scraped and the scratch treated with butter. After several months the tongue becomes detached and can then be reversed inside the mouth. Eyes shut, the orifices of the body closed with the heel, fingers and tongue, levitation should be possible. If nothing happens, it is not the fault of yoga. The practitioner has not purified himself sufficiently.

When I asked the Swami in Delhi if he had ever levitated he said he had tried but had only managed to hop around a little. The Poona Yogi's tongue could be extended nearly to his navel. His fee for filming, he said with some difficulty, would be one million pounds and two tickets to the Albert Hall. I said the tickets were possible but not the million pounds. After several days he relented and was paid the usual fee for sticking out one's tongue. At another centre a Yogi's tongue had been surgically split down the middle like a snake.

The life-cycle of the soul involves 8,400,000 rebirths. The aim of Hatha Yoga is to liberate oneself from this great chain. But if the perfected practitioner evades death, where does that leave him? The mystic East has a lot of dilemmas like that. Meanwhile, *breathe –* and look after the snake in your pelvis.

119

IT WAS 1965 and I was fifteen. My father, a stern disciplinarian, had discovered that I was now too big for the slipper, cricket-stump or being sent to bed early. A job was the answer.

Down at the local labour exchange they were advertising for porters at the General Hospital. The pay was about £5 a week, plus as many hospital lunches as you could eat. My friend Gerald and I signed up straight away.

Bromsgrove General Hospital was a series of cream-coloured, single-storey buildings with corrugated roofs. Covered walkways connected the wards and asphalt roads ran in and out and round about. Our job, explained Paddy, the senior porter – an Irishman who could roll his own cigarettes with one hand while simultaneously explaining how to lift a bedridden patient onto the loo and marking his betting slip for the 2.15 – was to 'do any durrty job going'. He was going to enjoy having someone to whom he could delegate.

Gerald and I soon got used to the work. It was simple enough manual labour, with only the occasional unpleasantness, like having to clear up someone's mess from the floor or throwing a particularly bloody lot of laundry into the sluice. A couple of times I had needles sink into my knee as I slung rubbish bags, but it was long before AIDS and no one gave it a second thought.

Often we were asked to help lift elderly patients in or out of bed, or into the bath. The sight of grey-haired genitalia when you were scarcely able to live with your own was a bit much first thing in the morning, but after a while you got used to it.

Sometimes, we'd be called to wheel a covered tin trolley from one of the wards down to the mortuary. Luckily, the top was always rolled down well over the corpse, although one time we caught Paddy in an uncharacteristically gloomy mood. He'd just come back from taking a trolley down to the mortuary. This one had no cover on it, just a sheet covering the contents. When a gust of wind got up, it blew off.

'Four babies,' he said quietly, all trace of his usual bravura gone. 'All just born and still covered in blood.'

He never mentioned it again, and Gerald and I, shocked, frightened and yet mesmerised, used to wonder if one day we'd get a similar call. We never did, but for months afterwards I used to impress friends with tales of the hospital, in which it had been me wheeling the dead babies down to the mortuary when the wind blew the paper off. An apparent ability to cope with death was some sign of adulthood.

If the corpses were our nightmare, the fun was the fleet of electric trucks which we drove around the hospital grounds, delivering washing or rubbish, or trailing a metal caboose stacked with over-boiled lunches from the hospital kitchen.

Walking on the Wild Side

If a bohemian is just a skiver, **Nell Dunn** *found it harder work than she'd hoped*

'BOHEMIAN! Just an excuse for being lazy.' So said Andrea, my Argentinian friend and neighbour. 'Perhaps you're right,' I said, falling about with laughter. She laughed too.

When I was fifteen I saw *La Bohème* at the Paris Opera House… 'My Tiny Hand is Frozen'. I was enchanted. She crouched by a flickering stove wrapped in shawls in an 'artist's' studio… I yearned for that artist's studio.

I think both my mother and my father were bohemians *manqué*. My father loved the company of Augustus John and collected his drawings, particularly the ones of dishevelled young women. But his dishevelled daughter sometimes worried him. My mother took in penniless painters and had them pay the rent in pictures, but she drove an ice-blue Mercedes SL300 with butterfly doors and was quite show-offy at the wheel. She also liked Balmain clothes when they happened her way.

When still quite young, I married a bohemian and my first child was born. The house was big but there was no heating, except for an open fire made from burning driftwood he sometimes collected from the Thames. We cooked on this fire and the smoke got in my eyes, so we usually went to the local café and ate egg and chips and fried bread. Lots of people came to visit or talk or spend the night – or even to move in. They used up my shampoo and finished the last of the milk that I had hoped to give the baby with his breakfast pap. One (Kasmin) even accused me of stealing the knickers he'd left drying in the bathroom. I didn't like it.

In 1884, when Alphonse Daudet was forty-three years old, he wrote *Sappho,* in order to warn his sons off wild women and the bohemian life. I wonder if it did the trick. The book is about the young protagonist, Jean Gaussin, up in Paris from the South to pursue his studies, with his bohemian mistress. I quote:

'And the intimacy of their sensual love was changing too. At first she had had reserves, out of respect for her youthful lover's innocence and illusions; but she no longer felt any need for restraint after seeing the effect that the sudden revelation of her sordid past had on him, the swampy fever that she had lit up in his blood. And the perverse caresses that she had so long suppressed, all the raving words she had clenched her teeth against, she now let loose, letting herself

There were four of these trucks, which you steered by standing on a platform at the front and wiggling a metal stick up and down. There was fierce competition every morning to unplug the fastest – obviously newer and still with some of its paint on – from its overnight charger.

After a fortnight Gerald and I had saved enough money to be able to splash out. For some reason – I suspect it was Paddy's idea, since he was one of nature's bon viveurs – we bought several bottles of sweet sherry and a couple of flagons of cider. By lunchtime we were doing 'Knees Up Mother Brown' down the main corridor.

The patients seemed to tolerate this equally enough, although we were less sure about the doctors. Paddy said it hadn't been a good idea to offer them a drink, so we retreated to our room and finished off the booze ourselves.

It was then that Gerald made the fatal suggestion. Outside, the electric trucks were lined up, one loaded with rubbish sacks headed for the incinerator, the other with great rolled-up

If justice truly were poetic, we ought to have ended up in casualty with both legs broken

balls of linen destined for the laundry.

'I bet I can make that old truck beat the new one.'

'Five bob says you can't.'

A gently swaying Paddy lined us up, calling out, 'On yer marks. Gesset. Gow!'

Out we staggered, in a weaving, slow-motion Le Mans start.

For the first few hundred yards, I had a comfortable lead, pulling steadily ahead of Gerald. As we rounded each corner, brown paper sacks spewed off the back of the truck, scattering soiled bandages, syringes and old plastercasts.

Occasionally, patients being taken for their first post-op walk would have to scuttle out of the way.

Several seemed to be shouting at us. Gerald, carrying a heavier load, was falling farther and farther behind until disaster struck.

Rounding the corner on the downhill stretch I saw, to my horror, two nurses – or was it four? – wheeling a stretcher across the road. An old lady lay on it, secure and comfy beneath clean white sheets. The nurses saw the two approaching horsemen of the apocalypse with an expression of blank terror.

In a fuddle of sherry, cider and fear, I leaned on the steering handle. The truck, unaccustomed to making sudden changes of direction, certainly never at this speed, wobbled on its two right wheels and then, in curiously slow motion, turned turtle into the ditch.

If justice truly were poetic, we ought to have ended up in the casualty ward with both legs broken, and been ignored by the passing nurses.

As it was, there were a few bruises and cuts, but most hurtful of all, a public bawling-out by the fearsomely stout matron. We collected our National Insurance cards and left by the back entrance.

---

go, yielding herself to the nature of her being – now utterly the courtesan, amorous, adept, living up to the dreadful fame that had earned her the name Sappho.'

Daudet was living in Paris at an extraordinarily rich period for the arts. He knew Flaubert, Zola, Mallarmé, Rodin, Degas and Baudelaire. In the *Goncourt Journal* dated January 1885, we are told how he became a writer:

'Daudet went on to say that during all those years he had done nothing at all, that all he had felt had been a need to sing, make music, to roam the woods, to drink a little too much and to get involved in a brawl. He admitted that at that time he had no literary ambition, but just an instinctive delight in noting everything down, in recording everything, even his dreams. It was the war, he declared, which had changed him, by awakening in him the idea that he might die without having achieved anything, without leaving anything durable behind him… Only then had he set to work, and with work came literary ambition.'

However, according to a story he told Zola, he still had problems over whether to spend his francs on a whore or a bunch of white lilac for his wife on their wedding anniversary. The lilac won, but he got scolded for being late.

I've always fallen for bohemians, with or without ambition. I have sometimes tried to knock them into shape. It doesn't work. At the heart of every bohemian is a bohemian. Bohemians are born not made, and at least they don't expect dinner on the table.

'Excuse me, do the Thatchers live round here?'

Philip Purser *delights in the refurbished Wigmore Hall.* *Illustration by* **Nick Baker**

HALL SWEET HALL

In the classified pages of *The Oldie* (or maybe it was the *Literary Review*) a lady was seeking a room in London for two or three nights a week. 'Must be near the Wigmore Hall,' she added. I do hope she found what she wanted, because nobody should be denied the pleasures of one of the few sweet haunts of gentlefolk remaining in the capital.

My wife and I started going there regularly about five years ago. I had always supposed the Wigmore would be too high-minded and sepulchral, especially for someone whose musical sensors reacted most readily to noisy orchestral works by Berlioz or Walton.

Up to a point I was right. A grim subterranean bar, the possibility of an earnest sandwich, an ice cream in the interval, hardly add up to conviviality. But then they shut the place for a year, and when it re-opened in 1992 it had two delightful restaurants and a smart new bar between them.

We have had a little something before the concert ever since, usually from the self-service counter. Yes, there is a vegetarian and wholefood bias, but not brandished at you in any evangelical way. It simply accords with the traditional character of the Wigmore clientele, which is drawn from that section of humanity which Michael Frayn usefully defined as the herbivores.

They wait for each other with only the mildest impatience, nursing a glass of Beaujolais Villages and catching up with last Saturday's *Guardian Weekend*: the salt of the earth, or even *das Salz von der Erde* – refugee dynasties established in Hampstead and Highgate 60 years ago are still strongly represented. There are women in bright smocks with their hair combed up if not actually wound round the head in a plait. There are incredibly well-behaved young children wearing shiny black shoes. There are men in velvet cord whose domed heads gleam above fringes of wiry grey curls – seen all the more dramatically as, ascending to the auditorium, they settle into their seats in front of you.

Ah, the auditorium! The seats are red plush; red marble and mahogany abound. Big vases of forsythia or chrysanthemums flank the stage. But the first time you will have eyes only for the mosaic which arches over the platform. Designed by Gerald Moira in 1900, it's a dream of post-Pre-Raphaelite, pre-Paul Raymond exotic symbolism.

The naked Soul of Music, his lower register discreetly veiled, gazes upon the fireball of Harmony while a chubby-bottomed nymphet of Love urges on a mortal fiddler. In the thorny foreground, a composer scrabbles to transcribe the heavenly notes onto a scroll under the full-frontal inspiration of Psyche. If that sounds as if it might distract, it doesn't really, except perhaps during passages for unaccompanied lute.

The Wigmore began as the Bechstein Hall, built by the German piano manufacturers as an adjunct to their Wigmore Street show-rooms. Busoni and Pachmann gave the opening recitals in 1901. The young Sybil Thorndike played Chopin and Liszt before turning luvvie. Saint-Saens and Percy Grainger played their own music, Beecham was the first to squeeze a (small) orchestra on to the stage.

In what sounds like a bit of war-time jiggery pokery, Bechstein UK was wound up by the Board of Trade in 1916 and all its property sold off.

Renamed, the concert hall survived under various managements until 1987. It was then taken over by the City of Westminster, who on this evidence can't be all bad.

Apart from the refurbishment, the programmes under their aegis continue to be imaginatively planned. There are series of concerts under such labels as Early Music & Baroque which can be booked well in advance, but also plenty of oddments which crop up only in the lucky dip of the monthly schedule.

Once we drove up from the country to hear the pianist David Owen Norris and were baffled to find a sinister black-glass coach from Geoff Amos Coaches, a familiar Northamptonshire firm, unloading outside the Hall. We only remembered then that Norris was a local musician and favourite – the point of which story being that the Wigmore audience (and with it the Wigmore atmosphere) does vary a bit according to the artists involved. Dividing the salt of the earth this night was a solid block of yeoman groupies.

The most evident, and in many ways the most uplifting, permutation occurs when young performers undertake a debut recital. Then the audience is packed with mummies, daddies, grandparents, brothers and sisters.

We went lately to hear Ruth Bolister, a wonderfully talented oboeist. She had assembled a crew of friends to accompany her, including a cellist who wouldn't have been out of place in the Moira mosaic. In the interval other friends loudly exchanged college gossip – all seemed to have been at Cambridge together. But so fresh was the playing, so infectious the enthusiasm, that the crustiest oldie would for once have had to applaud youth. This one did anyway.

Still Life with Tractor

Com-a-ti-yi-yippy-i-yay! That ghastly din shattering the peace of the bluebell woods is **Naomi Sim** *riding the range with Will Hawes, alias Wheelhorse the scarlet tractor. He's a cantankerous old galoot and he ain't made for stopping...*

Years ago I would leap gracefully on and off the saddle. Nowadays, when I get off I put one foot on the ground and must then use both hands to lift off my other leg. Some people would think I was past it

FOR A SHORT TIME last week the skies cleared, the sun came out and at last I was able to go riding the range on my Wheelhorse again. This animal is a garden tractor, and we have been working together for 21 years. Our relationship is complicated. On my part it is 50 per cent pride and joy, and 50 per cent trepidation and exasperation. On the part of my Wheelhorse it is ten per cent a cheerful will-ingness to work and 90 per cent bloody-mindedness.

I can't blame it entirely for this attitude since I am told by engineers that the normal working life of a Wheelhorse is about ten years. If I, too, had to double my life expectancy I would be a hundred and forty, and might possibly feel sour when faced with really heavy work.

The chief problem we face is a large area of rough grass to be cut on very un-even ground, and in May this is covered in bluebells. Each year there are more, and from every window of my bungalow I can see deep, dark blue, in the open and under the trees, stretching into the distance.

I refuse to cut any grass until the bluebells have quite faded, but by then every-thing is at least two feet high and at that point, sure as eggs is eggs, down comes the rain. By the time it stops the grass is flattened, the roots tangled and sodden, and it is then that I ask my Wheel-horse to do its first cut of the season. It doesn't take kindly to the idea nowadays and usually refuses to start.

As this is not the cutting season, all I wanted to do last week was to hitch up the trailer and make three or four journeys up into the wood to pick up logs and bring them down to the woodshed. I greeted it lovingly. I checked petrol, oil and tyres, and cleaned the plug; the equivalent of the ingratiating manner in which people try to catch a live horse that has quite different plans. Preliminaries over, I switched on, pulled out the choke and the accelerator, and made my first pull on the starting rope.

A strong man should be able to start the engine now with one good yank, but I have to take the rope in both hands and hurl myself backwards to its full extent. Nowadays, I find that six pulls like that is my limit. After that I am liable to have a seizure. This time it started after five. A good day.

I backed it out of the shed, hitched up the trailer, and we started off with me singing joyfully, 'I got spurs that jingle, jangle, jingle'. Unfortunately the other occupants of the valley were not stopped in their tracks by the beauty of my voice because the sound, as always, was drowned by my Wheelhorse.

It doesn't like competition. It makes such a racket in its old age that if anyone wants to speak to me when we are working I have to stop, dismount and walk away several paces before we can make ourselves heard. On no account must I switch off the engine for it will refuse to start again. It will stall if the blades strike a hidden mole hill or fallen branch in the deep grass, or if the engine overheats, or for some reason beyond my comprehension.

Through the years various bits of it have fallen off, the brakes are practically non-existent and the gear lever slips into neutral if not held manually in position. An outing with Wheelhorse is always an Adventure.

This day all went well. We brought in four loads of logs and got back to the shed with no mishap. It hadn't stalled, it hadn't run away with me as it has done more than once, it hadn't unseated me as it has frequently tried to do, and as I dismounted I was filled with gratitude.

Years ago I would leap gracefully on and off the saddle. Nowadays, when I get off I put one foot on the ground and must then use both hands to lift off my other leg. Some people would think I was past it.

In the days before I had Wheelhorse I used to drive an Allen Scythe. This creature had a blade in front which moved rapidly from side to side, while I, in theory, walked behind at a reasonable pace guiding it with the two long handles.

In practice it hurtled madly forward, cutting everything in sight and usually making for the nearest tree. It had no idea that I was 'guiding' it and I never grew to love it.

Alastair disliked physical labour and he didn't like to watch me doing it either. It kept me away from our fascinating discussions and, anyway, he didn't see why nature should be disturbed.

When he was stretched on the swing seat and I was cutting the lawn he would say 'Aw, the little daisies'. This filled me with guilt but didn't stop me from cutting. He also thought I worked too hard and was always asking me to get help. But I enjoyed the work and didn't want anyone.

However, in time a neighbour told me of his wonderful new machine on which he actually sat, and I went to see it. A Wheelhorse, of course, painted bright scarlet with a purring engine and a comfy saddle. Love at first sight.

I went home and told Alastair that I had met my neighbour's garden help, that his name was Will Hawes, and that he was prepared to work for us too. Alastair was delighted.

When my own Wheelhorse was delivered I left it in the back drive, rang the back door bell, and went to tell Alastair that Will Hawes had arrived, and would he please come and say hello. 'Oh, must I?' 'Yes, he's a bit of a red. You'll like him.'

Alastair was always frightened of first encounters and needed a lot of persuasion, but when he finally met the person he would be utterly charming. He enjoyed the encounter, though, when he realised he could save his charm for another day, and he always laughed whenever he saw me riding Will Hawes.

These days the Wheelhorse and I may not look such a pretty pair but we must look, shall we say, experienced. Its scarlet paint has faded to a dull red and it is covered in dried grass and daubed with oil. I am in gum boots, filthy jeans, and an anorak that has stood with me on the top of most of the mountains in Scotland over the last 37 years.

For good or ill, I feel that I have an affinity with my Wheelhorse and that we shall probably go together when that happy time comes. The Wheelhorse to a museum, I to the winds.

'See - my horoscope says "Buy", yours says "Spend"'

PLACES NOT TO GO TO

A Guide to the World's WORST Dumps

SOHO

FOOLISH and misguided young people are still making the pilgrimage to Soho. Perhaps they think that Dylan Thomas is still propping up a corner of the French pub. He isn't, he is dead and Soho is in its hideous death throes. It is now as boring as Lanzarote, as squalid as Times Square, as porn-ridden as Amsterdam and as gay as San Francisco.

Newcomers to the square half-mile of decay wishing to become what is laughingly known as 'Soho characters' have missed the boat by 30 years. The trickle of advertising and TV commercial people that began some time ago has become a flood. Gays now promenade along Old Compton Street, where barmen in the Swiss Tavern are trained to spot heterosexuals and refuse to serve them. There are now exclusively gay cafés along that street, and even a gay barber's shop. And the pubs and clubs are in pathetic decline.

Ian Board still gives his bad imitation of Muriel Belcher to the new generation of alcoholics in the Colony Room Club, and Norman Balon's egomania and what passes for his wit has all but emptied the Coach and Horses. A few faceless customers remain from inertia, but gone are the days when one might look up at the sound of a door opening and think, 'Oh good. Here comes so-and-so.'

Where now there is a dirty bookshop or a strip club there was once a bistro, café or delicatessen. The rot set in years ago, when Lord Wolfenden banished prostitutes from the streets and so gave birth to the porn industry. Paul Raymond, a very unprepossessing creature, has polluted Soho; locust-like, he is eating up all that was good about it. It is a small mercy that he is not a member of the Groucho Club. When he got hold of the only good baker's shop in the area (in Peter Street) it was selling porn within 48 hours. Richards, the excellent fishmonger, had to close while they sought new premises.

Now even the restaurants are in sad decline. Only a man with an expense account can afford to eat in Frith Street, and only the Amalfi in Old Compton Street remains within the average pocket. Wheelers, once second home to various bohemians who boasted genuine talent, is no more than an expensive fish and chip shop for innocent, gullible tourists. The French House died when Gaston Berlemont retired. It smells of failure and attracts non-achievers who hang on to the past by their grubby fingertips. Paradoxically, next door the Golden Lion has been empty since they decided to get rid of the gay regulars such as Dennis Nilsen, who picked up his victims there.

Westminster council are reported to be keen on ridding the area of Berwick Street and Rupert Street markets, Soho's saving graces. Expect an influx of gay barrow boys any day now. **JEFFREY BERNARD**

I WAS MADE deacon in the Church of Wales at the beginning of the war and was sent to a parish comprised of a string of small villages on the edge of the South Wales coalfield. The parish was served by three churches, one of which was sold about the time of my arrival. It was made of corrugated iron and was later taken away section by section to become part of a factory.

The residents were miners, quarrymen, farmers and farm labourers. For many, Welsh was their first language. In some parts of the village were settlements of people who could be described as well-to-do. These were known as the *crachach*, a Welsh expression which translates roughly as 'the toffs'.

I remember the first adult I was asked to prepare for confirmation. He said: 'Curate, I need to make it clear from the start. I can never love my neighbour.' Seeing that this was likely to cut across aspects of the instruction I had prepared, I paused. He continued: 'Only yesterday she threw a bucket of dirty water into our back door.'

The following day more was to follow. I visited the wife of a farm labourer. She had been making bread but, doubtful of the written word, had included half a pound of yeast in the dough instead of half an ounce. One of my earliest parochial duties was to help her to remove the bread from the oven with the help of a spade and bury it in the garden.

It may be that I was something of a prig. I suppose that as an undergraduate I had lived a moderately sophisticated life and, at a theological college, an ordered one. So to be in the sort of parish in which I found myself was a considerable cultural shock. It was before the days of National Health. Even so, it was a surprise to come across two old ladies who shared the same pair of false teeth.

These were the days before what has been called the 'indiscriminate baptism' controversy. I soon found that many people did not ask for baptism. They were ordered to bring the child to baptism. The vicar would thunder at them in the main street, in

my first job

Reverend Laurence Tanner

the opening words of the 1662 baptism service, which I have heard on no other occasion: 'Has that child been baptised or no?' If the answer was no, the following instruction was given: 'Sunday week, 2.30.'

It was part of my job to call at homes where there had been a birth. I remember calling at one cottage and the baby, one week old, could not be found. 'She can't have gone far,' I was told. I never did see the baby, but she did turn up later in the day under a pile of washing. As I slunk away from the cottage, I saw at every window the faces of other offspring.

The most dramatic situation was apt to take place on Monday morning, washing day, in the village down the hill. A message would be sent: 'Curate, there is a bit of a fight going on among the women.' There were ten houses forming a right-angle served by a single

tap. Inevitably tempers got frayed and buckets of water went flying about. Some of the older men, technically unemployed at that early stage of the war, were nevertheless active enough on those Monday mornings to refill buckets for their women-folk to hurl. I suppose the sight of a clerical collar was expected to put a damper on things. My theological college had not equipped me for such a situation.

One night I was at my bedroom window when the air-raid siren sounded. Rows of lights went on at various points in the parish. As the village policeman lived a few doors away, I called to tell him. 'Right,' he said, 'I will report the situation straight away.' Some minutes later he told me not to worry '– it is in our interest.'

It took some days for me to realise we had been designated a decoy area. Before the blitz on London, German planes attacked ports in Wales and the West Country. Some, like Bristol and Cardiff, were not far distant from us. The lights were intended to represent harbours, factories and steelworks. Someone on high had decided that our parish was expendable and at times I could see the point. As a result, night after night the village was subjected to full-scale blitzes – chandelier flares like large Christmas trees, then incendiary bombs and high explosives. Surprisingly little damage was done. The only fatalities were a couple of heifers and a Herefordshire bull.

In some families there was great poverty, although most people were reasonably well-fed. Clothing was very poor – but better than that of the evacuees who arrived from Birmingham. Some boys wore dresses because they had no other clothes. Such evacuees had to be drafted into the church choir. All was well as long as they only had one tune. Trouble started when their repertoire increased. They would begin a hymn, singing flat out and end with a quite different tune. How the change came about I have no idea. It was as uniform as a flock of birds suddenly changing course.

It was a memorable two years. I look back on them with affection.

OF ALL THE CITIES of the Pianura Padana, the great plain of the Po – Parma, Reggio nell'Emilia, Modena and Bologna, all strung out along the Via Emilia – the most rewarding to visit, because it has so much to offer in a small compass that is either remarkable, or beautiful, or elegant, or bizarre, or a compound of these, is Parma.

It is good to sit at one of the café tables in the Piazza Garibaldi on an autumn morning. The holidays are over and the Parmigiani are back from the sea and the mountains; the university founded in 1601 by Ranuccio Farnese, the atrociously cruel but cultivated descendant of Pope Paul III, has re-opened, and drifts of leaves lie deep in the arcadian avenues of the Park of the Palazzo Ducale.

If it is a Wednesday, a market day (the other being Saturday) there will be lots of farmers in the piazza all gassing away beneath the sundial on the Governor's Palace, which gives the time simultaneously in Agra, Tobolsk, Isfahan and Moscow in the mornings, and in Lima, Quebec, Buenos Aires, Rio, Pico di Tenerife and Paris in the afternoons.

In spite of their 30s felt hats made by Borsalino and Panizza, the majority of them still vote Communist. In much the same way as the French believe that they invented the wagon-lit, the submarine and the suppository, the Parmigiani believe that they invented Communism, a sort of Communism that must make Lenin want to turn in his mausoleum.

Here, if you close your eyes and listen to the strange dialect, you can be transported in the imagination to some French province. In Italian a cork is *turacciolo*, in Parmigiano *bouchon*; a cupboard in Italian is *armadio*, here *armoire*; *vino* is *vin*.

In 1816, Maria Luigia, daughter of Francis I of Austria, Napoleon's second wife and mother of his son, the King of Rome, became Duchess of Parma. She married her handsome and intelligent principal minister, Count Neipperg – his death mask,

Ham AND Opera

Eric Newby *has taken Parma to his heart, with its love of food and music, and its atmosphere of mystery*

complete with eye-patch, shows him to be the double of the Man in the Hathaway Shirt.

It was she who inspired the women of Parma with the passion for dress which they still have to this day and it was she who caused the exquisite Teatro Regio to be built and appointed Paganini to be one of the directors of her orchestra, the finest in Italy.

Music is one of the two abiding passions of the Parmigiani – the other is food. Toscanini was born in Parma and studied at the Conservatorio, as did that rarity, the *lirico spinto*, La Tibaldi. Verdi was born near Busseto near Parma and the great composer Ildebrando Pizzetti, who died in 1968, was also a Parmigiano.

When it comes to the appreciation of opera the Parmigiani have the most critical ears in Europe. Their verdict, particularly that of those in the gallery, is absolute. Of some 14 productions, six will be by Verdi.

The atmosphere before the curtain rises is one of almost unbearable

tension for the performers. Applause for a Violetta at the end of Act 1 can, by the final curtain, turn to *il fischio*, a savage whistling. Sometimes it is the prima donna who gets the fischio while some unknown youngster is lauded.

The time to see the women of Parma at close quarters is during the *passegiata*, the promenade, at dusk when the clock on the Governor's Palace lights up.

You can see the living embodiments of those painted by two of the city's greatest artists, Correggio, whose entire output of frescoes can be seen in Parma, and his admirer and follower Il Parmigianino – women with the witty mouths and saucy eyes of Parmigianino's 'Turkish Slave' in the Palazzo Pilotta; or the sort that Coreggio might have used as models for 'Diana Returning from the Chase' in the Convento di San Paolo – soft, sensual, lovable women, but perfectly capable of devising a fate similar to that of Actaeon for anyone who wrongs them.

Here, as women choose what they wear with infinite care, so do they choose their food. There are innumerable dishes in which *grana*, otherwise *formaggio Parmigiano*, otherwise Parmesan, is incorporated. The most famous of all pasta dishes is *tortelli d'erbette*, little snacks of pasta stuffed with a mixture of *ricotta* (a cheese that is a by-product of making *grana*), long-leafed spinach, egg, butter and a little *grana*, served with grated cheese, *grana* of course, and melted butter. The *grana* gives off a sharp and appetising smell and when you put a piece in your mouth – a good way to end up the meal – you find embedded in it a hard, salty nodule, *il grana*.

Equally famous is the *salumeria* – everything made from pig. *Prosciutti di Parma*, the most famous of Italian hams, air-cured in barns in the foothills of the Apennines. *Spalla* from San Secondo, the shoulder, the part preferred by Verdi. *Culatello* from Zibello, part of the pig's bottom, a rare delicacy which Gabriele d'Annunzio,

129

that eccentric and erotic patriot compared in a cannabilistic moment to the breasts of a beautiful woman.

But in spite of all this homeliness Parma has a bizarre quality, especially in the depths of winter when the fog rises from the ditches and canals that irrigate the plain and comes down in the city, with church bells clanging out in the now invisible campanili overhead.

You feel it in the chapel of the black Madonna in the Oratoria dei Rossi to whom, with her equally black child, students have recourse to ask help in their examinations; and in the crypt in which the Farnese and the rulers of the house of Bourbon-Parma are entombed.

And you feel it in the Pilotta, the unfinished palazzo built with millions of thin pink bricks, a vast barn-like structure so named because *pelota* was played in one of its enormous courtyards.

Hidden inside it is the vast Teatro Farnese built entirely of wood and decorated with painted stucco mythological figures and life-size equestrian statues. For long the greatest and most splendid theatre in the world, only six performances ever took place in it, gigantic spectacles in which hydraulic machinery was used to simulate battles between sea monsters. It was destroyed during the war and subsequently completely reconstructed.

Mysterious rather than bizarre are the figures of the Seasons carved by the sculptor Antelami in the octagonal, five-storeyed Romanesque Baptistery which he began to build in 1196.

What are they thinking about, these twelfth-century men and women with their calm, inward-looking faces, as they ride out in the spring on horseback, reap the harvest and make barrels for the vintage?

What do we know of Antelami? Nothing beyond a Latin inscription: 'In 1178, in the second month, there appeared a sculptor named Antelami. That sculptor was this Benedetto.' That is all.

Acquainted with the Night

Nell Dunn, *no stranger to the darkest hour, reconnoitres in the twilit world of the insomniac*

I USED TO fear sleepless nights. When I lay awake in the small hours, my thoughts would be of the next day and of how exhausted I would be and a panic would settle in me. My body would ache and a sensation of despair creep through my heart and settle in my mind. Indeed I would wake exhausted and depressed, and driven to all the small businesses of the next day would find no pleasure, no pleasure at all in being alive.

However, since becoming an oldie, all this has changed. Sometimes I sleep alone, sometimes with my best friend. If I wake when he is there I lie and listen to his breathing and feel pleased that we are still together and alive. I even feel quite cheerful. Then I usually fall asleep.

If I am alone I have a more unpredictable time. I've got a bed I like and a very light goose-down duvet and a really comfy pillow. I have a good radio – not a battery one as they kept running out – but a plug-in one with several buttons for easy search of different stations. I've also got a bottle of mineral water and a favourite George Simenon, a writer who is such an ace at understanding night and aloneness, as

If I wake when he is there I listen to his breathing and feel pleased that we are still together and alive

is Graham Greene. I listened to Julian Glover reading *The End of the Affair* on the World Service the other night. What a writer, what a book. I lay there in my lovely bed, the room gently lit by the street lights shining through the blinds, listening to that marvellous passage where the bomb drops and the door falls on him and he frees himself and goes back into the bedroom to find his mistress naked, praying by the bed :

She turned quickly and stared at me with fear. I hadn't realised that my dressing gown was torn and dusted all over with plaster; my hair was white with it and there was blood on my mouth and cheeks. 'Oh, God,' she said, 'you're alive.'

Sometimes I go downstairs and make myself a cup of tea and then the dogs wake and want to come up to bed with me and I usually let them and we all snuggle up together. Jack Russells lie extraordinarily still in the night, although Ivy has a slight snore from a damaged larynx sustained as a puppy when she was dragged by her lead accidentally trapped in the car door.

By now I feel close to myself and warm and ready to drift off. Other times I fancy a bit of telly. There is often a film on at about 2.30am. It's *Chinatown* this Friday and I hope I wake up. Sometimes I do feel tired the next day but it is often the kind of tiredness I felt as a young woman when I had stayed up all night at a party or in a lover's arms – an exhilarated tiredness, the tiredness of time well spent, of having stolen a march on the sleeping population.

PIN-UPS

Jean Marsh

picks her top six

1 Philip White
He was my dustman and, on Thursday mornings, it was a treat to see his attractive strong beaming face as he carried away my rubbish and delivered my official, council issue black plastic bag.

2 Louis B Mole
My godson – good-looking and amusing, essential in a pin-up. And who could refuse any man who, the minute he sees you, puts up his arms and says 'cuggle'?

3 Nude male, Géricault
Serves the fantasist in me. He has taken me forcefully, gently, slowly, passionately and with the added advantage of having a different face every time.

4 Charlie Watts
Has a wonderful Plantaganet face and an appealing mystery and elusiveness.

5 Eric Rohmer
My favourite film director. I imagine him stopping me and inviting me to star in *My Afternoon with Jean*, or *Jean's Elbow*.

6 Ricardo Muti
A great conductor (an instant aphrodisiac for me) and stunningly good looking. Brooding, saturnine and, I hear, irresistibly unavoidable.

Right: actress Jean Marsh

The Gnome Spotter

It was not until he reached middle age that **John McEwen** *realised how much of his surviving sense of wonder he owed to 'BB', author of 'The Little Grey Men'*

'BB' WAS THE PSEUDONYM of the author and artist Denys Watkins-Pitchford. His favourite sport was wildfowling and 'BB' was the trade-name of the heaviest goose-shot cartridges. 'BB' was born on 25th July 1905 and died on 8th September 1990. He was always grateful for the luck to be born when he was: 'A few years earlier and I'd have been killed as a subaltern on the Western Front.'

His writing career began in 1939 with publication of the story of a fox, *Wild Lone*, illustrated – as all his books would be – by himself under his proper name, 'D J Watkins-Pitchford'. His most famous was *The Little Grey Men*, a children's adventure story about some gnomes who went in search of their long-lost

brother. It was inspired by his own incontrovertible sighting of a gnome at the age of four. He was a down-to-earth man and never budged on this issue; though latterly he felt that gnomes, like so much of the countryside, might have become extinct during his lifetime.

The Little Grey Men won the Carnegie Prize, encouraging him to give up his first and only job as assistant art master at Rugby. 'BB' published over 60 books plus a great deal of journalism, much of it as a columnist for the *Shooting Times*. He was most popular in the 1940s and 50s.

Brendon Chase, his own favourite from among his books, was published in 1944. It drew on his experience at Rugby and told the tale of three boys who run away from boarding school to live by their wits in an English forest. Its success could be gauged, to his amusement, by the number of irate letters from headmasters cursing him for yet another break-out. Certainly it was a bible to countless country-bred prep and public schoolboys.

At last, a selection of his writings and illustrations, introduced with a brief life by Tom Quinn, has been published. *BB: A Celebration* (Wharncliffe, £18.85) is in itself a cause for celebration.

I speak as a *Brendon Chase* addict, who had the good fortune to become a friend of the author. As a commissioning editor on *The Field* under Simon Courtauld in the mid-1980s I discovered that 'BB' was still alive and writing.

Shamefully I had long consigned him to oblivion. First the film-star 'BB' had supplanted him in my affections, and then London. Now it dawned on me in middle age that it was to him I owed most of the little wonder I retained. I fired off a passionate letter of thanks.

I anticipated his reply with the impatience of a schoolboy awaiting a love letter. It eventually arrived, typed and signed with both his names. 'I am just emerging from a dark valley having had an operation for prostate in the local hospital, a period of anxiety and discomfort which I hope will soon be forgotten. I am in my eightieth year, blind in my right eye, but feeling as young and eager as ever I did. What a pity the envelope which encloses us wears out so soon!'

This was to be a recurring pattern and refrain. Ill-health dogged him until the end, though not for one second did he fail to live by the old and anonymous valediction with which he prefaced all his books: 'The wonder of the world, the beauty and the power, the shapes of things, their colours, lights and shades; these I saw. Look ye also while life lasts.'

The day came when I, like many before me, made the pilgrimage to Sudborough in Northamptonshire. He was a short man, with an old-fashioned moustache, notably flat ears and the tinge of a Northamptonshire accent in his deep voice, which often broke into a gruff laugh.

The initials of 'Bill Badger', a later character of his, coincidentally matched his pseudonym. Badgers are always warriors in his books – significantly, the 'Bill Badger' series was particularly successful in Japan – and 'BB' was a warrior. He spoke with gusto of his time as a Special Constable in the General Strike, knocking sense into the skulls of Camden Town hooligans. And he had a badgerish taste for 'dens'.

'BB' lived in an old and conical gatehouse in Sudborough. The Round House was instantly recognisable as his abode by its weathervane – a wild goose of his own design. There he lived with his daughter Angela and twin brother Roger.

His wife had died 20 years before, poisoned – he was convinced – by inhaling wind-blown insecticide. On the mantelpiece was an early 50s snapshot of him with his son Robin, aged eight, both with guns. Robin had died shortly after it was taken of a painful and mysterious illness, the bitterest of blows.

'BB's own childhood had been spent entirely at home because of ill-health, which did not prevent him hunting with gun, rod or butterfly-net, on horseback or on foot, to his heart's content. This bred in him a reverence for the chase he never lost – from ignorance of it townspeople were for him 'only half alive' – and an attendant and instinctive knowledge and love of nature.

No one has drawn or painted Northamptonshire's landscape better, its shaggy hedges and ivy-muffled trees; or brought such 'moonlight witchery', as a New York reviewer called it, to scraperboard illustration. And his always poetic descriptions have an animal keenness of perception, sounds and smells as sharply evoked as any sight. Even from hospital he regaled readers of the *Shooting Times* with his sighting of a duck-shaped cloud, the manoeuvres of ants on his window-sill and the comforting com-panionship of a 'tall douglas fir, with its dark gloomy interior'.

It was no surprise to learn that readers would write or visit at the rate of at least one a week to thank him for saving them from suicide; that 1,000 carp fishers, a fraternity created by his *Confessions of a Carp Fisher*, rose as one to acclaim him at a surprise dinner; that he was the favourite author of Richard Walker, most legendary of post-War fishermen, Ranulph Fiennes and Julie Andrews. He was the last of the old poet naturalists.

Standing Room Only

This tale was handed down to **Michael Roberts** *by his father, a Methodist minister of 'formidable narrative powers and unshakeable standards of truthfulness'. Perhaps a detail here and there has been embroidered, but this is in essence the true story of one man's amazing journey from Kent to London*

ON A SUMMER'S DAY nearly 30 years ago, my elderly father boarded a London-bound single-decker bus which stood empty at a country terminus somewhere near Canterbury.

He was the first to board, ahead of the driver and conductor. However, the bus soon began to fill up, until eventually all the seats were occupied and several people were standing. Meanwhile the driver climbed into his cab and started up his engine. Moments later the conductor stepped briskly aboard – a thin-faced hatchet of a man, who needed no time at all to observe that his bus was full and that six people were standing.

'Sorry!' he announced loudly, not sounding a bit sorry. 'Only five allowed to stand. The last person to board is required to alight, if you please!'

The general hubbub of conversation swiftly died; but nobody moved.

'Come on now!' rapped the conductor, 'last one on – off!'

The standing passengers who had been struggling with their bags looked at each other questioningly. One or two shrugged; but no-one admitted to being last on, and nobody moved.

All the passengers were now silent. Against the background throb of the engine the conductor spoke more quietly, but with impressive finality. 'Regulations!' he declared. 'This bus doesn't move until the last person to step aboard steps off.'

The driver, who'd been waiting patiently for the starting bell, switched off his engine, clambered down from his cab and ambled round to the board-ing door. A huge man with a florid, amiable face, he looked up enquiringly at the conductor. 'What's up, Frank?'

'Regulations,' intoned Frank. 'One too many standing. Last one on won't say, and nobody'll get off.'

The driver looked at his watch and his expression became fractionally less amiable. He poked his head through

'I'd best go – they're getting impatient to use the phone'

VOICE from the GRAVE

'I doubt whether patriotism can stand the wear and tear and temptation of the front benches in the House of Commons. Men are flying at each others' throats, thrusting and parrying, making false accusations and defences equally false, lying and slandering – sometimes picking and stealing – till they become themselves unaware of the magnificence of their own position, and forget they are expected to be great. Little tricks of sword-play engage all their skill. And the consequence is that there is no reverence for any man in the House.'

From Anthony Trollope's 'Phineas Redux', 1874.

Contributed by Mrs Dorothy Jones

the door. 'Come on there!' he said. 'Can't wait all day!'

The passengers began to mutter among themselves. But still nobody moved.

'George,' said Frank, addressing the driver decisively, 'this is a job for the inspector.'

'Right you are,' said George. 'Where is he?'

'Don't know,' said Frank, 'but I'll go round the terminus one way and you go round the other. He'll soon sort this lot out.'

George readily agreed. Leaving their passengers to discuss the escalating crisis among themselves, he and Frank departed in opposite directions. Yet it was only a minute later when one of those rare but impeccably timed interventions of fate altered the whole course of events.

Unaware of anything unusual, an elegantly dressed but diminutive gentlemen, lugging a suitcase almost as large as himself, clambered laboriously aboard the bus.

To the best of my knowledge, no one has yet explained how a group of total strangers can suddenly think and act as one; but not a single person, including my father, opted to inform this hapless latecomer of the bizarre circumstances surrounding his arrival. Instead, he was greeted by a great burst of unexplained laughter.

The first appalled reaction of a gentleman so elegantly attired might have been to steal a furtive glance at his trousers. But whatever nightmare images came unbidden to his mind, they were banished almost immediately by the arrival of an irate inspector in the company of big George, the driver. The inspector mounted the boarding step and addressed the assembled passengers in the manner of the captain of an ocean liner.

'All right,' he said grimly, 'the last person to board this bus will disembark immediately.' Without a word of protest, the recently-arrived gentleman picked up his suitcase and struggled off the bus.

'Might have done that in the first place!' snapped the inspector, and instantly switched his gimlet glare on George.

'Where's Frank?'

'Looking for you,' said George.

Clearly a man accustomed to taking quick decisions, the inspector called out to another conductor strolling nearby.

'Harry,' he rapped, 'take this bus out! It's way behind schedule. Frank can take yours out later.'

Without another word, the inspector turned on his heel and strode off. Big George shrugged, ambled round to his cab and started his engine for the second time.

Harry, the new conductor, boarded the bus and put his finger to the bell. Pausing for a moment, he looked down at the solitary figure patiently minding his suitcase.

'Where yer goin' mate?' he inquired in cheerful Cockney tones.

'London,' came the quiet reply.

'Don't just stand there then. 'Op on!'

ALTERNATIVE BIOGRAPHY
CLIVE JAMES

COL. VIVIAN ('CLIVE') JAMES: Born in Sydney, New South Wales, in 1939, and educated at Sydney University, James arrived in Britain ostensibly to continue his studies at Cambridge. On graduation he flourished as journalist, songwriter, television critic and finally a celebrated television performer of a waggish nature.

Only on his precipitate escape home in 1995, via Luton Airport and Alicante, was it learned that under his code name of 'Clive' he had been an agent of the Ozintern, the undercover organisation set up in 1960 with the object of bringing all suitably sophisticated countries under Australian cultural domination.

After an initial setback when his cover was almost blown by the publication of satirical poems so feeble that even the London literary set noticed, James became an assured and successful operator. In addition to casting ridicule on British television for 12 years, he is believed to have contributed to the popularisation of Rolf Harris, Australian dental hygienists and kangaroo-based petfoods throughout the UK. On his return home, a grateful government accorded James the rank of Colonel in the Australian Secret Intelligence Service, the dreaded Ockerana. **PHILIP PURSER**

Memories are made of this

Sir: One of the best things about an oldie reading *The Oldie* is that, given a day or two, when reading it for the second time one has no recollection of having read it before. This is particularly useful when one wants something to read and there is nothing else lying around. Turn to *The Oldie*, and there is absorbing new material.

Maureen Rivett
Guildford, Surrey

Pook meets Puck

Sir: I enjoyed John McEwen's article about the writer 'BB' (see page 132). Like the latter I too only ever saw one gnome, when rather older than four, I think.

Although for years I had scoured the garden for fairies which I expected to look like illustrations by such as Margaret Tarrant, when I was suddenly confronted by this creature indoors it was all wrong: too tall, in drab-coloured shabby clothing, and extremely ugly. We glared at each other for a minute or two before it either vanished or ran off.

I never saw another fairy but the order of beings is not – as 'BB' concluded – extinct, because I know a very rational-minded gardener who sees fairies so frequently he can't understand why everybody does not.

As with sightings of that other order of beings, angels, it seems more usual to have only one experience, if that. Once is enough to make one open-minded and indeed open-eyed, but not foolishly gullible.

Mary Pook
Brighton

Gnome sweet gnome

Sir: In my youth, my friend and I cycled at weekends (as a change from to and from work) for anything up to 50 miles from where we lived in London. Our main interest was aircraft and aviation. We knew every airfield and landing ground within our reach.

On Sundays we would leave home early and make our way into the country – in those days not too far. Even

now I see reminders of those journeys in the surviving pubs and cottages along the old Great North and Great West roads. One morning we were meandering through the Hanworth/Feltham area. An empty road, glorious sunshine, some cottages across to the right, some trees and fields to our left.

We cycled together quietly, enjoying the experience. Just ahead we saw a figure standing by the side of the road in the open grassy area towards the trees. As we got nearer it appeared to be a rather small person – maybe about four feet tall. Dressed in green as a pixie might be (according to the story books), he had a small and not unpleasant face, a little grey beard and sharp, bright eyes. He watched us go by as we nodded to him. A little fur-

'I wonder if I could interest you in a gold-embossed, leather-bound copy of the Maastricht Treaty?'

ther on we both looked back, and he was still there.

A while on we stopped for a sandwich. My friend's mother always put an extra chocolate-spread into his bag for me. He asked me, 'Did you see that back there?' 'Yes,' I said, so we agreed that he must have been there. Who he was or what he was doing we could not imagine, and we could hardly tell anyone about it – could we? We never ever saw him again.

N W Byrne
South Oxhey, Herts

Poof pastry

Sir: I realise that *The Oldie* is a haven for outdated sentiments, particularly homophobia, so I wasn't surprised to note that Jeffrey Bernard's criticisms of his once-beloved Soho (see page 126) focused on the increased number of gay bars, restaurants and hairdressers in the area.

It was his assertion that 'the only good baker's shop in the area' had been replaced by a porn shop, implying that you can't get so much as a decent sticky bun in Soho these days, that made me gasp. I can only assume that if and when Mr Bernard gets out he is so blinded by prejudice that he fails to notice the elevation in culinary standards that has accompanied the proliferation of poofs in Soho.

As a heterosexual woman who visits Soho regularly with gay friends, I can also recommend the view.

Pauline Brown
London SW2

Virol: The madness begins

Sir: A small point on the excellent account of Virol (see page 81), a ritual for many between the wars, especially at school breakfasts. It did not claim to be needed by anaemic girls. That message came from Iron Jelloids, mainly on hoardings lining the railway lines.

Henry Swanzey
Bishops Stortford

Virolmania: 2

Sir: With respect I beg to disagree with Henry Swanzey on the subject of Virol.

The walls of the now defunct Exchange Station, Liverpool, were once adorned with brightly coloured enamelled signs. I saw these so many times over the years as my commuter train pulled in that they are imprinted on my memory. Among these signs were 'Virol. Anaemic Girls Need It'; 'Phyllosan Fortifies the Over Forties'; and possibly the most negative advert ever – 'Monkey Brand: Won't Wash Woollens'.

Monkey Brand was a small abrasive brick, used for cleaning doorsteps, so its alliterative advert was accurate.

Walter Greenwood
Levens, Cumbria

Virolmania: 3

Sir: Pace Henry Swanzey, I do not remember Iron Jelloids being advertised except at railway stations. Seventy years ago the fields beside the lines on which I travelled were largely occupied by billboards promoting Carter's Little Liver Pills.

Adverts for Iron Jelloids appeared at a convenient height to catch the eye of travellers ascending the stairways across the lines at such stations as Fenchurch Street. There was one line on each 'riser' of the steps. The message was:

'Well Marjorie, he still looks like a Nazi war-criminal to me'

> *Take Iron Jelloids*
> *Now and then*
> *The tonic for women*
> *The tonic for men*

The fifth line was something of an anticlimax: *And children*

Michael Reilly
Yelverton, Devon

Virolmania: 4

Sir: Concerning Virol; the stuff was made in a factory near Hangar Lane, in west London. Adjoining it was Brentham station, on the Paddington-High Wycombe Line. Brentham was a typical wood and corrugated iron GWR

'How about Pea Green then?'

halt and it was entirely covered – bedizened might be a better word – with blue-and-white enamelled iron advertisements for the product, informing the traveller of the classes of persons who would benefit from its use.

Among them, I am pretty sure, were anaemic girls, despite the claims advanced by Mr Swanzey for Iron Jelloids. They may have helped too, of course.

R K Bluhm
Marple Bridge, Stockport

Virolmania: 5

Sir: Virol was delicious but Yadil (1924-5) was revolting. It, also, was a cure of absolutely all, and people who had thought themselves dying claimed to be restored to robust health by it.

I suffered daily for several months after severe bouts of pneumonia, and I've no doubt it did me good. Some scandal (a quarrel between the press and the advertisers, I think) caused the truth to be revealed. It was merely concentrated and unadulterated garlic juice. I have often thought it was a great pity that Yadil was taken off the market immediately, garlic being one of the healthiest of plants!

H Wyatt
Goodnestone, Canterbury

A modest proposal

Sir: Would it not be more convenient for shops and customers if a new coin of 99 pence was added to our coinage?

Norman Garrett
Leigh-on-Sea, Essex

THE WORLD ACCORDING TO
Enfield Senior

IN OUR SEARCH for a Saturday paper that does not think we want to waste the weekend reading boring articles about uninteresting people, we tried the *Financial Times*. It said that Japanese whalers are popularly portrayed as feisty fishermen; that Tutti Frutti stools come in funky colours; and that Joan Collins has chutzpah. I read somewhere that a leather-clad Marxist professor of English at Oxford is bent on destroying the language and I think he has infiltrated the *FT*.

Being as ready as the next man to jump on a bandwagon as long as it is not moving too quickly, I am thinking of spearheading a movement with a new language called Interchangeable. 'The feisty fisherman sat on the funky stool and helped himself to chutzpah'. 'Feisty Collins's tutti-frutti made the fisherman funky.' These very vivid scenes are described with words which, to me at least, are devoid of meaning and therefore a great advance on the elitist practice of requiring sense or accuracy.

This lends itself particularly well to advertising, as in the slogan: 'Feisty cats love Funky'. This can be used as a caption for anything – cats eating cat food, bond dealers drinking lager, housewives eating ice cream. You can turn it round and use the plural if you want: 'Funky cats love Feisties' for

'Feisty Collins's tutti-frutti made the fisherman funky' – a great advance on sense or accuracy

children eating potato crisps or nubile women in state-of-the-art designer jeans.

As the leather professor is bound to agree that advertising copy is as worthy of serious study as *Jane Eyre*, I think he will be tickled more pink than he already is with my contribution to the destruction of English as the ideological apparatus of the capitalist state.

I GENERALLY READ theatre reviews as a prophylactic measure to innoculate myself against the risk of seeing the performance. I read an account of a new Pinter play and it said he had had a bad attack of writer's block before he wrote it. To borrow a joke from George II, I wish he

would bite some other of our writers.

If I were condemned to run a bookshop I should have a small section for Fiction and a large one for Pornography, to accommodate the bulk of modern novels. It would give me a certain satisfaction to say: '*Polo*, madam? Certainly, madam. Under Pornography, letter C.'

This would be fair as the dictionary defines pornography as the 'description of the manners etc of harlots' and I understand from the reviews that there is lots of etc in *Polo*, though I believe the harlots may be acting on an amateur basis.

There would also be a large section for Vulgarity, in which would go those melancholy works which are classified as Humour. Above all it would provide for those that are piled high and sold cheap just before Christmas, known as Adult Humour and amusing only to adolescents.

On the left of the door would be a section called Folly, reserved for the works of those whom Lord Chesterfield had in mind when he said 'When you hear a man of what rank soever swearing, cursing, talking obscenely and even

boasting of the vices of which he ought to be ashamed, put him down as a fool.' Political memoirs in which the writer tries to boost sales by obtruding his private vices upon the public gaze would fit nicely into this category.

While there would be plenty of female authors in the Pornography section I would not have expected to put many under Folly. I would not, for instance, have supposed that if Mrs Currie came to write her memoirs she would choose to portray herself as a kind of female Alan Clark, but having read the reviews of her novel I am not so sure. Writing books which sell on the strength of their indecency is a poor way of making money, and for a Member of Parliament you might think it undignified if dignity were something you associated with Mrs Currie.

This shop I would run merely as a front and to make a living, but the real business would be at the rear and all the authors would be dead. If you wanted something decent you would need to come round to the back where I could let you have *Northanger Abbey* in a plain brown paper wrapper so no one knew what unfashionable stuff you read.

'Did you say this was your first christening?'

Lucky **Frank Barnard** *comes from sturdy pioneering stock.*
That's why he has wonderful distant relatives like the Canadian cousins
who will evermore be evoked by the elusive…

Odour of Raspberries

IT STARTED unpromisingly and got worse. 'Hi there. I'm phoning from Edinburgh. You don't know me but I'm your cousin Nancy from Canada. Your grandfather was my grandfather's brother. Al and me would love to see you. We've heard about your quaint little cottage in the Cotswolds…'

'Chilterns.'

'…and we'd like to call and catch up on all the family news and tell you about your relatives in Vancouver and kinda get to know you and your lovely wife Joan…'

'Jan.'

'…'cos we've seen the photos and she's gorgeous. Al's got the hots for her and Al's got taste believe me. You're gonna love him. Just a ball of fire. He's the guy who came up with the scenario of networking my relations. Al's your man for saving a buck but it makes sense, right?'

'Uh, right.'

'So how's Tuesday for English tea and muffins? Seriously, don't go to any trouble. This is family, know what I mean? We'll call you from the train station, cousin Frank. Bye now.'

'What was all that about?' asked the gorgeous

young woman who was doing the sprouts.

'We've been networked,' I said, 'by Canadian cousins. That's the bad news.'

'And the good news?'

'Al's got the hots for you.'

Tuesday came and they didn't. We'd thawed out the muffins for nothing. Actually they were crumpets but we gambled on it going unnoticed by someone who confused the Cotswolds with the Chilterns.

'Maybe they also confused the Barnards with the Bernards or some such,' said the gorgeous woman.

'Maybe they've been involved in a serious coach crash,' I mused.

'Maybe it was a wrong number. Soggy crumpet anyone?'

Nancy and Al came the next Tuesday when we'd forgotten all about them. I was up a ladder cleaning gutters, Gorgeous was checking the cesspit.

'Cousin Frank? We're here, at Reading train station. Excited? You'd better believe it. Guess you're consumed with curiosity to clap eyes on these crazy Canadians, right?'

'Uh, yes indeed,' I said, like Harry Enfield's Cholmondley-Warner.

'What automobile's he got?' I heard an odd voice shouting in the background, 'So we can spot the guy.'

'A Fiat Panda,' I said, adding to make it more interesting, 'black.'

'That's okay,' said Nancy in a soothing way, 'that's fine. No problem.'

I was relieved it was no problem. I heard the odd voice asking cousin Nancy how long I was going to be. 'It's kinda cold just hanging around, know what I mean?'

Gorgeous was replacing the cesspit cover. 'Got any crumpets left?' I said. 'The Canadians are in Reading.' It sounded like a bulletin from the battlefront. 'They don't mind the Panda. It's not a problem. One more thing.'

'I know. Al's got the hots for me.'

'Not that. Remember to wash your hands.'

I spotted them immediately: a small figure in a red windcheater and blue jeans sitting on a yellow suitcase with wheels; a gangling character in a purple turtle-neck carrying two grey holdalls and pacing to and fro like a trapped moose. I didn't like the look of all the luggage…

139

'Hey hey hey,' said my cousin Nancy as I walked round to open up the back of the car. 'Look at that. The Barnard nose.'

'Dat nose sure travels,' said the ball of fire with the odd voice. 'I seen dat nose on your grandpa, baby.'

The nose and I got back into the Panda. 'You okay for space dere, sugar?' said lovable Al endearingly. 'I been in bigger toilets, know what I mean?'

I allowed a goofy smile to descend on my chops and headed west... We pulled into the drive. Al unfolded himself, grunting with trapped-moose spasms. Cousin Nancy sprang onto the gravel.

'... So I guess that kinda takes us up to 1902 and Auntie Ada, well she was one hell of a woman, they sure made 'em tough in those days and where she met Uncle Wilfred nobody could figure out, but he was down from the Yukon where he was building bridges and why, they settled in DC and oh, this was two years later, maybe three and they had kids I'm telling you. Ten was it, or twelve? Hey Al, Aunt Ada's kids...'

'Loadsa kids,' said the trapped moose unloading – I saw with a pang of fear – all their luggage.

Gorgeous materialised at the front door, bathed in the glow of the porch light, smiling a worthy semblance of a welcoming smile. I thought it would be too much for Al but he nodded at her briefly and said, 'Hey, how you doing?' He had the hots well under control.

'... Now uncle Perec, well it all went wrong for him. He was in construction, met this Doreen creature at the golf club. Boy, did he fool around. Aunt Jessy was a saint and she forgave him but this gold-digger had got her claws into him and Jessy was history after 43 years and she just upped and died of cancer and Perec he never even came to the funeral, just sent a wreath from him and his floozie. Then his heart gave out and she came in to the lot...'

'Another crumpet?' said Gorgeous. Cousin Nancy didn't want another crumpet. We were up to 1924.

'What do you do, Al?' I said quickly.

'I drive da trucks,' he said in his odd voice.

Gorgeous was grinning like a chimp back from space. I recognised a dangerous light in those blue eyes that had given Al the hots

I saw Al at the wheel of a mighty Mack thundering over a Rocky Mountain pass, pulling a chain to make the klaxon go.

'Rugged,' I said, dropping – I thought easily – into the North American idiom.

'Not really. I drive da trucks for da Vancouver post office,' said Al, and suddenly Postman Pat was yanking at the klaxon chain.

Gorgeous was grinning like a chimp back from space. I recognised a dangerous light in those blue eyes that had given Al the hots. 'I've got a treat for you,' she said, springing for the door as cousin Nancy reached for 1925.

'Now Aunt Amelia, she was a sweetie – Jeez did she have a tragic existence...'

'That accent, Al,' I said, 'I can't quite...'

Al hailed from Trinidad and as Gorgeous came back in I told her Al hailed from Trinidad. 'Is that right?' she said, looking at me boss-eyed. 'Dat's right,' said Al. 'Hey, what's dis I see?'

I stopped myself saying dis was raspberries. Not any old raspberries, but ones we had grown and stored for a special occasion. Gorgeous had got cross in the kitchen, then felt mean and was out to make it up to people who didn't even know they'd been offended.

Al looked at her offering. He stirred them about with his spoon. 'Sure is a lotta raspberries,' he said to Nancy, not to us. He glanced at Gorgeous. 'You trying to get rid of da things, or what?'

Cousin Nancy laughed. 'Al, you crease me up...'

Al looked at Gorgeous, his brows in trapped-moose mode. 'It's a good ting Chuck ain't here,' he said.

'Why's that?' said Gorgeous, her smile apparently meeting at the back of her head.

'Chuck, he hate da raspberries,' said the moose...

I took them on a drive. Gorgeous was expecting the man who mends the telephone. I told her in the kitchen: 'You're expecting the man who mends the telephone.'

We have a route that covers the delights of Bucks and Oxon. I helped Al out with the luggage and put it in the Panda while he said, 'Sure is cute here. Just da spot for a break.' 'Yes, well,' I said.

Dorchester, Stonor Park, Hambleden, Henley – I did the circuit. Cousin Nancy and the moose rubbed the mist from the windows and peered out at the gathering gloom.

'That's the Thames,' I said. 'This is Hambleden. Old Catholic family, the Stonors. They've got a priest's hole.'

'What?' said Al.

The tour could take two hours. I did it in 25 minutes. 'So here we are,' I said. Their fingers squeaked on the glass. They stared out, expecting to glimpse quaint Chiltern prospects. The stuttering blare of a high-speed 125 gave them a clue. 'Dis is der train station,' Al told cousin Nancy.

'You'll be back in London in time for dinner with your friends,' I said.

'But we ain't having dinner wid da friends,' said Al.

'I must have misunderstood,' I said. 'What a pity. They might have had da raspberries on da menu.'

Gorgeous was supine in the sitting room, an empty bowl of raspberries balanced on her chest. She held her hands up in a gesture of defeat: 'Don't... say... anything.'

'One thing,' I said. 'Future plans. Networking, that's the scheme. I'm the guy for saving a buck. Besides I've got the hots for cousin Nancy. And there's another person I'm particularly keen to meet.'

'Who's that?'

'Chuck,' I said, and we added in perfect unison, 'He hate da raspberries.'

PIN-UPS

Ken Loach

picks his top six

1 Ann Leaburn
Just one of many women who changed from housewives to superstars during the Miners' Strike. (*NB None of the sources we contacted could provide a picture of Ann Leaburn, so this one of miners' wives will have to stand in for her.*)

2 Arthur Scargill
Ref the above – unique among Trade Union leaders, the one who didn't betray.

3 Jewell and Warris
Up there in the gallery of great comics, alongside Frank Randle, Norman Evans and Jimmy James, not to mention Hyda Baker.

4 Billie Holliday
Obviously. Or it could have been Piaf. They both cheer you up.

5 James Connolly
His analysis of Ireland's British problem is still the definitive one. Go to the Sinn Fein bookshop and buy his books.

6 L Trotsky
However predictable, it's hard to leave the old man out. He still has things to say about how we get out of this mess. (I hope Tony Benn will understand!)

Right: Ken Loach, hard-hitting film director

Desperately Seeking Simba

A man-eating lion is on the loose somewhere in England, and he hasn't had a meal for nearly a century. Fearless **Paul Pickering** *is dogging the trail of the cat that ate Uncle Elrington*

I HAVE been hunting a particular man-eating lion across the shires of England ever since it slipped from the grasp of an elderly businessman. Maurice Hopkins was indefatigable in his quest and was prepared at the drop of a hat to spend 'several hundred pounds' to secure the stuffed mammal, whom taxidermy does not seem to have slowed down at all.

'The closest I came was in 1935, at a Hertfordshire café,' he told me some years ago. 'There had been a sale at Hatfield House and the café owner had bought it, only to sell it on the next day. It's quite easy to identify. And that's what makes it so special. The plaque on the case states it murdered my Uncle Elrington: "This is the lion that killed Dr E F McKay." Apparently, there is a very peevish look in those green glass eyes.'

The tale begins, of course, in darkest Africa. The uncle was eccentric elephant hunter and ship's surgeon Dr Elrington Francis McKay, a pioneer cyclist who had once won the 50-mile race around Phoenix Park in Dublin. Unfortunately, Dr McKay had an equal passion for big game hunting and set out on 22nd October, 1894, along the shores of Lake Nyasa with both barrels primed.

Maurice recalled: 'He was a surgeon on the gunboat *HMS Pioneer* and had taken a few days off to go hunting. Two lions confronted him in a clearing and the bearers, expecting elephants, not lions, ran away. They went straight up the nearest tree. Elrington was left standing there all on his own. The bearers would not come down. Who could blame them?'

Elrington stood his ground and wounded one of the cats as they took off into the jungle. Then, foolishly, the Dublin doctor followed the punctured Simba. Unbeknown to Elrington, the lion had taken the large bullet in the backside from his Holland and Holland elephant gun very personally. In fact, as Elrington strode into the bush, it was waiting behind a mango tree for the champion cyclist – 'a jolly un-lionlike thing to do, if you ask me,' according to Maurice.

The last thing Uncle Elrington saw in this life was a huge maned head which smashed the heavy weapon out of his hands. The bearers, safely above, watched in fascinated horror as

The bearers watched in fascinated horror as the lion settled down for a well-earned snack. All they could do was throw mangoes

ALTERNATIVE BIOGRAPHY
BRIAN CLOUGH

Elrington's mother was not amused when her servants opened the case and she came face-to-face with the beast that had eaten her son

Elrington's arm and jaw were broken and the lion settled down for a well-earned snack. All they could do was throw mangoes.

At last the cat was distracted from tucking into the tough cyclist by the hail of fruit. This gave a faithful bearer, Musa, the chance to prove he really *was* a faithful bearer. He scrambled down the tree and, as the lion disengaged from his meal to charge again, snatched the gun from the mess that was now Elrington and shot the cat. 'You could say it was draw,' chuckled Maurice. Both cat and man died from their wounds and the captain of the *Pioneer*, Mr K Everett, was called to the scene. His problem was that there was not really enough of the Anglo-Irish cyclist left to send home.

So, in the best possible taste, the captain decided to have the lion stuffed by a Lake Nyasa taxidermist and placed as a *memento mori* in a large glass case bearing the legend: 'This is the lion that killed Dr E F McKay.' The grinning beast, caught in his moment of triumph, was thus dispatched to the surgeon's mother. Even given the more robust attitude to death at that time, Elrington's mother was not amused after her servants opened the large packing case and she came face-to-face with the savage wild animal that had eaten her son.

'The lion was brought to my uncle's parents and presented with profuse naval apologies and a picture of the "grave" by Lake Nyasa,' Maurice added. 'It was one of those formal occasions that quickly became the contrary. His mother was furious and shouted: "Take that horrid thing away!" '

Cast out into the world the simba, by all accounts a splendid cat, began a tour of English country houses and salerooms that it could never have dreamt of in its jungle days. Its impish, satisfied stare in death assures one that gentleman cyclist and Trinity man McKay is not remembered with any of the respect he possibly deserves. Accidentally getting eaten does not help a reputation for speed or erudition.

'One of my uncles came face-to-face with it in another road-house in 1935,' continued Maurice, before retiring from the fray somewhere in the direction of Brighton. 'My uncle stopped for a cuppa and saw the lion, who seems fond of cafés, looking at him over a tea urn. Right in the eyes. He stalked out in a fury. Well, it did gobble up his brother.'

Maurice always maintained he wanted the thing as a 'burglar alarmer' to put in front of his French windows. I'd like it myself – because I hate cyclists.

HIS 18 YEARS at Nottingham Forest between 1975 and 1993 established Brian Clough as one of the outstanding forest managers of our time. In that span – 'a mere drop of a leaf in the lifetime of any tree worth calling a bloody tree,' as he characteristically put it – he extended its area, cleared away much dead wood, planted thousands of saplings and, with the aid of an imaginative sponsor-a-squirrel scheme, quadrupled its small quadruped population.

Five years after Clough took over, Nottingham beat Savernake to win the English Woodlands Championship, and in 1987 was named European Forest of the Year. Tree-lovers clamoured for him to be appointed national forest supremo and take on the challenge posed not only by EEC woods but also by the newly deregulated East European forests.

Alas, 'Cloughie' had not gone out of his way to win allies in the higher echelons of silviculture. He was too outspoken on television shows such as *Name That Tree*. Rumours were circulated of fibre-glass elms he had erected to replace those lost to Dutch Elm Disease. The *News of the Wold* published the story of an airman who alleged that Clough had hired him to rain litter and used contraceptives onto rival woods. On the day Nottingham was relegated in a local derby by Sherwood Forest, the great man retired. **PHILIP PURSER**

Smoke on the Water

Adam Moore *visits Varanasi, the departure lounge for the Hindu afterlife*

FROM THE TOE OF VISHNU pours forth the Ganga; so say the Vedic hymns. In which case the Lord of Creation should wash his feet – the Ganges is filthy. Nevertheless these waters are sacred to Hindus and can, apparently, cure a number of complaints, such as being born poor and lowly. To receive its holy blessing one travels to Varanasi, a city which draws its life from the water's edge. Consequently the best place to view it is from the river itself.

In the half light of dawn we wound our way down to the ghats, or landing stairs, to negotiate a price with a boatman. Then, with the sun piercing the horizon, we sat back as our faded wooden rowing boat pushed off into midstream. The bustle, noise and smells of the city recede, leaving one simply to watch. While the muddy Ganges slopped our boat's side, the humanity of Varanasi came down to bathe.

Groups of women, quietly chatting, wash with practiced skill, leaving in place the covering of their saris. Gangs of men, boastfully posing, dive into the waters to splash and be splashed. Elsewhere the routines of life continue. Boys bully their water buffalo to the water's edge. Dhobi wallahs, submerged to their knees and with their backs to the river, beat out the stains and buttons of other people's clothes.

Slowly the boatman guided his craft down to the Burning Ghats, so named for the half-dozen or so log fires which cremate the the discarded husks of Hindu souls. In terms of reincarnation, having the cinders of one's mortal remains committed to the Ganges at Varanasi looks good on your eternal CV. Therefore Varanasi is a popular place.

This creates a problem. The country is generally very hot, and corpses cannot easily, or rather hygienically, be transported across it. Even in India there is a limit to what can be strapped onto the roof of a bus.

The solution then, for attaining this leg-up into the next life, is to travel to Varanasi alive and leave it dead. Hence the large number of ancient beings shuffling painfully over the worn cobbles and marking time with prayers. Such devotees stay at one of the many hotels which litter the town. One such was advertised with a sign saying 'Hotel Shiva, stay here and die'. This could be a signwriter's error, but it is just as likely to be a form of niche marketing.

Our boatman, meanwhile, had brought us to within six feet of the steps to the Burning Ghats. Five fires were already roaring away while a sixth pyre awaited the final ingredient. It did not have to wait long. Down the steps came half a dozen men supporting, in various ways, a wooden stretcher, upon which multi-coloured silks covered a small mound. This was manhandled to the river where it was completely submerged, then propped up against the steps.

With the boatman keeping our craft steady, we watched the mourners peel back the silk coverings to expose a grey shrunken face. In turn, each of the deceased's relatives poured river water into his mouth. The silk was replaced and the stretcher layed on top of the pyre. Finally the priest played his part and, with the eldest son, absent-mindedly torched the kindling wood.

Sacred rites in India are performed with a degree of nonchalance. The priest carelessly throws another log on one fire, aims a kick at one of the wild dogs which are scavenging around, and, in one movement, fishes out the indestructible hip bone from a smouldering pile and throws it into the river. Behind the ghats loom enormous piles of wood, cut, ready and waiting. The alien observer, prepared to be reverent, may find the scene more bewildering than beatific. Though of course cremation is taken very seriously here. It is big business, cornered by closed-shops.

To be done properly costs upward of 1,000 rupees (about £30) – a major investment for most Indians. However, the government has tried to undercut the wood-burners' union. Standing on stilts over the river, joined to the shore by a short bridge and high-tension electricity cables, squats the official electric cremation building. But despite posters advertising 'Electric cremation, 100 Rs a body', the site is rarely visited. No doubt traditions take time to change, or perhaps they just do not trust the power supply.

There are also other, unsubsidised competitors, dotted up and down the river shore. Cheaper, no doubt, than the Burning Ghat and more acceptable than electricity, but the workers here do tend to leave their jobs early; as soon as the cortege has disappeared, in fact. Meanwhile the dhobi wallahs bash away at the water's edge, among the organic froth.

The Hindu method for disposing of the flesh no doubt has its merits, and it is certainly less gruesome than the Tibetan 'sky burial'. There is, however, one drawback, in that Indian cremations do not bequeath to humanity the benefit of an epitaph. But then if you are coming back anyway, what would you say?

> **Even in India there is a limit to what can be strapped onto the roof of a bus. The solution, then, is to travel to Varanasi alive and leave it dead**

Miles Kington

A FEAST OF FRIENDS

WHEN I MOVED from London to the country in 1987, I not only left lots of London friends behind, but left behind people I had just met and with whom I would have become friends, I felt sure, were it not for this mad move to Ruralshire. One of them was the playwright Alan Plater, whom we met at the opening of an exhibition at the Royal Academy, I think. My wife Caroline and I immediately took to Alan and Shirley, but when they suggested meeting again, we said we were moving to Bath, which must have seemed unfriendly at the time…

Cut to six years later. Alan Plater is fed up at the idea of spending all summer in London. But he doesn't want to move to the country. He sees an ad, offering large house for let for the summer. Brilliant! He rents a house in Somerset for several months where he can work undisturbed. However, he doesn't want to be *too* undisturbed, so he sends a friendly letter to friends and relatives, saying it's open house and everyone come and stay if they want to.

The place is only 20 miles from us, at Somerton, so it doesn't make sense to go and stay – instead, I ring up Alan and suggest we come over for lunch one day. Brilliant! he declares, in the tone of one whose day is spoilt for not having people to lunch.

But when we arrive there one Wednesday, I realise he greeted our self-invitation so warmly for another reason; we were guests who were *not* staying the night. He had not seriously thought that many people would accept the invitation to traipse all the way to the Bristol Channel for a night or two. He was wrong. People have arrived from all over, and I got the impression that he and Shirley had found themselves learning the logistics of running a small country-house hotel, willy nilly.

It's only mid-week, but already the house is full of guests – son Paul, who runs an arts service in Durham, Alan's Aunt Lil from near Hull, scores of other people whose names I didn't catch, and Lenny Henry, for whom Alan Plater has been doing some writing. I have never met the great Lenny Henry before, but I once (as I hasten to remind him) shared the stage with him on the same bill at a charity concert in Oxford 12 years ago. He frowns and goes through his memory bank. His frown clears.

The White Horse Morris Men wasn't quite the Edinburgh Fringe, but not bad

'My God,' he says, 'you must have been in Instant Sunshine!'

What a memory! What a star! Sadly, that's not all he remembers.

'Didn't something go strangely wrong in the middle of your act?' he inquires. Yes, as a matter of fact. The bridge fell out of my double bass with a tremendous bang. It amused everyone in the audience intensely, but it gave

me a shock and took 10 minutes to put back while the act continued around me. Embarrassment for years. Then I forgot about it. Now Lenny Henry has brought it all back.

Later, as we leave after a wonderful lunch, Alan confides to me that it has been a fine experience, but next year he intends to rent a one-bedroomed cell somewhere and just work. He probably thinks that living in the country is always like this, but in my experience people are very lazy about coming to stay from London if they know they can do it any time.

I think it's because Alan put a time limit on it that people flocked in droves. Otherwise, people stick to their London habits. We once lured our friends Phil and Lynn down here for dinner and the night, and they drove 190 miles, had dinner, then drove back again, not realising they were invited for the night.

And there is also culture in the country not found in London. The other night the White Horse Morris Men came to our pub to dance in the street for an hour. It wasn't quite the Edinburgh Fringe, but not bad.

My wife was invited to take part in their last number, as they needed a woman. She didn't realise that she would end up hoisted in the air by all eight dancers, like Joan of Arc above the unlit bonfire. When she was returned to us, the lead dancer said: 'Perhaps you ought to know that the dance in which your wife has just taken part was an old and very effective fertility dance, and we will be surprised if she is not with child by Christmas. If it fails, we will gladly come back and try again. Here is our card…'

I took the card and still have it. It is nice to know that if your wife becomes pregnant, there is someone you can sue.

Richard Usborne

BRINGING IT ALL BACK

I WAS STILL a vomiter, liable to be sick in trains and closed cars, at the age of fifteen and at public school.

Thanks to a prep-school that all other prep-schools called a crammer, I had got a junior scholarship to Charterhouse in 1923. I was a 'hash-pro' – 'hash' being Charterhouse jargon for work, books, classroom stuff. This took £30 a term off my bills, and, if I passed high now, through my end of summer term exams, I might get a senior scholarship – another £15 a term off. This would be much appreciated by dear Mama, with four sons and one daughter to get educated on my father's pension.

I had worked hard that term, and I think they could juggle with the awards in favour of worthy widows. Anyway, on the last day of term I learnt from my housemaster that I had got a senior scholarship. Mama would not have approved the expense of a telegram or a telephone trunk call, so I had to take my good news with me next day: the 0630 train from Godalming to Tonbridge by the South Eastern, change for Battle on the South Eastern and Chatham.

I had reached the status at Charterhouse of being allowed to arrive and leave each term in 'sportings' – home clothes rather than the school city-clerk uniform of black coat and striped trousers, black shoes and bowler hat. There were rich boys who knew the name of Jack Buchanan's Savile Row tailor and at what width he had last ordered his Oxford bags. I got mine made 3" wider at Winsborrow's, haberdashers of High Street, Battle.

That last morning of term I dressed carefully into hoarded 'sportings' for the usual before-dawn greasy-sausage-fried-bread-and-tea breakfast in the House Buttery, and lit my first cigarette going up the steps to the bus that was picking up boys for the station. (Some of us tried to arrive at the beginning of term with nicotine stains on our fingers to show that we were heavy smokers.)

The bus brought my first presentiment of nausea. By Tonbridge, after a second Gold Flake, I was glad of a wait of a quarter of an hour on a platform in the comparatively open air. As we approached Battle I was in a cold sweat, but reckoned I would just make it. From the carriage window I saw Mama waiting at the end of the platform, with Buzz straining at his lead.

Back-from-school days of us four brothers and one sister were exciting occasions for him. He knew them because Mama turned left out of the house to walk to the station (you turned right for the town). He endured

Near Battle I was in a cold sweat but reckoned I would just make it

'I'll try the Bitter Gourd with Onion Stuffing followed by Cauliflower with Coconut Milk, Fried Spiced Prawns, Curried Pumpkin and Mango Soufflé'

term-times stoically but lived for the holidays. Now he spotted me down the platform, Mama let him off the lead and he shoved his way past people and milk-churns and luggage towards me.

I was embracing him and rehearsing my good tidings for Mama… 'I got the scholarship'… when she got her greeting in first. 'Dick, you look green!' My words got caught in a rush of nausea and shame. I was comprehensively sick.

I went back to Battle a few years ago, and I identified exactly the spot on the platform where I disgraced myself that summer morning. I told Mama about the scholarship on the walk up from the station. It was not quite the greeting I had planned for her.

David Ransom

'Is it too early in the interview to ask if you'll sleep with me, Ms Dobbs?'

FOOTLOOSE, FUNGUS FREE

THERE must be many ex-public schoolboys who suffer from chronic athlete's foot – a condition born of years of padding about concrete-floored changing rooms permanently awash with slime, Valderma and Sloan's liniment, a perfect culture for the unchecked growth of the dreaded fungus.

At my school, athlete's foot was taken seriously only if it got as far as the scrotum. This didn't mean it had to crawl all the way up your leg, but since scratching one's athlete foot was one of the few pleasures one could indulge in openly at school, the medical staff felt that other, covert habits of small boys meant that the infection might be transferred by itchy fingers to any warm, damp part of the body.

Matron waged war on athlete's foot by periodically conducting what we called football inspections. This involved us stripping from the waist downwards, to enable her to rummage about in our pubic hair with a pencil torch for signs of the infection, followed by a lavish painting of our feet with a noxious purple unction.

If, as happened occasionally, some rather forward boy became a little excited by the probings, a vigorous slap from matron's purple paint brush did the trick.

Happily, I never suffered from the extended form of athlete's foot, but my schooldays have left me with a tendency towards a persistent itch between my toes, which plagues me from time to time on the train. The problem is not being able to scratch it. A really satisfying scratch means being able to get off a shoe. Any other attempt at relief is short-lived.

I've tried stamping. This not only makes a lot of noise, it also attracts attention. An alternative is to squeeze one foot on top of the other. The drawback here is that what were perfectly cherry-blossomed shoes when you left home are not up to lunching in the chairman's dining-room.

It's not at all easy to remove a shoe surreptitiously on the train, as I found recently when a mild tickle turned into an all-consuming itch. The only escape from it lay in removal of my shoes. I was sitting at a table seat. My travelling companions were occupied with the evening paper. I reached down slowly to undo my shoelaces.

At my school, athlete's foot was serious when it got as far as the scrotum

This meant my face being drawn nearer and nearer to the table top.

Just as I was turning my face to one side to achieve the final inch of room, the newspaper opposite me gave a noisy twitch, and I saw its reader's face glaring at me. I grinned fatuously. The man, thinking I was trying to read the back of his *Evening Standard*, snorted, and briskly re-folded his paper.

I sat up, hoping desperately that the itch would go away. Not a bit of it. I tried a new technique. I drew up each knee, and wedged them against the table edge. This manoeuvre forced the table towards the man opposite. Once again he rattled his paper huffily and glared, but I was able to reach my shoes.

In no time, ecstatic relief was flooding my body. Feeling I'd drawn enough attention to myself I left my shoes off, and was soon dozing happily.

I awoke to the sound of cursing. In getting out of his seat, the man opposite me had stumbled on one of my discarded shoes. 'I'm sorry,' I mumbled, as he hopped painfully out. 'I don't suppose you went to St John's, Leatherhead, by any chance?'

EVELYN Waugh was at his eccentric best in 1953 when we arrived to record an interview for Far Eastern listeners at Pier's Court in Stinchcombe, known to friends as 'Stinkers', its brass plate announcing 'No Admittance on Business'.

I once met...
Evelyn Waugh

As the recording cable was run in to the house he expressed concern that his wife's cows, chewing the cud in a field a hundred yards away, should not be electrocuted by accident.

After some confusion the interview began. He sat behind his desk in the library, wearing a grey suit, waistcoat, watch-chain and a Brigade of Guards tie. 'My original ambition was to become a painter and after that a carpenter,' he declared. 'But I found that I was too lazy to acquire very much facility in either of these crafts, while my whole education had gone to make me literary.'

Drink had been his main interest at university. All music was painful to him, with the possible exception of plainchant. Decent architecture ceased about the time he was born.

This visit preceded publication of *The Ordeal of Gilbert Pinfold*, a name borrowed from an earlier owner of Pier's Court. Pinfold was harassed by the voice of a BBC interviewer. Yet in 1960 Waugh agreed to go on television in *Face to Face*. He wanted a huge fee and a contract was devised including every conceivable right. He accepted. Had he agreed the original offer the total would have been greatly increased by repeat fees.

I went with Felix Topolski to Combe Florey, near Taunton, a house without a television and a radio only in the servants' quarters. Waugh showed surprise that we had not arrived, as gentlemen normally did, by train.

Over lunch he asked what would be required of him. 'Will the studio be very hot? Would I need to wear my tropical clothes?' I assured him that the black drapes of the set would keep him cool.

When Topolski started to sketch Waugh was aghast. 'But where's your easel, Mr Topolski? What! You don't use an easel?' As Felix sketched, Waugh discussed, among many things, buggery on Mount Athos.

Then it was time for afternoon tea. As we got up I admired the chandelier. 'That's not a chandelier – that's a gasolier! Are you interested in gasoliers?' and off I was taken to admire the gasoliers.

We arrived in the dining-room where a large tureen of green-tufted strawberries was waiting. Too late I saw the problem. Put the strawberries on the plate, add the cream, take the spoon – and you were trapped with the strawberry tufts. My attempt to spear one shot it under the sideboard. Topolski, seeing what had happened, did the socially unthinkable – dipped a strawberry into the cream with his fingers. 'Ah, Mr Topolski,' Waugh observed helpfully, 'you need a spoon.'

When he arrived at Lime Grove it became clear that his illness had not completely evaporated. 'Where's the hidden microphone?' he enquired. His eyes settled on the wire of the electric clock. 'Ah yes. I see.'

When John Freeman arrived I introduced them. Waugh stepped back horrified. 'The name is Waugh – not Wuff!' he protested. 'But I called you Mr Waugh,' Freeman smiled. 'No, no, I distinctly heard you say "Wuff",' said the great writer, lighting a cigar. I read later that he had checked for any defamatory information about his interviewer in case he needed it for defence or offence.

When asked why he was appearing on television he replied: 'Poverty. We are both being hired to talk in this deliriously happy way.' Freeman challenged him on this pose of poverty. Waugh replied: 'Never saved a penny. And of course no honest man has been able to save any money in the last 20 years.' His worst fault, he said, was irritability. With? 'Absolutely everything. Inanimate objects and people, animals, anything.'

A postcard arrived after the filming, addressed to 'The Director General of *Face to Face*'. He had found a cigar cutter in his pocket which was not his. Was it mine? I replied that I was not missing a cigar cutter. Another card arrived after the film was transmitted. 'Thank you for your letter. I did not see the exhibition but somebody who did remarked that it seemed to end abruptly. I assure you I don't care. EW, SS Peter & Paul 1960.'

It had indeed ended abruptly. Freeman had asked as a closing question whether, looking back on his mental breakdown, he could see a conflict between the way he had been brought up and the lifestyle he had chosen. 'Oh, I know what you're getting at. That ass Priestley said that in an article... Poor old Priestley thought that.'

BBC lawyers decided the reference might take us all into court, so it was cut out. A pity because Priestley *v* Waugh on whether Priestley was an ass would have been worth every penny of a legal action. **HUGH BURNETT**

'You mean we get to choose?'

149

A Gardener's World

Christopher Lloyd is a guru to gardening writers and his home, Great Dixter, a horticultural Mecca. So green-fingered **Patricia Morison** *leapt at the chance of a first-hand encounter*

BEFORE I WAS MARRIED, Christopher Lloyd was a Sunday morning treat. Propped open under my cereal bowl would be his *Well Tempered Garden*, an endlessly re-readable classic now nearly a quarter of a century old. It was the launch of his latest book that gave me the opportunity to visit Lloyd in his lair.

Christopher Lloyd is the most admired of Britain's gardening grandees. Readers of *Country Life* know him from the distinguished column he has been contributing these past 30 years. Until recently Lloyd could be read more cheaply in the *Observer,* but now the new brooms have swept him away. Oh, the blindness of newspaper editors! By comparison with Lloyd, other garden-writers are displaced persons, and the difference really shows. Thousands of people have visited Great Dixter. From Lloyd's writing – peppery, quizzical, endlessly informative – thousands more *feel* as if they know both it and, in some measure, its owner.

Lloyd was born at Great Dixter in 1921. In 1910, his father left his business in London and bought a spectacular late-medieval, timber-framed manor house standing alone on a ridge of Sussex Wealden clay. He had Edwin Lutyens restore and extend it into an imposing yet comfortable house of glowing red tile and brick.

The famous garden is therefore as old as the century, the creation of Lutyens's genius and two generations of Lloyds. Christopher's father laid out and trained the topiary with its voluptuously shaped hedges and whimsical birds, 'a parliament' as they were called by Mrs Lloyd. Her influence made young Christopher a gardener.

Getting to Great Dixter should be simple – train from London to Eastham Station, 80 minutes from London on the Hastings line, and an £8 taxi ride. That particular morning London's tube service imploded, so I walked up the garden path two hours late. The oak front door opened and two dachshunds poked out their

noses. 'Are you *very* disorganised?' inquired their master.

Things warmed up with a sherry in front of the fire. Lloyd put aside his lap-top computer, to the satisfaction of the dachshund Dahlia who instead took his lap. Great Dixter appears to be one of those rare country houses still untouched by the heating engineer. Moving from sherry to the dining-room was like a journey from Algeria to Alaska. Yet although this is a house for long-johns, Lloyd himself is an epicurean, with scant sympathy for English killjoy attitudes.

A constant theme of his writing is that although good gardening means doing the job efficiently and with skill, it is all pointless without enjoyment. So he reminds us to plan our winter's day gardening according to where

A constant theme of his writing is that although good gardening means doing the job efficiently and with skill, it is all pointless without enjoyment

Far left:
The master
with Dahlia the
dachshund

Left: The Long
Border in
high summer,
Euonymus
'Silver Queen in
the foreground

the mind. He also appreciates the insights that come from friends' reactions to his garden. 'I am always learning, always changing my mind,' he says. Tastes can and must enlarge, he says, citing his discovery of Japanese gardens – in their habitat. 'All those Japanese gardens they are making over here, they are just so badly done!'

Writing about gardening is another way in which Lloyd shares what he has, writing for experts and amateurs alike. However, there are well-defined limits to his generosity. Woe betide anyone who transgresses them. Ladies who beard him at table with horticultural queries he understandably sees as ill-mannered cadgers. He suffers terminal boredom from people who drone on about their gardening problems.

I suspect he thinks much the same of being interviewed. He certainly ignored most of the questions I had thought up. 'Which have been the most valuable plant introductions...' I began. No good. Lloyd is adroit in deflecting conversation. I saw the point; it is all there somewhere in the books, the articles, and most clearly of all, in the garden itself.

I did better asking whether English gardens had not become too bland of late, too much 'good taste' grey and pink and lavender. He agrees, for he is a plantsman whose tastes are admirably, excitingly catholic. His eye esteems cannas (one of the plants which has replaced roses in the Old Rose Garden), orange gazanias, golden doronicums, and tricolour phormiums.

Lloyd caused a storm on a recent lecture-visit to Australia when he described Canberra as a blot on the landscape. But then, he is no pussy-footing please-all. 'I get very bored with people who won't make value judgements. But if you do, you are thought arrogant.' Lloyd's fans, at least, know the difference.

Nearly four o'clock, light going, and still I had not seen the garden. 'Oh, you surely don't want to see the garden?' said Lloyd mockingly. But I did, badly, and so we made a brief excursion together in the intervals between being photographed together for the umpteenth time. It was not how most people see Great Dixter, on a bitterly cold afternoon, the garden just emerged from an untimely blanket of snow. But it was marvellous, all the same, as any Lloyd fan would expect.

If you are sceptical as to what late autumn can be like in a great English garden, just look at the photographs and read the closing

Here, then, is not your caricature oldie. Lloyd in his seventies is more convinced than ever that balking at change leads to sclerosis of the mind

the sun will be shining. People who weed without a kneeling-mat he calls daft.

Lloyd cooks for himself and gives as much care to do it well as he does to gardening. After all, they are complementary activities, if one has the time. Meals at Great Dixter are devised to delight the eye as much as the gullet. The late November salad all came out of the garden, green and purple leaves scattered with the pale gold blossoms of unseasonable wall-flowers.

Never have I been in a house where spoils from the garden were so imaginatively shown inside – this, moreover, in November. Enchanting small vases stood on the dining-table, with others dotted through the great hall and drawing room: rust-red chrysanthemums in a flame-coloured lustre pot by that great English potter, Alan Caiger Smith; a dozen sugary pink nerines put together with scarlet fuchsias and silver honesty; a third vase brilliant with the berries of hips and stinking iris, cooled by periwinkle, green and white euonymus leaves, and plumes of silver grasses.

Lloyd, a fortunate man, delights in sharing what he has. He loves to entertain, filling Great Dixter of a weekend. But doesn't that get in the way? I asked, thinking of more harried gardeners reluctantly forced to be amiable to London guests when they long to be turning the compost. But Lloyd, living alone, sees contact with quick-minded people as a necessity. Especially, too, he likes contact with young people. They won't be up for Sunday breakfast, and that is fine by him.

Here, then, is not your caricature oldie. Lloyd in his seventies is more convinced than ever that balking at change leads to sclerosis of

Above: The Sunk Garden, appearing from beneath a thin covering of snow. 'Yes, grasses really are beautiful...'

chapters of *The Year at Great Dixter*. The end-stop to the Long Border was one of the most gloriously declamatory plants you could ever see, a Golden King holly, 14ft tall, thick with berries. It has been growing slowly upwards and outwards since Lloyd planted it in the year of my birth.

On all sides, there were things read about but not seen, such as the sterling silver worth of Helichrysum splendidum, and the excitement of shiny-leaved Arum pictum, pushing up through a drift of brown leaves. If only all you obsessive autumn sweepers and hackers could see Great Dixter now, you would surely change your ways!

I saw other things which have been my own modest discoveries, such as how smashing a luridly bright rose (in this case, orange Comtesse de Cayla) looks all alone on a declining winter's day. Better still, I saw things read in Lloyd but never till that moment believed. He wins. Now I truly know that there is a place in this world for spotted laurels – given only the space and the right variety. Yes, grasses really are beautiful and rustling bamboos an adornment we should all consider.

It was too cold to stay out long and besides, I had grossly over-stayed my welcome. Damn and blast London Transport, I thought as Christopher phoned for a taxi. No footling Citizens' Charter rebate would compensate for what I had missed. Yet how much I had learned – and so can we all, so long as Great Dixter is there and its owner too, celebrating it in print.

'Writing must be such fun'

The Death File

Veteran Test umpire **Dickie Bird** meditates on the failing of the light and the final drawing of the stumps

My ideal way to go
Umpiring out in the middle at Lords, because it has become almost like my second home now.

My life expectancy
Whilst I'm still fit, I am going to keep going. After retirement, as long as I can stay in good health so I can travel the world to watch cricket, I really won't think about it.

My last words
'I hope they play cricket in heaven.'

My method of disposal
Buried in my village cemetery. I don't think they'd allow my ashes to be scattered at the Nursery end at Lords.

My funeral arrangements
Nothing too grand. I've been a bachelor all my life. I have little time for women because I'm married to my cricket, so I'm leaving the arrangements to my amazing sister.

My special effects
I'd like to take my MBE with me because it means more to me than my life. It was a wonderful, wonderful surprise.

Memorial service
Whether I have a memorial service or not, I'd like to be remembered by the comment made by the Australian bowler Mervyn Hughes. I took him to one side at the end of a particularly bad over and told him to bowl line and length. He turned to me and said, 'Dickie, you're a legend.'

Who would you like to meet on the other side?
My Mum and Dad. They did a lot for me and brought me up the right way. My father never saw me achieve what I have as an umpire, so it would be wonderful. Oh, and also Barbra Streisand, although I might have to wait a bit.

My thoughts on life and death
I know there is an afterlife. I am a big believer and as long as I get to eighty I won't be scared of death.

Compiled by
Richard Middleton

Parrots in the Springtime

If you thought Paul Pickering's raven, Hector, was a smart bird (see page 88), prepare to be astounded by the brilliance of Bertie – or was it Roberta? – the African Grey parrot who owned **Hugh Cudlipp** *for 30 years. Acting as a roving publicist for the newspaper that his pet human edited, he survived shipwreck and kidnapping, became a French media star, gave a press conference, was suspected of having an affair with a hen, and then laid an egg…*

If you promise not to fall off your own perch in the meantime, I'll tell you later the bizarre story of how my parrot Bertie vamoosed in France clutching the wig of a screeching lady, hid in a wood all night, was abducted by a toothless hag who owned a medieval pet shop, reappeared triumphantly at a TV press conference in Paris, obliged me to be economical with the truth at a grilling by a Hitlerian customs officer on our return to Merrie England, and underwent a sex-change after the trauma.

It's a fair bet that 75 per cent of *Oldie* readers of all ages have a domestic pet barking, purring, twit-twitting, or blowing bubbles in a glass bowl somewhere around the homestead. My problem has been parrots, and it may help if I clue you up on parrotology. When on the fifth day, as it is said in Genesis, God created winged fowl that may fly above the earth in the open firmament of heaven, and invented the whale the same day as an encore, who knows whether He included *Psittacus erithacus*, the African Grey? I suppose so. They were certainly around when civilisation emerged in the scheme of things. The ancient Chinese were aware of a variety of species. In 328 BC Alexander the Great presented live Indian parrots to his tutor Aristotle. Seamen brought parrots to England as gifts for their families, and King Henry VIII, when not otherwise engaged, was fascinated by their antics, chatter and sociability.

Le docteur, frock-coated, thumbs in waistcoat, delayed his treatment of Madame to pronounce that the beaked one was obviously the vicious Coco, escaped from the workman's bistro, the Café Chez Coco

Parrots aren't just any old bird. They are often in the local headlines, escaping, being stolen or appearing in pantos. In recent months they have hit the nationals for more significant reasons. A tape recording of a parrot mimicking an au pair's passionate sexual cadenza as she frolicked with the master of the house clinched a divorce case. In America a Downy Grey named Max may be the crucial witness to the murder of his thirty-six year old mistress Jane Gill. The defence hopes to establish that Max's shrieking of 'Richard, no, no, no!' proves the innocence of Gary Rasp, the man on trial. A serious piece in the *Times* by David Pannick, QC, discussing the legal implications was entitled 'Will Parrot Squawk before the Beak?' In Britain the *Daily Telegraph* has reported that Axa, a green Amazon parrot, is encouraging patients under treatment at Walsgrave Hospital in Coventry for speech impairment after a stroke. They are chatting with Axa in a way they find more difficult with a speech therapist.

Legal and medical duties apart, I have it on the authority of the *Encyclopaedia Brittanica* that 'the sharp angle of attack of the jaw muscles on the bony elements closing the bill combine to produce one of the most powerful crushing mechanisms in nature'. An African Grey can crack nuts in a jiffy with his black bill, or leave the bloodstain on a finger that will remind the foolish that *Psittacus erithacus* is no cheep-cheeping love bird. It is the best talker, and there are other attributes and eccentricities that rank it among the élite of God's winged creatures. Parrots have four toes, the centre two pointing forward and the first and fourth pointing backwards. Combined with the hawk-like beak this equipment makes the performance of highwire acrobatics without a safety net risk-free. Come to think of it, with training they could cock a snook in a gesture of contempt.

They are big heads in more senses than one. Their cranium is huge in relation to their body, a necessary asset to encase their large brains. Of all parrot species African Greys are the most intelligent, capable of flaunting a vocabulary of 200 words with tonal quality and mastering a complicated sequence of tricks. Curiosity may have killed the cat but it explains the parrot's longevity – so much to learn, so many new tricks to perform, so many boarders to repel. The record for a Grey in captivity is claimed to be 100 years, and 50 or 60 is the norm.

Here's the sex bit, without which, in the licentious 90s, no article, play, TV film or papal encyclical can hope to grab the audience or congregation. My knowledge of ornithological gender is slender. True, at a Washington dinner I once sat next to a Japanese ambassador who partially relieved my ignorance. Nobody wants to bring up the past, or for that matter the present or future, with a Japanese diplomat. There are some subjects one avoids during the social small-talk over the *terrine de canard à l'orange*. I stifled in the nick of time the spontaneous question, did he enjoy Alec Guinness in *The Bridge on the River Kwai*? We exchanged bare-tooth smiles until, whack-o, I got it.

'Your Excellency,' I ventured, 'would you kindly enlighten me on a matter, a Japanese matter, that perplexes me? Your nation is renowned throughout the civilised and uncivilised world for several cogent reasons... ' His immutable smile flickered until I completed the sentence. 'Why are the Japanese pre-eminent at sexing chicks? What is the secret, or must it forever be hidden in a lacquered padlocked chest under a bed in the Emperor's Palace?'

'Ah so. Quite simple,' said His Excellency. He cupped his right hand as if it were cradling a day-old fluffy chick and blew into the centre of gravity. 'Quite simple, no Oriental magic.'

Ah so, but the wiliest Jap couldn't sex a parrot, even with a blowlamp or a high-powered water jet.

Parrots are lousy lovers. We are indebted to Dr Matthew M Vriends and Dr Herbert R Axelrod for this no-kiss-and-no-tell revelation: 'Unlike pigeons, chickens, peacocks and certain other highly social birds, parrots have a very weak and limited courtship procedure. They may have some movements of the wings and feathers, accompanied by eye dilations, but it is usually over very quickly. They don't even sing each other a song!' The doctors, Mat and Herb, offer a plausible explanation: 'This is probably due to their monogamous life. Most courtship rituals, including songs and special breeding colours, are nature's way of helping breeding birds find and recognise each other. With parrots and their high intelligence, this may not be necessary.'

My own theory is less highfalutin. Sexual dimorphism (the occurrence in a species of two distinctive types, male and female) is absent in parrots. Maybe that's the trouble. An African Grey male with the best of matrimonial intentions may find himself flirtatiously fluttering a wing at an African gay, or a female targeting an eye dilation at a lesbian *Psittacus erithacus*. They all wear the same suits and vivid red tails. Some breeders believe the size of the skull is a clue, but not decisively so. One can hardly expect a randy African Grey to go courting with a calliper in his beak when he is not at all sure whether he personally is a 'he, she or it' (the enigma immortalised in Liberace *versus* Cassandra, the funniest libel case of the century). The fact that the dark grey iris displayed by very young birds gradually turns yellow is a sign of maturing and has nothing to do with the birds and the bees.

T he first parrot I saw and heard of as a kid was screaming 'Pieces of eight!' on the shoulder of Long John Silver in *Treasure Island* at the New Theatre, Cardiff, *circa* 1920. Since then I have owned two African Greys – or, so help me, have been owned by two African Greys: Bertie, who dominated our household for 30 or more years, and Bobbie, one year old last June.

Bertie's first and last professional assignment was in the publicity department of the *Daily Mirror*. He would appear in his super cage at public promotions urging the populace to read the newspaper that kept him in fruit, nuts and veg. The fact that he was adventure-prone, specialising in survival, was established when he was earning his keep aboard a massive raft towed along the south coast seaside resorts for the entertainment of teenagers. It was equipped with water slides, games, refreshments – and Bertie; that is, until it broke up in a sudden storm. The piece to which the parrot's cage was fixed drifted and eventually floated ashore at Shoreham, with Bertie screaming 'Read the *Daily Mirror*!' until he was rescued by the police. He knew how to pull the Power of the Press.

The French press played a decisive part in tracing and rescuing our survivor after the second adventure in his life. It began when we were sailing westwards along the River Oise in my cruiser *Laranda II* on a pleasant August day fortified by chilled Chablis, awaiting the confluence with the Seine where we would steer to port for Paris. The next day we were to moor at the bridge at the end of the Place de la Concorde, there to be met by Monsieur Pierre Lazareff, illustrious chief of *France-Soir* and his wife Hélène, editor and founder of the magazine *Elle*. A dinner at Maxim's was to follow drinks on board.

'Why are you all so sad?' asked Pierre. 'Have you lost somebody overboard?'

'Well, yes,' I said, and told him the reason for our shattered morale. We had lost Bertie the previous day and

The parrot flew onto Virginia's head of hair, which, until that moment, all had assumed was her own. It wasn't. She let out a piercing shriek, terrifying Bertie who soared upwards with her blonde wig

it was my fault. Virginia Vernon, an elderly but spirited lady from our Paris office, had joined the cruiser at Champagne-sur-Oise to accompany us on the last lap. In a moment of aberration I had released the parrot from its cage, confident it would fly as usual onto my head. It didn't. It flew onto Virginia's head of hair, which, until that moment, all had assumed was her own. It wasn't. The Vernon lady let forth a piercing shriek, terrifying Bertie who soared upwards with her blonde wig tangled in his claws, vanishing into a wood I identified on the map as Fôret de L'Isle-Adam. After a patient wait, we had no alternative but to continue the journey to Paris. Who could find an English parrot in a French forest?

> **In the heartland of British conservatism he was still urging all within earshot to read what most of them abhorred as 'the bloody lefty rag'. I coaxed him to add 'And the Daily Telegraph' but he would have none of it**

'Fear not,' said M Lazareff on the quayside. '*France-Soir* will find Bertie, I promise you.'

The next day his newspaper announced on the front page: 'Lost in L'Isle Woods, An English-Speaking Journalist-Parrot'. 'If you find Bertie,' said the story, describing his grey suit and red tail, 'bear in mind that he eats nuts, fruit and vegetables and drinks water. You will be handsomely rewarded.'

The saga is rich in Maupassant characters who played their parts as the news drifted through a network of villages. Jacques, the *jardinier* of the riverside villa 'La Rive' warned his employer there was a bird in the acacia tree speaking English. Monsieur Bloch-Carrique, a respected civil servant, Agent d'Information à l'Imprimerie Nationale, reproved Jacques for being *un peu zig-zag*, and then himself perceived the miscreant with his treasured binoculars through which, as he often retold, he had seen much of strategic significance during his years in the Resistance. His wife Madame Bloch-Carrique, *malade* abed, was scared out of her wits by the entry through her window of a parrot with a grey suit and a red tail urging her to read an English journal. *Le docteur*, frock-coated, thumbs in waistcoat, local doyen of the profession whose wisdom is known to encompass all from constipation to the secrets of the cosmos, delayed his treatment of Madame to pronounce that the beaked one was obviously the vicious Coco escaped from the workman's bistro, the Café Chez Coco, where to the curiosity of the clientele the *très distingué* Monsieur B-C later parked his up-market Renault among the bicycles and barrows.

La patronne informed Monsieur that there was Coco swinging happily in his cage, and advanced the possibility that the English-speaking parrot might have escaped from the bird-seller's shop on the Parmain side of the Oise. The bird-seller's wife, questioned on the phone from Café Chez Coco by Monsieur B-C as to whether she had lost a grey parrot with a bright red tail, replied '*Mais oui*, that is my *perroquet*. I will collect it immediately. *Merci beaucoup*, Monsieur.' Any woman fit to be a bird-seller's wife knew that Berties were selling at £150 (now £550).

Young Pierre Collier, district road surveyor, joining the apéritif drinkers at Chez Coco in his blue overalls, was first to disclose *France-Soir*'s interest in the errant bird. His wife was concierge at the L'Isle-Adam town hall and she knew that the mayor had been requested to display a 'missing' notice and to instruct the gendarmerie to do likewise. Then the paper itself arrived at Chez Coco, and then, within two hours the excitable Virginia Vernon materialised at the head of a motorcade propelling a posse of journalists and cameramen, interviewing witnesses and finally laying siege to the bird-seller's fortress.

'*Mais non*,' said the bird-seller's wife, through the grille in the door, 'there is no English-speaking *perroquet* here. Never heard of such a thing. An English-speaking parrot?' From a covered cage at the back of the shop came the desperate call: 'Read the *Daily Mirror*! Read the *Daily Mirror*!...'

The next day M Lazarreff's newspaper announced '*Bertie, "perroquet journaliste" retrouvé à L'Isle-Adam grâce à France-Soir*'. Bertie explained what had happened as best he could at Monsieur Lazareff's press conference. Some penetrating questions were put to me by the TV team: What did I feel when Bertie was lost? How did I feel now? With Bertie shouting in the background 'Read the *Daily Mirror*!' I replied with feeling: 'He will soon be saying "And *France-Soir*!" '

There were two sequels to the French adventure. On our return to the River Hamble an officious customs cuss in dark spectacles ordered me to assemble all on board to be quizzed about booze and cigarettes, warning me that if he doubted our assurances, the Rummage Crew would search the boat and take it apart, plank by plank. When the inquisition was ending, a raucous voice from the forward cabin advised the company which newspaper to read. 'So,' said Customs Cuss, 'there is someone else on board.' I produced the culprit in his cage.

CC: Are you aware it is illegal to import parrots?

HC: No, I am not. It is not illegal.

CC: Are you teaching me the law?

HC: Yes. I consulted the Min of Ag and Fish before I set sail. Here (*producing official signed form*) are the current regulations. The signatory must declare that while abroad the bird has not consorted with poultry. I have signed on the dotted line overleaf.

Only one of those aboard *Laranda II* knew for sure what happened on that fragrant summer's night in Fôret de L'Isle-Adam on the River Oise and, just this once, he wasn't talking.

The other sequel to the trauma was a physiological phenomenon. A few months after his rescue, Bertie, to our embarrassment and probably to his, laid an egg. We changed his name temporarily to Bertina but didn't tell the neighbours why. Some secrets are better kept within the family, don't you think?

There were lamentations when he finally fell off his perch, as eventually all oldies do. He had the grace to take his final curtain call with dignity in a vet's surgery while we were away in Spain. The silence was eerie on our return. No squawking, no talking, no parrot, just the memories of half a lifetime with a handful of feathers.

I could swing Bertie by the tail and once delivered a speech to the National Pets' Club with my friend on my head, amusing the audience with his interjections. He enjoyed his hols at sea, enchanting French children in Honfleur harbour by jabbering in the language they were learning at school and then perfectly intoning one of his party pieces. He drew blood from the four fingers and thumb of a pissed Pole in a Thames-side pub who insisted that parrots would eat out of his hand (delete out of).

When I moved to Chichester in the heartland of British Conservatism he was still urging all within earshot to read what most of them abhorred as 'the bloody lefty rag'. But you can't de-brief a parrot. I coaxed him to add 'And the *Daily Telegraph*!' but he would have none of it, he was bolshy to the end. Even when the *Mirror* was obscenely shattered by Captain Robert Maxwell, Bertie still blazoned his pride in a nobler era.

He wolf-whistled at the monks in their brown habits and sandals and at the seminarians in their cassocks studying at the Theological College next to our apartment. Oh, and he once disconcerted his admirers by embarking on a spate of feather-plucking, diagnosed by a leading vet as caused by anxiety, loneliness or idleness; the truth was we had stupidly moved his cage near a radiator and it was too darned hot. Conspiracies by friends to teach him four-letter words failed. He knew how to behave in a cathedral city.

The ornate Italian cage was empty. The bird had flown to rejoin his Maker, hoping that after all that time he would still be remembered. The void was as saddening as the passing of a favourite comedian who was also a personal friend. The only answer was to find a worthy successor, a young African Grey who could mimic but perhaps never emulate the late and great Bertie, who staged a sex-change just for an extra laugh. Bertie, or Bertina, would have been proud of Bobbie, or Roberta, bilingual in English and Spanish before his second birthday, a lock-picker and escapologist who would astound Houdini. Frankly, he's a genius.

Modern Life

What is... Lip-Synching

HOLD ON to your bedcaps, readers, for I am about to tell you something rather shocking. You remember that scene in the screen version of *West Side Story* in which little Natalie Wood twirled about in her party frock singing, somewhat immodestly: 'I feel pretty, oh so pretty, I feel pretty and witty and gay...'? Well, the awful truth is that Miss Wood wasn't actually singing that at all! For, sad to say, the raven-haired actress was as inept at warbling as she was later to prove at swimming, and the lovely voice you heard was that of one Marni Nixon, one-time MGM messenger girl and formidable chanteuse. So all Natalie had to do was mouth the words with her fragrant lips: she was, to use the technical term invented by the American film industry in the 1940s, 'lip-synching'.

Lip-synch: ugly word, from 'lip' (one of the fleshy parts forming edges of opening of mouth) plus 'synchronise' (occur at the same time, be simultaneous) with the last two syllables chopped off.

Hollywood musicals were ever awash with the lip-synch practice. Joan Crawford couldn't sing for toffee so, in *Torch Song*, she had to pretend to be all melodic to the pre-recorded sound of one India Adams. Lauren Bacall, she of the deep and rusty *spoken* voice, was absolutely useless when it came to holding down a tune so, in *To Have and Have Not*, she had to fake it to the seductive tones of... Andy Williams! And do you really imagine that it was Audrey Hepburn singing

'Dammit, I am smiling'

'Just you wait, 'Enry 'Iggins, just you wait!' in *My Fair Lady*, or Deborah Kerr going 'Give a little whistle, phweep phweep' (or however the silly song went) in *The King and I*? Of course not. Auds and Debs were 'lip-synching' both, to the delightful flutings of our old friend Marni Nixon.

In America, where several generations have been raised on horrible popcorn in what they call 'movie theaters', the artifice that is Hollywood has always been accepted readily. Nobody ever objected to the fact that when Margaret O'Brien

burst into song in *Big City* she was only lip-synching to something the film producers had prepared earlier – something chirped by (you may have guessed this) Marni Nixon.

However, in England, the land of cricket and fair play, we have always thought that lip-synching was a bit of a cheat and not quite on. For many years we resisted the adoption of the term – it arrived on our shores, inevitably, in the 1980s.

In olden times we English youths would cluster around our TVs in various states of excitement to watch *Top of the Pops* and guffaw at popular 'beat' combos who never seemed to have their guitars plugged in and whose singer, quite clearly, judging from the embarrassed and wonky lip motions, had forgotten the words to the song he was 'lip-synching' to. 'He's *miming*!' we would cry. (For that's what we brave little Britons called 'lip-synching' – *miming* – until recently when we all succumbed to the debilitating affliction known to doctors as Dreadful-Made-Up-American-Word-Syndrome.) 'He's bloody hopeless, hahaha!' we would weep...

In the mid-60s, the Musicians' Union decreed that there was to be no more lip-synching on the telly, on *Top of the Pops* in particular. It was perfectly all right, the union declared, for the drummer of a group to feign the rattling of his percussive things or for the electric guitarist to affect, rather preposterously, that he was, indeed, a-twanging away – but the singer had to be, as they say, 'live'. The singer had to *sing*! Oh, calamity!

'*Your father and I are just having our Sunday joint*'

This odd directive fell to bits in August 1967 when peculiar pop 'legend' Jimi Hendrix turned up at BBC premises to perform his latest chart-busting experience for the excitement of the nation. What was *supposed* to happen was this: the backing track of Mr Hendrix's song, 'The Burning of the Midnight Lamp', would come wafting from the loudspeakers in the studio and he would lean into the microphone to provide words and 'melody'.

What *actually* happened was this: the backing track of 'The Burning of the Midnight Lamp' failed to issue forth because the BBC engineers had got all muddled up and were playing Alan Price's jaunty piece 'The House That Jack Built' instead. Red faces all round! 'I like the voice, man,' waffled Jimi into his microphone, 'but I don't know the words.'

The nation was horrified by this grand mishap. To lip-synch or *not* to lip-synch became the roaring issue around the playgrounds and

the sixth-form common rooms of the day.

But now we have moved swiftly on to 1993 and nobody gives a hoot about the lip-synch 'debate' either way. Tiny tots with wayward hair-dos toddle into Wembley Stadium to gawp, from a great distance, at Madonna in her awkward underwear. Upon the stage Madonna is lip-synching to backing tracks of her 'greatest' hits but it really doesn't matter anymore because, 50 years on from the invention of lip-synch, we are living in a society that happily *embraces* all things phoney.

Reality is redundant, so who *gives* a fig about the miserable fact that Marni Nixon – glorious provider of notes high and low to so many so-called 'Silver Screen Goddesses' wobbling their lips less than convincingly in CinemaScope – appeared bodily in but *one* film? Yes, Marni Nixon played a bit-part nun in *The Sound of Music*. But if you blinked you missed her altogether... **TOM HIBBERT**

VOICE from the GRAVE

'In time past men were full of pity and compassion; but now there is no pity; for in London their brother shall die in the street for cold; he shall lie sick at the door between stock and stock (that is between the door-posts), and then perish for hunger. In times past, when any rich man died in London, they were wont to help the scholars at the universities with exhibition. When any man died they would bequeath great sums of money towards the relief of the poor... Charity is waxen cold; none helpeth the scholar nor yet the poor.'

From a sermon preached by Hugh Latimer in 1548 and quoted by Winston Churchill in his 'History of the English Speaking Peoples'

Contributed by Mark Rhodes of Derby

Roy Hudd

picks his top six …

1 Dolly Parton
Two obvious reasons.

2 Samantha Fox
See above.

3 Sabrina
See above.

4 Maria Whittaker
See above.

5 Otto Preminger and Telly Savalas
What a team they would
have made!

6 Kate Moss
She'll grow…

Right: Comedian Roy Hudd